Kathy Battista is Director, Contemporary Art at Sotheby's Institute of Art, New York, and Senior Research Fellow, Winchester Centre for Global Futures in Art Design and Media at Winchester School of Art, University of Southampton. She is a regular contributor to *Art Monthly* and *Brooklyn Rail*.

'*Renegotiating the Body: Feminist Art in 1970s London* by Kathy Battista does much more than its title suggests. It is an assiduous study of the founding generation of feminist artists in Britain. The book is timely both because so much of this emergent feminist movement was ephemeral in its day, and were it not for Battista's careful excavation it would be in jeopardy of extinction, and because only now with the historical perspective of four decades is it possible fully to contextualize and assess the significance of the work done in the 1970s. Through interviews with the artists, investigation of primary source material, and onsite research, Battista brings an historical period back to life, documenting exhibitions and performances that were groundbreaking in their time and shows how this work was linked to the feminist art movement in America at the time, and now it continues to influence a younger generation of women artists working today.'

Professor Jo Anna Isaak
John L. Marion Chair, Department of Art History
Fordham University

Kathy Battista

RENEGOTIATING THE BODY

Feminist Art in 1970s London

I.B. TAURIS

LONDON · NEW YORK

Published in 2013 by I.B.Tauris & Co Ltd
6 Salem Road London W2 4BU
175 Fifth Avenue, New York NY 10010
www.ibtauris.com

Distributed in the United States and Canada
Exclusively by Palgrave Macmillan
175 Fifth Avenue, New York NY 10010

ISBN: 978 1 84885 905 0 (hb)
        978 1 84885 961 6 (pb)

A full CIP record for this book is available from the British Library
A full CIP record is available from the Library of Congress

Library of Congress Catalog Card Number: available

Printed and bound in Great Britain by T.J. International, Padstow, Cornwall
from camera-ready copy edited and supplied by the author

CONTENTS

LIST OF ILLUSTRATIONS

CHAPTER 2

CHAPTER 3

CHAPTER 4

ACKNOWLEDGEMENTS

First and most important thanks are to Liza Thompson at I.B.Tauris for having the vision to make this book a reality and the patience to wait for it to take fruition. The freedom and independence allowed to me was much appreciated. Thank you to Cecile Rault at I.B.Tauris for smooth handling of the production of the book. And sincere gratitude to Kim McSweeney for all her patience in the final stages of the manuscript.

I would also like to thank my colleagues at Sotheby's Institute of Art in New York and London, including David Levy and Carole Feld, Anthony Downey, Tony Godfrey, Lesley Cadman, Mary Rozell, Melanie Mariño and Stephan Pascher. Your collegiality, advice, and friendship have been vital to my ability to produce this book while creating and maintaining the MA Contemporary Art program in New York. I should also thank my students, past and present, for being a continual source of inspiration.

The formative discussions, support, encouragement and kindness of many of my colleagues at the London Consortium must be acknowledged, including Lorens Holm, Catherine James, Mark Morris, Charles Rice and John Tercier. Special thanks to Barbara Penner, who so thoroughly read early drafts of this work, and whose enthusiasm and insight were crucial to the completion of the project. Jon Bird and Jane Rendell also gave wonderful feedback on early drafts of this research. Thanks also to Mark Cousins and Steve Connor for their dedication to making me a more critical thinker. I would also like to acknowledge the support and enthusiasm of the late Paul Hirst, who never wavered in his belief in me.

This research would not have been possible without the financial support of various people and institutions. I am indebted to the Overseas Research Scholarship, the British Federation of Women Graduates and the Hugh Gaitskell Foundation Grant. Lastly I am grateful to the London Consortium for providing a post-doctoral Research Fellowship, which provided income during two crucial years of this project.

Thanks are due to the librarians and curators of the following institutions for their assistance and guidance at various stages in the project: Adrian Glew at the Hyman Kreitman Research Center, Tate Britain; Simon Ford, formerly at the National Art Library, London; Althea Greenan, Women's Art Library, Goldsmiths University; the British Library, especially the staff at the Rare Books & Music Reading Room and the Colindale Newspaper Library; Birkbeck Library; the Fawcett Library; the Getty Research Institute Library, Special Collections and Visual Resources; the MIT Architecture Library & Document Services department; UCLA Department of Art Library; Space archive; Acme archive. And in New York, thanks to Tom McNulty at NYU Bobst Library, as well as Erin Elliott and Melissa Wagner, Librarians at Sotheby's Institute of Art.

I am also greatful to the assistance provided to me by Pauline Daly at Sadie Coles Gallery, London; Irene Bradbury at White Cube, London; Anke Kempkes and Lauren Pascarelli at Broadway 1602 New York; Monica Manzutto at Kurimanzutto, Mexico City. Also, huge thanks to Pippy Houldsworth at the eponymous gallery and Richard Saltoun at Karsten Schubert for inviting me to mount exhibitions around this body of work.

The openness, encouragement, flexibility and kindness shown by the following people have made the project pleasurable and memorable. My sincere gratitude to all of you for opening up your archives and memories to me: Parveen Adams, Bobby Baker, Barry Barker, Kelly Barrie, Ray Barrie, Anne Bean, Jon Bird, Michael Bracewell, Guy Brett, Dr Juli Carson, Judy Clark, Mary Dinaburg, Cate Elwes, Rose English, Sharon Essor, Rose Finn-Kelcey, Theresa Gleadowe, Charles Harrison, Alexis Hunter, Tina Keane, Mary Kelly, John Latham, Linder, Kathleen Madden, David Medalla, Jacqueline Morreau, Laura Mulvey, Hayley Newman, Hannah O'Shea, Clive Phillpot, Carolee Schneemann, Penny Slinger, Jemima Stehli, Barbara Steveni, Anthony Stokes, Lisa Tickner, Monica Ross, Kate Walker, Marina Warner, Jack and Nell Wendler, and Silvia Ziranek.

I would also like to thank those people who have invited me to speak on this body of work: Jonathan Harris and August Davis at Winchester School of Art, University of Southampton; Beverly Fishman at Cranbrock Institute MFA Painting; Mark Morris at Cornell School of Art and Architecture; Jovana Stovic from Location One and Art Basel Miami Beach for inviting me to participate in a panel on performance art at the College Art Association conference 2012; Anke Kempkes at Broadway 1602 in New York; Catherine James at St Bede's School; Naomi Salaman at Brighton University and New York University Study Abroad Center; and Sophie Howarth at Tate Modern for hosting two courses on the topic. Thank you also to the editors of the following publications for commissioning pieces based on my research: Patricia Bickers at *Art Monthly*;

Mat Smith at Phaidon, and Doro Globus at Rindinghouse; Richard Dyer at *Third Text*; Keith Patrick formerly at *Contemporary*; and Althea Greenan formerly at *Make*.

Loving thanks to my family for their unerring dedication and support of this project. Also, Tracey Ferguson, Nina Krieger, Bridget and Polly Pierpont, Giora Polushko, Dr Fifi Battista and Nigel Talamo, whose friendship and love sustained me and continue to do so.

INTRODUCTION

How has feminism created a legacy in today's art practice? What role did feminist art play in London during the 1970s? How has British feminist art been integrated or selectively ignored by mainstream art history and museum practice? While feminist art has been acknowledged and even celebrated in America and some European countries, this practice and its history have been largely occluded in British institutional history. And while an encyclopedic history of this movement would not be feasible, this book aims instead to begin the recovery process. It seeks to remember significant works by artists informed by the women's movement. In particular it examines how the female body became a contested site in feminist art practice and how alternative sites fostered such work. It also seeks the legacy of this founding generation of feminist practice in the work of artists coming of age at the end of the twentieth century in London, revealing that the issues and themes of the 1970s are still relevant in recent decades.

It is widely accepted within art history that the women's liberation movement and theories of feminism significantly affected fine arts. However, the same period also saw a more general shift occur in contemporary art practice, one which challenged the traditional means of classifying art by placing a new emphasis upon the dematerialized form. This shift means that the emergence of a feminist practice cannot be considered in the same way as previous art historical movements. For what is a feminist work of art? Unlike, say, abstract expressionism, there is no singular style, means of expression or look to any given feminist work. I would also stress that in many cases feminism alone did not determine the nature of a given work, but was just one of several preoccupations that the artist was attempting to explore, leading one to wonder if the term "feminist-influenced" art might be more appropriate. For the sake of convenience, I use the term "feminist art" but acknowledge from the start that this generic term actually encompasses a wide range of practices. The resistance of feminist art to easy classifications and its lack of any signature style no doubt helps explain why it has been both marginalized in art history, and grossly under-represented in institutional archives and collections.

It is my intention to place feminist work of the 1970s firmly alongside other major currents of contemporary art at the time. Doing so promises not only to enrich existing discussions of feminist art, but also of 1970s art practice generally, as feminist art occupied a unique position during this period. As I will establish, feminist art practice straddles the categories of conceptual, body-oriented and political or theoretically based art. The reader will find that much of the work discussed centers on the themes of trace, memory and embodiment; this reflects the larger ethos of the book, which is committed to bringing these events to light, especially the lesser-known exhibitions and performances, and inserting them into any existing art historical account of the 1970s in London.

Given the dearth of specific studies of this period, the first task of this book is necessarily the historical recovery of primary evidence, using a variety of methods, from archival research to interviews. The context for this activity is a general body of literature on the subject of women artists. Since the beginning of the women's movement art historians and artists have re-examined the role of women in the visual arts. In the United States Linda Nochlin, Whitney Chadwick and Lucy Lippard paved the way for further generations of feminist writers such as Judith Butler, Laura Cottingham, Amelia Jones and Juli Carson. In the United Kingdom Rozsika Parker, Griselda Pollock and Lisa Tickner laid a foundation for a history of work made during this time. However, there has been a notable absence of a younger generation of writers like Amelia Jones and Juli Carson in the United States to retrospectively examine work from the 1970s in Britain.

In addition to historical recovery, this book attempts to build on the original art historical groundwork laid by writers such as Pollock, Parker and Tickner, in order both to examine some of the themes of 1970s feminist art from a contemporary perspective, and to make a bridge between feminist art of the 1970s and art produced in the 1990s and early 2000s. It attempts to situate 1970s feminist artists in the wider context of their contemporaries to remedy one of the deficiencies of the earlier writing the tendency to examine women's work on its own, removed from the history of other art movements. With the exception of Susan Hiller, Mary Kelly is arguably one of the most recognized artists in this canon, possibly because the work has been most thoroughly documented (Kelly is one of the few female artists to have a meticulously organized and maintained archive of her work) and because it has received institutional support and recognition (for instance, she is one of the few feminist artists who can be found in Tate's collection). This book attempts to challenge the very narrow canon of feminist artists in existing histories, the creation of which itself goes against the original non-hierarchical credo of feminist institutions.

PART I: ORIGINS

WOMEN'S WORK: A FEMALE AESTHETIC?

The impetus for writing on this topic came from two main sources that are discussed in this introductory chapter. The first is a founding body of art historical literature including *Why Have There Been No Great Women Artists?*, *Old Mistresses* and *Framing Feminism,* which attempted to consider the lack of writing on female artists. These seminal feminist texts provided a necessary examination of why women had been marginalized in the annals of art history. Linda Nochlin's seminal article "Why Have There Been No Great Women Artists" first appeared in the UK in *Studio Magazine* in 1971. In this pioneering work Nochlin exposed the intellectual distortion of perceiving any history from solely a white male point of view. Arguing that one could substitute any discipline (composer, scientist, philosopher) into the question "Why have there been no great women artists?," Nochlin pointed out the ineffectiveness of answering this question through either excavating women artists in history, or in suggesting an aesthetic particular to women. Instead, she asserted that it was institutionally impossible for women to achieve success at the level of men in any discipline because of integral elements of social structures, including academies, systems of patronage and class structures.

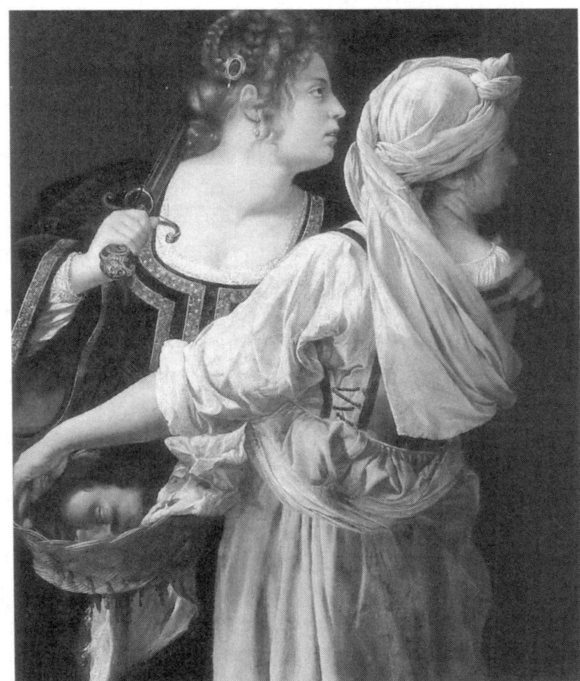

Figure I.1
Artemisia Gentileschi,
*Judith and her
Maidservant with the
Head of Holofernes,*
oil on canvas, *ca*
16251612–13.

Parker and Pollock, in *Old Mistresses,* adopted a similar stance to Nochlin. In this book they acknowledged artists such as Artemisia Gentileschi, Judith Leyster, Angelika Kauffman, Louise Élisabeth Vigée Le Brun and Gwen John; instead of attempting to provide a history of women's exclusion from art history, they evaluated the ideological basis of the writing and teaching of art history. Writing in response to a wave of feminist writers such as Betty Friedan, Kate Millett, Juliet Mitchell and Sheila Rowbotham, Nochlin's article and Parker and Pollock's book made significant art historical contributions, which were followed shortly thereafter in film studies by Laura Mulvey's groundbreaking article "Visual Pleasure and Narrative Cinema" in 1973.

An important early observation made by Nochlin, Parker and Pollock is that there is no essential feminist aesthetic. As Nochlin says there is no "distinctive and recognizable feminist style, different both in its formal and its expressive qualities and based on the special character of women's situation and experience". Parker and Pollock trace how the notion of a women's art as biologically determined and quintessentially "feminine, graceful, delicate and decorative" emerged within a nineteenth century bourgeois ideology. They quote a passage from a Victorian critic to emphasize their point:

> Let women occupy themselves with those types of art they have always preferred, such as pastels, portraits or miniatures. Or the painting of flowers, those prodigies of grace and freshness which alone can compete with the grace and freshness of women themselves.

This book continues in the vein of Parker and Pollock, presenting feminist work from the 1970s in London, and recognizing the differences in styles, production and reception of such work. In my research I examine how economic and social conditions in London during the 1970s affected the choice of themes in feminist art. If there is no essentially female aesthetic, then what of the possibility of a feminist aesthetic? I will argue that although much of feminist work contains similar themes—domesticity, the body and its traces, sexuality—feminist art has no one stylistic representation. I discuss works like Mary Kelly's *Post-Partum Document* and Judy Clark's *Menstruation*, which rely on a conceptual paradigm for their formal structures, alongside works such as Carolee Schneemann's *Up To and Including Her Limits*, a performance-based piece that comprises random marking and chance elements. I argue that all of these pieces might be described as feminist works of art, as they were influenced by sociological and psychoanalytic theory and revolved around the female body and experience, yet they nevertheless each have a unique aesthetic and could not be easily grouped according to formal style.

Feminist art historical writing in the 1970s was tied to the political aim of understanding the exclusion of women from the field of art production, and therefore, largely from art history. The earliest writing on feminist art history came from writers who were involved with political activism as well as academic research. There was evident in such early work an ambition to rectify the absence of women from art historical discussion. Writers such as Nochlin, Pollock and Parker unabashedly took on large sweeps of history that included a variety of media and nationalities. "Women" was not yet a contested category, as it would become in later feminist enquiry. In the 1980s and of course today, art historians are increasingly detailed and refined in their choice of topic, typically deciding on a specific period of time, geographical location or a specific theme in the work. And with the discussions surrounding other forms of difference since the 1980s, "women" today is not seen as a homogeneous identity. It is here that the work of women from non-Western viewpoints and alternative sexuality becomes prescient for contemporary debates. In this genre of writing, activism once again plays a central role.

In the same way that there is no one female or feminist aesthetic, it is impossible to have a universal point of view. Like Nochlin and her British colleagues, I write from the point of view of a white middle-class woman, but have benefited from the significant contributions to the field from lesbian and non-European-centric feminists: bell hooks, Harmony Hammond, Adrian Piper, Sonia Boyce, Renee Cox, Adrienne Rich, Tinh T. Minh-ha, Coco Fusco and Laura Cottingham are writers whose works in the last two decades have been crucial in opening up the discussion of feminist art to discussions of difference of race, class, age and sexuality. These artists and writers encourage readers and viewers to embrace difference, something often misinterpreted as "otherness." (Post-feminist critiques of sexual difference in part help to provide a basis for the on-going study of cultural identity politics.) Amelia Jones recently discussed the importance of history's accommodating artists whose work combines a feminist critique with a critique of racial and ethnic identity, as well as sexual orientation. Lesbian studies, too, have adopted a similar stance. As mentioned earlier, my work does not attempt to encompass all feminist artists of the 1970s, but represents a selection of work that is specific to particular themes. While a history of "other" feminist artists in Britain—lesbian and non-Western artists, such as Sonia Boyce—may be essential, it is something that I have not specifically undertaken here.

My work is more consciously aligned with Parker and Pollock's later effort, *Framing Feminism: Art and the Women's Movement 1970-1985* and Lynda Nead's *The Female Nude: Art, Obscenity and Sexuality,* in its presentation of a wide range of original material rather than a single theoretical argument. The latter's chapter on "Breaking the Boundaries" provided an important reference point for my work. Nead's discussion of the boundaries of the body, and in turn, of good taste, helped me to understand what was at stake for feminist artists in representing female sexual organs. As she observed, certain feminist work "challenged the aestheticization and sanitation of the female body within patriarchal culture and broke open the boundaries of this regime of representation to reveal woman's body as matter and process as opposed to form and stasis." This led to my interest in the work of Mary Kelly and others such as the American artist Judy Chicago, and sparked my interest in knowing more about this period in British art history. Parker and Pollock's book was a less theoretical and more structural reference; it included a framework and a time-line for the events, exhibitions and performances that took place in Britain in the 1970s and early 1980s, as well as essays. These afford an important archive of the period, and many feminist works would be forgotten without this book.

While the initial ambition was to create a historical record of this period in Britain, I quickly learned that I needed to narrow my approach to London, and have refined it even further to artists who use the body and its traces, performance, and who work in alternative sites. There are two reasons for this selection: first, regarding location, given the sheer numbers of activities it hosted in the 1970s, London emerged as an important center for feminist art and indeed an incubator for such work. The second decision, to focus on performance-based practice and alternative sites, seemed important as these practices encompassed works that were ephemeral and thus, less well-known. Painters and sculptors have an advantage as their works endure longer than a performance or site-specific installation.

I also realized that younger, internationally recognized artists like Tracey Emin, Sarah Lucas, Andrea Bowers, Rachel Lachowicz, Ellen Cantor, EV Day, Agathe Snow, Elke Krystufek and Patty Chang were now replicating this type of sexually explicit and gender-specific work around the world in art fairs and exhibitions, though the connections were in most cases not conscious or acknowledged. One of the aims of this book is to understand why there are similarities between contemporary practice and feminist art and to reconnect current art practice with earlier works.

WOMEN'S WORK: THE NEW FEMINIST ART HISTORY

The second starting point for the book came from a younger generation of writers, largely based in America. Two books published by Amelia Jones in the 1990s were important benchmarks for me. The first was an exhibition catalogue with essays that re-examined Judy Chicago's *The Dinner Party* from the contemporary perspective of mid-1990s America.[1] This presented the work of fifty artists from the middle of the 1970s who were working in Chicago's circle and that of her colleague Miriam

Schapiro. This seemed a model for the type of contextual project that I had in mind for 1970s Britain. While Pollock and Parker, as well as other historians such as Lisa Tickner, had recorded events for posterity, they, like Chicago, Kelly and Schapiro, were involved in the women's liberation movement. Thus, while to some extent this is an exercise in recovery, it also represents a shift. While I am interested in the history of the women's movement, I am of a different generation who looks in retrospect at these activities.

The terminology of feminist debate has shifted since its earliest incarnations. Gradually, as feminist studies has begun to overlap with studies of queer culture and questions of sexuality and class, it has increasingly become part of the larger category of gender studies rather than of women's studies. Jane Rendell writes about the implications of feminist work on studies of representation and gender in other fields like psychoanalysis, philosophy, cultural studies, film theory, and most importantly for my work, art history.[2] She notes that the shift in gender studies corresponds with a shift in interest from production to representation; this shift represents a move away from a representation of politics towards a politics of representation. While she is an architectural theorist, Rendell's point is well placed for any discipline concerned with feminism.

The aim of this piece of work, like that of Jones's, is to present historical activity in a way that is relevant to art practice today. I am not politically aligned to any strand within the women's movement: instead, this is written from the point of view of a cultural historian of a specific period. Nochlin has recently written:

> Perhaps 70s feminism, powerful and necessary though it was, is now outmoded; feminism has transformed and is itself transformed in contemporary practice. Feminist politics today is far more multivalent and self-aware; the battle lines are less clearly drawn. The binaries—oppressor/victim, good woman/bad man, pure/impure, beautiful/ugly, active/passive—are not the point of feminist art anymore. ... Feminism is not only overtly present but has over the past thirty years irrevocably changed the way we think about art, the body, the relationship between the viewer and the artwork, and the standing of the various media.[3]

Nochlin's contemporary writing resonates with my research and thinking. Her views on the move away from binaries in feminism are particularly important for my work, which attempts to understand the intersections between psychoanalytic, body-oriented and conceptual practices.

Jones's ambition, in *Sexual Politics*, was to look at work that had been "legislated out of dominant narratives of feminist art history,"[4] specifically in the context of feminist art in California. She also acknowledged important factors that were overlooked in the production of feminist art—for example, the collaboration that was necessary to create *The Dinner Party*—although the authorship is often attributed to only Judy Chicago. In much the same way, I have attempted to reconstruct lost works from the 1970s in London, to understand the trajectory of feminist art in the UK. In the same way that Jones excavated West Coast American practice, I have uncovered London-based events that were long forgotten, including the important project *A Woman's Place,* which took the West Coast American example of *Womanhouse* as its model.

Juli Carson's work has also been influential for my research. Carson has re-examined works from the 1970s and 1980s such as Mary Kelly's *Post-Partum Document* and Richard Serra's *Tilted Arc*.[5] Carson adopts a psychoanalytic approach, and writes from the perspective of a lesbian author. While my method and orientation may differ from Carson's, her commitment to understanding recent art practice and her relational approach to art writing was an important model for my work.

METHODOLOGY

This book was developed largely from primary research. Much of the research involved exploring personal archives and looking at work that had been stored in drawers for years. Women artists—as well as curators, writers, gallerists and practitioners—hold a vast resource of information and material that has not previously been published as a cohesive account of the period. The vast array of interviews conducted in London during the first few years of the millennium began as an effort to speak to a few key figures of the period in order to provide background information and as a way of understanding missing links in the available secondary sources. There were some surprises: my original choice for an inaugural interview declined on the basis that she did not want to be associated with feminism because that meant "career death". The first person that agreed to be interviewed was Guy Brett. Brett then urged me to speak to artists including Rose English, Rose Finn-Kelcey and Silvia Ziranek as key players in the 1970s London performance scene. And thus a growing network began.

Charles Harrison, from Art & Language, was an obvious starting point as Mary Kelly was interested in the work of Art & Language, specifically its conceptual approach. During this discussion, Harrison stated that Art & Language (in its English constituency) had no interest in her work or feminism in general. This type of discovery was vital to the research, and refined the direction of enquiry. Though such statements should not always be treated as the gospel truth, they are crucial to understanding the intellectual cross-currents of the period, and the tendency (of academics as well as artists) at times to "rewrite" history.

After the first round of interviews, I realized that I was building my own, retrospective archive of this period. It did not begin as an archive of any specific genre, for example, of women artists who paint or who make textile work. It is rather a network that grew organically out of connections that were made as I spoke to people. Each interview was built on the one before it, and by the end of the process, it had become a valuable resource in itself, which I hopefully have translated into a more easily digestible book form.

The interviews also reflect William Furlong's idea of "conversation as a creative process."[6] Furlong has spent a career conversing with artists in order to record oral history in the form of interviews. In large part each conversation was unique. It might have been useful to ask the same questions of each practitioner; however, the approach that I took allowed for each interview stand on its own and to be as free-flowing as possible. They evolved over time, which paralleled an evolution in approach. As I began to understand the significance of the discussions, the questions became more focused.

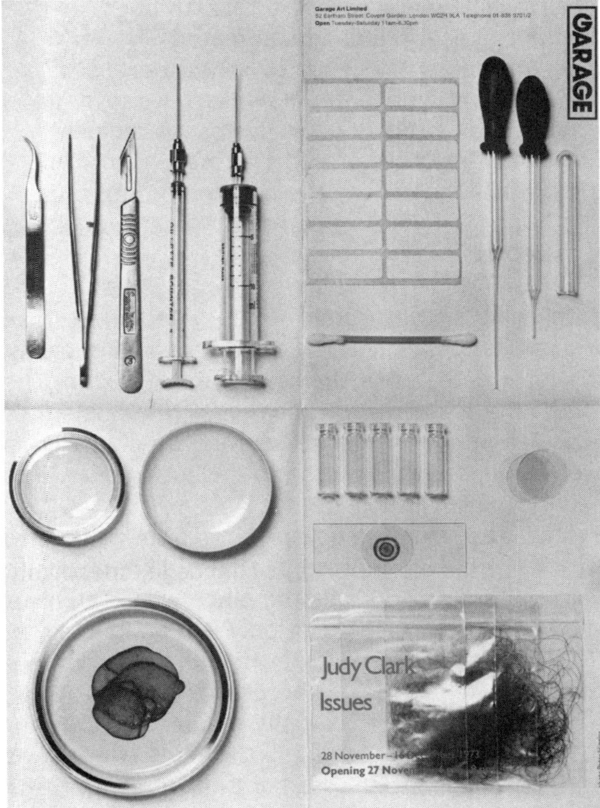

Figure I.2
Garage poster for Judy Clark's *Issues* show, 1973. Courtesy Anthony Stokes.

While I was flexible in my approach, my interviews were not random; for each one, there were certain key questions, which were usually concerned with gaps in archives and facts that were not in the available literature. Yet sometimes it was the digressions of the interviewees that contained the more surprising and valuable nuggets of information. One example was when I learned that there had been a reinterpretation of *Womanhouse* in London. This was not widely known or published, and therefore, the oral history was central to the discovery.

The notion of archive suggests an obvious reference to theorists such as Michel Foucault and Jacques Derrida, and as Griselda Pollock states, indicates the necessity for self-consciousness in all historical study. She writes:

> "Archive" insists on the social determination of that which we study, resisting ideological notions of the self-evidence of the historical document, or the work of art as the obvious, given self-present object of study. It also represents a break with the natural forms of art-historical writing, the monograph and the catalogue, which uncritically elevate the Author through the focus on the artist as auto-genetic individual creator. The term archive embeds us in the necessary sense of self-critical, self-reflective scrutiny as we engage with materials which have several pasts: a historical moment of production, a historical moment of consumption, a historical moment of entry into art-historical discourse, into the museum, the canon, the classroom, into our cultural "patrimonies," into a myriad of discursive frameworks, into our formations as subjects.[7]

As Pollock views it, engaging with an archive has several historical moments: that of the original work as well as the excavation and re-examination of that work at a later date. Much the same can be said for the interviews. For within each there are several moments: the moment of the interview, the historical moment of the actions that are discussed in each conversation, as well as hopefully, this archive's eventual entry into the discourse of visual culture in 1970s London.

This archive of interviews also enacts a spatial shift from private to public, as the act of historical recovery represents the shift from private knowledge to public information. Derrida calls the place where archives exist the "domiciliation", or "house arrest".[8] Not only is it an ideological shift, in the sense that this information is now available; it is additionally a physical shift, from the memories of the practitioners, to this, the book in which this information will eventually reside. The psychological shift from public to private is compelling in this body of work, as many of the artists interviewed had not discussed or thought about these early works for many years. This has had the effect, in some cases, of providing impetus for the artists to make monographs and to re-create past work. Also, the growth of online resources has made the digital archive an increasingly popular option for practitioners of this generation. For example, Helen Chadwick's notebooks, which are now digitized and available through the Henry Moore Institute in Leeds.

As one reads through the interviews inaccuracies and personal agendas come to light. In some cases relationships with the artists that were built over time allowed for further access and information. As far as possible, I attempted to create a fair and unbiased account; however, any work has its own implicit biases and prejudices.[9] It is important to remember that, as Joan W. Scott writes, the production of knowledge is not about the origin of the historian's explanation, but rather about what we want to explain.[10] For choosing what one wants to categorize in history is inevitably political. That I chose to document feminist artists is a result of my personal circumstances: of growing up in a male-dominated family, of my mother's desire to go to university, which was cut short by her marriage and birth of her first son, of my desire for female role models. While the history may be in places partial and contain absences or holes, it reflects the contradictions, discrepancies and half-forgotten stories that were related to me in interviews and found in my research.

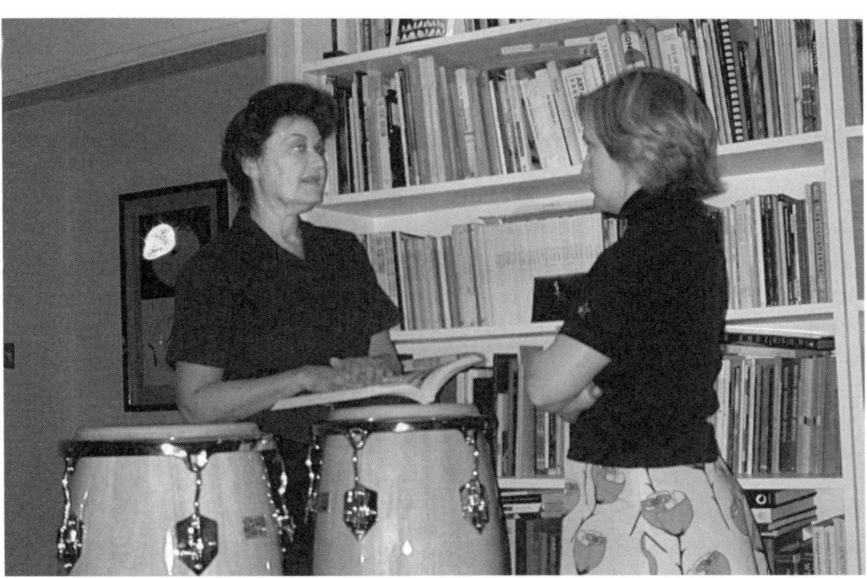

Figure I.3
The author in conversation with Mary Kelly, Los Angeles, 2001.
Photograph: Nigel Talamo.

PART II: THEMES AND TERMS

WOMEN'S WORK:
THE DEFIANT BODY, OR THE PERSONAL IS POLITICAL

In the post-war period, the hegemony of the art object was breaking down. The white, heterosexual paradigm of the artist was also disintegrating.[11] The political climate of the 1960s, with its anti-war protests, demonstrations and student uprisings,[12] gave rise to new forms of art practice. By the end of the decade minimalism, conceptual art, pop and fluxus, as well as body-oriented practices, became predominant. Anti-Vietnam politics led to agitprop agendas and the rise of politically motivated art. The body, which played an active and performative role in the protests, sit-ins and demonstrations, also became a central issue for much of this new art. For feminist artists the body was more than an ideological issue; it also became an important site for making and exhibiting work. In America Hannah Wilke, Carolee Schneemann, Adrian Piper and Ana Mendiata, and later Karen Finley, Cindy Sherman and Renee Cox used their bodies as both material and site.[13] This book illustrates how in the UK Bobby Baker, Rose Finn-Kelcey, Catherine Elwes, Anne Bean, Silvia Ziranek, Hannah O'Shea, Rose English and Sally Potter concurrently used similar tactics.

A significant debate emerged around the use of the artist's body in the work. Some women artists like Mary Kelly[14] and Susan Hiller[15] avoided depicting their own bodies in work that adopted, as they intended, a conceptual strategy. For others, however, the body was a liberating tool, which could be used to make a powerful statement on gender and sexuality. For those that opted to use the body in their work, a further deliberation was whether to be clothed or naked. Take for example, Carolee Schneemann, who found the naked female body empowering. She said "They were resentful. Friends of mine said every time they went to an event, or a party or something ... they lived in dread." They said "Here comes Carolee. She's going to take off all her clothes and distract everybody."[16] Rose Finn-Kelcey, however, would avoid getting undressed in performances. She said, "And I didn't take my clothes off in public as a performance artist. ... It was always this question of why haven't you taken your clothes off? I mean no one actually said that to me, but you haven't been brave enough if you haven't taken your clothes off in public, which now to me seems amazing."[17]

There were also many male artists using their body in work—including Dan Graham, Bruce Nauman and Paul McCarthy in the United States and Stuart Brisley, Richard Long and John Latham in Britain—but for female artists, the issue had an added layer of meaning. The female body had iconic status as muse and model; hundreds of years of art history attested to the depiction, idealization and fetishization of the female form. For feminist artists, the body then became a contested site, a problematic locus for work. Was the female body a form to be liberated from its position as submissive model? Or was this tipping dangerously close to self-exploitation? Amelia Jones has described the latter position:

> The feminist articulation of this turn away from the corporeal was particularly vehement about the absolute need to remove the *female* body from representation; *any* presentation or representation of the female body was seen as *necessarily* participating in the phallocentric dynamic of fetishism, whereby the female body can only be seen ... as "lacking" in relation to the mythical plenitude represented by the phallus.[18]

This feminist stance resists positioning the female body as the subject of the male gaze regardless of context or intent. Jones rightly expresses discomfort with such blanket condemnation as it presumes all viewers will have just one response. How can one approach to feminism be right? This type of view has led to certain types of feminist art being undervalued, again replicating the canonical approach of so-called white western art history. I aim to redress this here by including works that encompass a wide variety of approaches.

The first feminist studies that focused on the recovery of women's history necessarily focused on the body. Sheila Rowbotham's *Hidden from History* concentrated on the conditions of women's labor in society, both as procreator and as sole bearer of domestic duties. Betty Friedan continued this discussion of "the problem with no name" in her seminal book *The Feminine Mystique*, although her primary interest was in socialization.[19] Germaine Greer's *The Female Eunuch* related the history of women as sexual objects for use by other sexual beings, with her own sexuality misrepresented as passivity. Greer wrote of the obliteration of the vagina from images of femininity, and exposed the praising of castrate characteristics of women: timidity, plumpness, languor, and delicacy.[20] Jane Rendell sums up this generation's concerns about women, their bodies and their rights, when she writes, "Second-wave feminism recognized that, of equal significance to political and institutional forms of discrimination is discrimination experienced on a personal level—for example within the home—leading to the phrase 'The personal is political'."[21] This theme became a slogan for the women's movement, often seen on banners and badges. This slogan gained huge popularity in the mainstream culture, but it was underpinned by serious historical research and political ideology. If one thinks of debates over legalized birth control and abortion that took place in this period, one recognizes that "the personal is political" was central to feminist activism, and that the body is central to these issues.[22]

At the time when Greer, Rowbotham and other feminists were reconsidering the female body and its political, social and economic implications, artists were increasingly incorporating the body into practice. From action paintings to happenings and performances, the body played a new central role in contemporary art. And for feminists, the body as a shifting and unstable site offered further potential. If one believes that "the personal is political" then using one's body in an art piece is the ultimate political act. However, the body is an unstable medium in that one cannot control how it is perceived. For how can an artist guarantee her continued self-ownership amid the conditions of exposure to which the body is subject? What if viewers find her nudity titillating? Does the use of the nude body distract from a larger main point? In these cases, is the subversive element lost? This leads to the most difficult question of all: how does one display the body without being reduced to it? Most of the artists in this book engage their bodies in the work in some form though again their tactics vary greatly. In Chapter One, a discussion of artists Mary Kelly, Carolee Schneemann and Judy Clark will further develop this discussion.

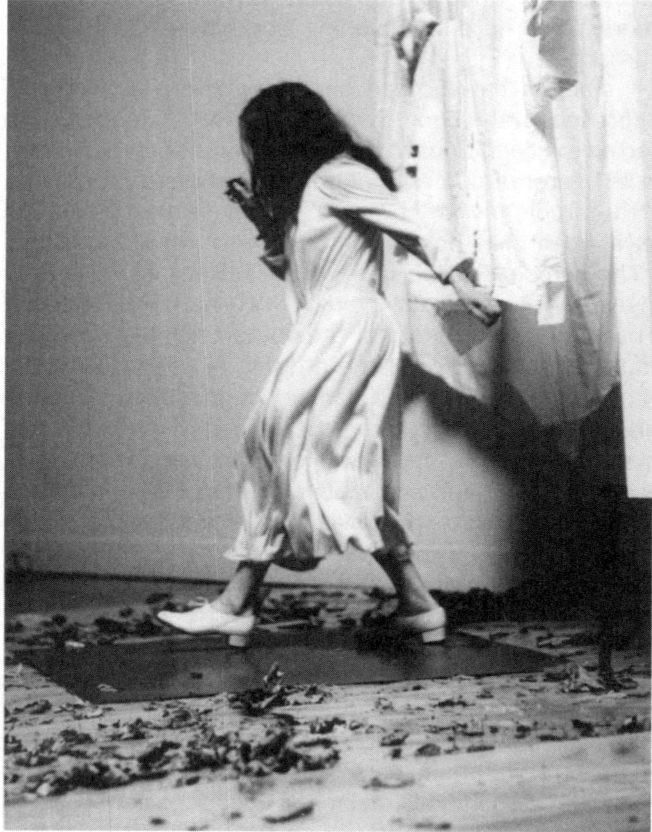

Figure I.4
Hannah O'Shea
Hannah's at Home, 1985.
Courtesy of the artist.

PERFORMANCE ART AND PERFORMATIVITY

Following from discussions around the body, the notion of performative practice and performance art became an integral element of alternative practice in 1970s Britain. Performance art has its origins in Dada and futurist events in the early twentieth century. In the 1960s, performance art became a viable alternative to a practice centered on the trajectory from studio production to gallery exhibition. Some historians see the burgeoning of body-oriented practices as beginning with Jackson Pollock's bodily engagement with his canvases. Performance became a way for artists to use their bodies as material and site. It most often included an artist and an audience, and at times included other performers.[23]

The relationship between performance and performativity, is not straightforward. Performance is by far the simpler term to define: an action that is done for a specific reason. This action can vary greatly from the carrying out of a duty to a ticketed theatrical performance. Performance art is perhaps neither and both of these. Many performances were based around the carrying out of a task or set of instructions set by the artist. I opt to use the term "performance" in this work as it remains the least problematic term and is most appropriate to the work discussed here.

Performativity as a theoretical term is a contemporary concept, begun by linguistic philosopher J.L. Austin and further explicated by others.[24] Performativity is also used as an art historical term that grew out of postmodern, art historical and performance studies. It is a contentious term,[25] one defined differently by various writers. For example, Michael Fried, in his essay, "Art and Objecthood" discussed the theatricality of postmodern art including pop and minimalism.[26] Fried asserted that the new "literalist" art forms (minimalism) required a more dynamic engagement from the viewer; instead of the passive viewing of paintings and objects, the new art forms demanded more commitment from the viewer. In some cases the viewer would need to physically move around or even over the objects, which were often not located on the walls; generally one could rely less on the formula of standing in front of a painting or work of art. Here performativity is enacted by the audience rather than the artist. For Amelia Jones a shift in art process towards the performative happens even earlier. She writes about the "Pollockian performative," that is, the images of Pollock creating his art by dripping, slashing and daubing, as producing a new engagement with the subject. This new subject is "dispersed, dislocated, and open to spectatorial engagement."[27] While Pollock was certainly not engaging in performance art, Jones sees his action painting as a bridge leading to body-oriented practice: Pollock is aligned with modernist conceptions of the artist as heroic individual, yet his dripping, squeezing, daubing actions open up the disruption of painting through performance.[28]

How do both of these terms relate to gender identity generally and to feminist art specifically? Feminist performance art brought to the forefront the idea that being a woman is always a performed role and seemed in many ways to anticipate Judith Butler's argument that gender itself is a role that is performed, rather than biologically determined. Butler poses the question, "Does being female constitute a 'natural fact' or a cultural performance, or is it 'naturalness' constituted through discursively constrained performative acts that produce the body through and within the categories of sex?"[29] For Butler, gender is not a static identity, given at birth, but constituted over time. Performativity, then, is a term that explains how one becomes one's gender.

Butler's "Performative Acts and Gender Constitution" most successfully synthesizes the terms performance and performativity. In this work she cites Simone de Beauvoir ("one is not born, but rather, *becomes* a woman") and Merleau-Ponty ("the body is not only a historical idea but a set of possibilities to be continually realized") to argue for the distinction between sex and gender.[30] Her point is that the acts by which gender is constituted are similar to performative acts in theatrical contexts. Butler writes:

> to be a woman is to have *become* a woman, to compel the body to conform to an historical idea of "woman", to induce the body to become a cultural sign, to materialize oneself in obedience to an historically delimited possibility, and to do this as a sustained and repeated corporeal project.[31]

If gender itself is a construction, as Butler sees it, what does that mean for a performance artist? As seen above, philosophers, art historians and theater historians each find their own meaning for the performative. If women have always been performing their gender, then how does a life model differ from an active performer? For that matter, how does any artist's performance differ from an ordinary performance? Perhaps performance art is at once overtly naive (in that it makes no attempt to disguise the performance) and more reflexively knowing. Performance art might be said to perform its own act of performance.

While the artists discussed in Chapter Three perform in some way in their art practice, it is notable that the discussion of performativity, like the development of gender studies, is a recent phenomenon; although it is useful for understanding the work that was produced, any such theorization would not have directly influenced the artists at the time of production. It represents more than a shift in terminology, however, as it also illustrates a shift in how we understand these earlier works of art today. This is an important point: despite many similarities between art of the 1970s and current work, we should acknowledge the difference between conditions and concerns of the former at the time of its production and current preoccupations. For example, Judy Clark's work might be an important predecessor to an artist such as Tracey Emin, but perhaps not for the same reasons as it might have been to her colleagues in the 1970s. The same point must be made about the reception and understanding of these works.

THE SPACE OF FEMINIST ART: DESTABILIZING THE SITE

Alternative practices in the 1970s, and feminist art especially, are significant for their shift away from a gallery-based exhibition space. This is no doubt related to the trend toward using one's body in performance art, which moved art out of the predictable confines of the gallery, both exposing the work and forcing a reflexive framing of it in the new space it occupies. At the time artists—performance and otherwise—chose to site their work in non-gallery spaces such as in nature (Richard Long, Ana Mendiata, Michael Heizer, Robert Smithson, Walter De Maria),[32] magazines or print (Dan Graham, Robert Smithson)[33] or domestic settings (Kate Walker, Bobby Baker, Judy Chicago, Miriam Schapiro).[34] In New York a network of alternative structures, spaces and artists groups (such as Black Emergency Cultural Coalition, Art Workers' Coalition, Apple, Women Artists in Revolution, etc.) developed in the 1970s.[35]

In London an abundance of alternative spaces for art and performance also flourished. For example, David Medalla's Artists for Democracy held monthly events and spaces such as Acme and Air provided important sites for new work. In the 1980s Brian O'Doherty wrote of the sanctity of the white cube.[36] This essay posed legitimate questions around art spaces that were raised in the 1970s. The organizations and alternative spaces of the 1970s, although at times still containing white spaces, defied the notion of elitist culture and took art to new and increasingly radical venues. This was the era of consciousness-raising groups of all sorts: from women's and men's groups to history and family groups. These in themselves should be seen as embodying an important spatial shift. People were re-organizing themselves through their own initiatives, often taking local action to discuss international politics and events. The pages of journals such as *Red Rag*, *Shrew*, *WIRES* and *FAN* were additional sites for activism. Through these publications one could learn about women's issues, world politics, alternative art projects and public demonstrations and events. They became a vehicle for connecting like-minded people.

For feminist art practice, concerned with an ideology and often resistant to traditional media, alternative spaces and sites for showing work were absolutely essential. In Los Angeles Miriam Schapiro and Judy Chicago's groundbreaking Feminist Art Program was consolidated through the *Womanhouse* project. This was followed in London by *A Woman's Place* by Kate Walker (and others) in Radnor Terrace. In New York artists such as Ana Mendiata and Adrian Piper were using domestic settings and taking to the streets with their work. For the artists discussed in this book, three types of spaces were essential: alternative art spaces, alternative public sites and their own domestic settings.

Before the women's movement, galleries and museums were for the most part male-dominated institutions, run by men, showing the work of men.[37] The development of a feminist art practice was necessarily linked to the questioning of such "patriarchal" space and of the ideology of a separate sphere which aligned men with the public sphere (production) and women with the private (reproduction).[38] As Doreen Massey, a social geographer, writes:

> space and place, spaces and places, and our senses of them (and such related things as our degrees of mobility) are gendered through and through. Moreover they are gendered in a myriad different ways, which vary between cultures and over time. And this gendering of space and place both reflects *and has effects back on* the ways in which gender is constructed and understood in the societies in which we live.[39]

The only female presence within the public space of the museum was the female model, often nude. Feminist artists destabilized the patriarchal space of museums and galleries by inserting themselves—their bodies and their work—into those spaces. I will show how alternative spatial structures, including galleries and collectives, also provided an important forum for feminist artists. This move away from the gallery also had an unfortunate underside: in moving art away from these patriarchal institutions, these artists also moved away from visibility, remuneration, documentation and acclaim.

PART III: FRAMEWORK

This book is a starting point. It presents a cross-section of feminist activities in the 1970s through the themes of documentation, the body and space. This introductory chapter has established the main themes and their context within feminist art history: documentation and trace, the body and performance, notions of subjectivity, the personal versus the political, spatial theories of feminism and the idea of a feminine aesthetic. It positions feminist practice as a complex and disparate entity, one that overlaps several art historical groupings and periods, and one that has evolved since its initial activities.

Chapter One begins by focusing on Mary Kelly, an American artist who lived in London during the 1970s and 1980s, and whose work is most often cited in critical treatises on feminist art. Her exhibition *Post-Partum Document* at the ICA in 1976 will be discussed, as well as the artwork of the same title. This series-based work is an ideal place to begin because through the first four sections of this project, one is able to identify the central influences on and preoccupations of the women's movement in London, including psychoanalytic inquiry, Marxist and socialist politics, film theory, the role of documentation, the question of patriarchy and the role of the female body and sexuality in art practice. The work of Judy Clark and Carolee Schneemann is also discussed in relation to Kelly's. In the debate around the body of the feminist artist, Kelly, Clark and Schneemann represent opposing viewpoints. Clark's work, like Kelly's is concerned with the trace of the body as the work of art, but differs from her American colleague in that it is based on her own body as well as that of others. And, where Kelly avoids any depiction of her body in the work, Schneemann celebrates the sexually explicit female form as a provocative affirmation of women's sexuality. This chapter also discusses the public reception of contemporary art practice and feminism at the time by considering the scandals caused by Kelly's *Post-Partum Document*, Clark's *Issues* exhibition in 1973, and the notorious *Prostitution* exhibition in 1976. The materials used in this chapter are supported by primary research, including lengthy interviews with key players in these exhibitions.

Chapter Two focuses on the body—oriented practices in women's art of 1970s Britain. Following on from the previous engagement with such topics, I illustrate examples of early body-oriented art—for instance, the Gutai group in Japan, as well as the European artist Yves Klein and American artist Bruce Nauman—in an attempt to explain how performance became a vehicle for artists in general at that time, and specifically for women artists. I will examine what this type of art entails, including the possibility of an unmediated effect on the viewer, the representation of the domestic and female aesthetics, the question of sexuality and the alternative sites of performance work. Again, my aim is not to create a complete history of women's feminist performance during the period, but rather to tease out some of its most powerful and important themes.

Any history of live work lacks adequate documentation, due to its ephemeral and fleeting nature. This chapter relies on primary material or material close in time to the primary events, especially performance notes and interviews with the artists who created the events; these interviews are integral to the research since little of the work was recorded, and much of it was not even scripted. Some performance art left traces that existed only in people's memories. As many artists noted during my discussions with them, the importance of the live event superseded any need to document, or so it seemed at the time.

However, the abiding argument of this book is that the period examined is characterized by extreme fluidity. While some artists ultimately did not want documentation and attempted to resist commodification, they still would like to be remembered and rewarded as artists. This places the work in an ambivalent position historically, for how can one resist the commercial art market yet ensure a place in the history of art of that period? For certainly a place in history is secured by being part of the public institutional system, which relies on the art market for guidance and for work.

Chapter Three looks at the alternative spatial structures for exhibiting feminist art in London at the time. While artists such as Mary Kelly and Cosey Fanni Tutti were able show work in major public galleries, most women artists were not so fortunate. One of the main concerns of feminist art in 1970s London was the problem of getting shown in mainstream spaces; thus, many artists like Bobby Baker, Anne Bean, Silvia Ziranek, Catherine Elwes and Annie Wright chose to circumvent this system by showing in alternative gallery spaces. There were also several commercial galleries who were sympathetic to avant-garde work. In addition, a discussion of Acme, Space, AIR and Garage will show how key non-profit galleries opened up an arena for women to show their work alongside avant-garde male artists, giving the work the context that it required. I will also discuss galleries that were specifically dedicated to the work of women artists, for example the Women's Free Arts Alliance in London.

In this chapter, I also present examples of activities and work that took place outside of any organized gallery, including the *Feministo* women's postal exchange, Bobby Baker's mobile home, *A Woman's Place*—the house that was converted into a one-off exhibition by feminist artists—and the use of public buildings and sites by the artist Rose Finn-Kelcey. These alternative spaces were physical embodiments of the political activism of the period. Other relevant sites, for example, radical journals from the period, will be discussed here.

Chapter Four returns to themes of the earlier chapters, but in relation to contemporary women's art. Here the discussion of the spatial politics of women artists showing outside of galleries is continued with reference to Tracey Emin and Sarah Lucas. Their *Shop* as well as Emin's self-dedicated museum is discussed in relation to projects from the 1970s such as *A Woman's Place* and the Women's Free Arts Alliance. These projects from both decades (1970s and 1990s) chart in multiple ways the spatial shifts that are articulated in and around women's art. In terms of architecture they represent a move from the gallery to the home, and in Lucas's and Emin's case, back to the gallery. Culturally, these contemporary projects represent a shift from marginal sites to the mainstream art world. Such shifts can be measured in distinctions between the early 1970s to the mid-1990s revealing the larger differences of the economics of the art world, as well as the smaller individual notions of how an individual can navigate her way through such a world. For example, an artist in the 1970s who elected to show in alternative sites would have great difficulty crossing over into the mainstream commercial market. Today, artists move more easily between the two spheres, as the market welcomes and incorporates new and emerging artists. This then leads one to consider the changing role of the artist, as well as the role of the spaces that they occupy. What was a radical statement in the 1970s is now wholly integrated into the commercial London art world.

On the theme of the body and performativity, Hayley Newman's performances will be examined in relation to those discussed in Chapter Three. Jemima Stehli's work is also discussed in regard to strategies of appropriation from male artists and the use of the artist's body. These artists are examined for their continuation of themes and tactics (performance, the body, ephemerality, documentation) found in 1970s feminist art. I hope to draw connections between the generations of artists, but, it is important to emphasize that these young artists would possibly not label themselves "feminists". For many of the generation of artists working in the 1990s and today suffer from a cultural amnesia regarding feminism, which has in turn become more implicit in art practice. Lisa Tickner, in 1995, wrote, "This is the first significant generation of artist-daughters of artist-mothers. Perhaps only in the last twenty years have women as artists grown up with both parents (and artist-siblings and a feminist audience)."[40] Her point cannot be overestimated. For the generation of artists discussed in Chapter Four, being female and being an artist was not as problematic as in earlier generations. Role models in the form of mothers, sisters, college tutors and colleagues are available, perhaps making the earlier emphasis on protest and enfranchisement less explicitly necessary.

Yet, while the influence of the 1970s feminist works on the later generations may not be visible or intentional, I will argue that it nonetheless should be acknowledged. As Laura Cottingham has written, "it seemed to me that the feminist art of the seventies was being lost and obscured— even as it was having a completely unacknowledged revival in the work of younger artists in the nineties".[41] Amelia Jones makes a similar point, noting that feminism's "insights have become so central to our understanding of the world that it informs most modes of visual culture analysis at this point, whether this dependence is acknowledged or not."[42] The great legacy of 1970s feminist art was to ensure the relevance of certain themes, for example, the domestic and the artist's body, to contemporary artists.

It is the intention of this book that the reader will have an insight into a selection of the major themes and practices of women's art in 1970s Britain. The research is less about influence and trajectory than an attempt to set a context for multiple activities within the visual arts related to the women's liberation movement and to come to terms with where that has brought us in regard to women's art today. It is my wish that this work will inspire other academics and curators to continue on from what is presented here with more exhibitions and books devoted to art of the 1970s and feminist art in particular. I would like to think that this work will itself become a trace and a memory of activities that should not be forgotten. Hopefully it will provide not only a memory, but a resource for more active and informal processes of remembering and recollection in the future.

Chapter 1

FEMINISM AND CONCEPTUAL PRACTICE

The day before I went to Paris this guy came in and asked me to tell him about the show, saying he was a journalist for the *Evening Standard*. I told him about it but said that there was no need [to review it] because Richard Cork was going to review it. What he'd done was to see Cork's copy in his tray on his desk, saw the word "nappies", and got straight around to the ICA. And that's how the shit hit the fan ... and I think it was the first time that questions were asked in the House of Commons about art.[1]

INTRODUCTION

Mary Kelly's *Post-Partum Document* occupies one of the defining moments of feminist art in London during the 1970s. She is the first artist mentioned in discussions on the women's movement and the visual arts in this city during that decade.[2] Part of the reason for her centrality is the amount of attention that the public, and especially the press, paid to her first large-scale exhibition at the Institute of Contemporary Arts in 1976. The debate that ensued brought unprecedented attention to her work, as well as to the larger world of contemporary art, the role of governmental funding, and its relationship to the viewing public.

Given its notoriety and importance, Kelly's work in the ICA exhibition *Post-Partum Document* is a logical starting point for an investigation into the London art world and the impact of feminism in this period. In particular, *Post-Partum Document* helps to identify the central debates and key concerns of 1970s feminist artists, such as the representation of the female body, the use of everyday materials, conceptual and documentary strategies, as well as an interest in feminist politics and psychoanalytic theory.

This book attempts to situate Kelly's work in the feminist debate around the body and to establish a wider context for Kelly's practice. Catherine Elwes remarks that it is important to "think about the wider implications of what Kelly represented and how she fitted into the general pattern of what was going on and what people were saying and feeling and thinking about the body. And how she was part of the division."[3] Elwes refers to the dichotomy between women who used their bodies in their practice and those who did not. Elwes, whose use of her own body will be discussed in a later chapter, reminds us that Kelly's resistance to depicting her body represents a decision taken by some feminists to use textual theory over visual form.[4] Other women artists such as Elwes, Carolee Schneemann (in some works) and Cosey Fanni Tutti adopted the opposite strategy.

Post-Partum Document embodies traces of the body—both of the mother and the child—in its material. It does not, however, explicitly depict the body of either the artist or her child. Again, one can consider this strategy in relation to Judy Clark's work of the same period, which also incorporated traces from the body, in this case that of the artist and her lover. Both Kelly and Clark used the serial form, reflecting the influence of both avant-garde film production and conceptual strategies. Finally, Kelly's and Clark's works will be considered alongside the work of Carolee Schneemann, whose provocative work during her stay in London made overt use of the nude female body. It is not my intention to provide a comprehensive re-reading of Kelly's work, but rather to examine it in the context of other practitioners in London during this period.

THE ART OF EVERYDAY LIVING:
DOMESTIC MATERIALS AND TRACES OF THE BODY

An important hurdle that feminist artists in London faced was the lack of spaces that were willing to host exhibitions of their work. The opportunity for a feminist artist[5] to show in the ICA, or any major art gallery, was not typical.[6] Kelly's exhibition came about through her affiliation with the ICA's Director of Exhibitions, Barry Barker, who she met through her partner Ray Barrie.[7] Barker was a member of the Artists Union.[8] Kelly remained active in the Union longer than Barker, but the latter kept abreast of the progress of her work. When he was made Director of Exhibitions[9] at the ICA he offered her a show, which was part of his curatorial policy of showing younger British artists in an international context. Kelly became one of a prestigious list of exhibitors that included Marcel Broodthaers, Lawrence Weiner, Dan Graham, Daniel Buren, Richard Hamilton and Dieter Roth, all members of an international avant-garde that Barker associated with, and was responsible for bringing to England at the time.

The ICA exhibition consisted of three parts of *Post-Partum Document*, a series-based work that documents Kelly's son's development from infancy into language.[10] This included the sections titled "Documentations I–III"

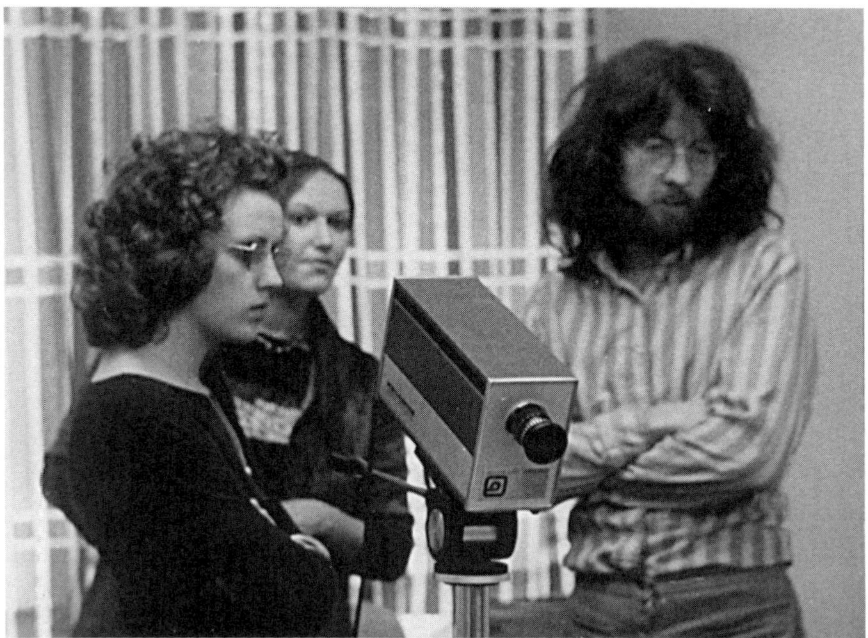

Figure 1.1
Mary Kelly (center) teaching at the London College of Furniture.
Courtesy Mary Kelly Archive.

and a copy of Kelly's introductory notes. Located in a simple grey binder these notes[11] offer the viewer assistance in reading the piece and understanding the various diagrams. The notes, like the larger work, are divided into sections, and hence only four parts existed at the time of her show at the ICA. (Kelly would in subsequent years create three additional Documentations, numbers IV–VI.) Each section comprises a series of units, hung in Perspex boxes in the gallery. In total there would be 135 individual units in *Post-Partum Document* by the end of its gestation.

While *Post-Partum Document* is not about the physical manifestation of the mother's form, parts of it clearly represent internal economies between mother and son, such as feeding, digestion and defecation. Writers such as Winnicott have remarked on the mother/baby unit; that is, during the breastfeeding months the traces of the baby's faeces are traces of the mother's milk, which is in turn a result of her diet. During the time of Kelly's preparation of "Documentation I" Kelly[12] was no longer breastfeeding, but the stains cannot be seen as simply an autonomous trace of the baby. They are also traces of the care provided by the mother, in this case, the artist.

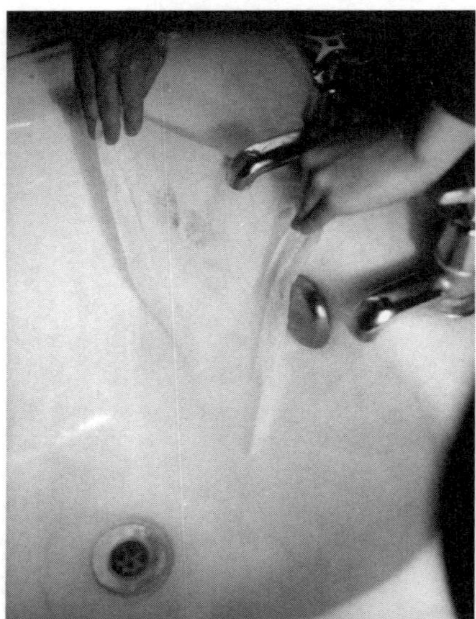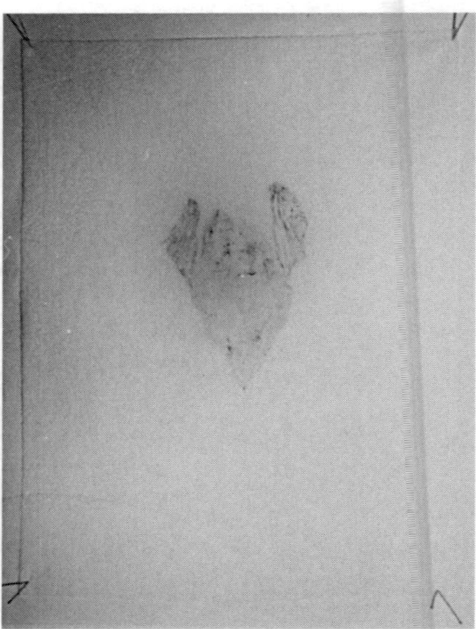

Figure 1.2
(left) Kelly washing nappy liner, 1973; (right) Stained nappyliner drying, 1973.
Courtesy Mary Kelly Archive.

"Documentation I: Analyzed fecal stains and feeding charts" is a section of *Post-Partum Document* that encompasses two elements important for this chapter: first, it is an example of Kelly's decision not to depict her own body; and second, it caused a furore when exhibited at the ICA. The section opens with a chart (as each section does) that documents the body weight of the child over the course of twelve months. The look is quasi-scientific or medical.[13] The scientific appearance of the graph, however, was not what the public[14] objected to when the work was exhibited. Instead it was the twenty-eight other units in this series.

The nappy section (as it has come to be known) of the first documentation contains one unit for every day of the baby's infancy in his sixth month, during February 1974. These were made from liners, which were washed by the artist, and left to dry, with stains intact. Kelly, who had recorded the child's food intake for three months, would decide to use the period of February because it illustrated the most drastic change. During this interval the artist, like most new mothers in England in the 1970s, diligently noted every morsel that the baby ate and drank and these feeding charts provide the basis for the text that is typed on the dried liners. In the lower half of each liner is the daily intake, including feeding times and type of food. A total at the bottom of each liner provides a breakdown of the amount of solids and liquids that the child has consumed.

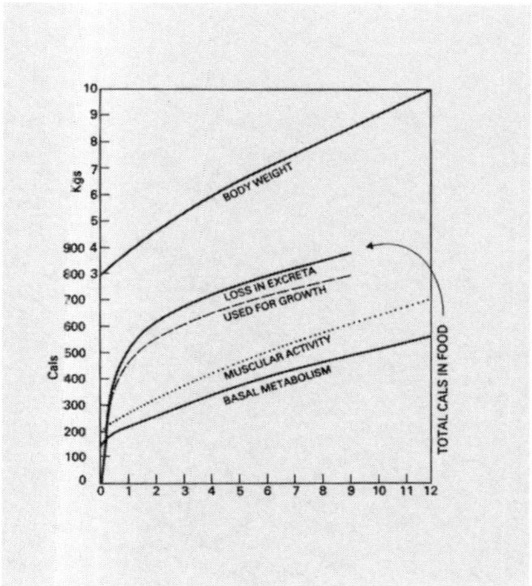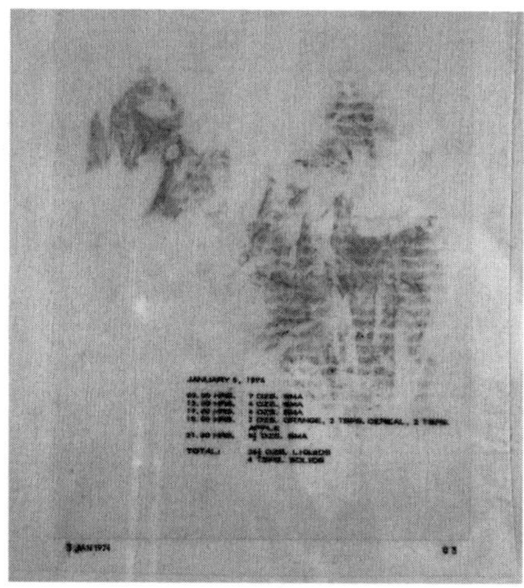

Figure 1.3
(left) diagram of infant metabolism 1974; (right) *Post-Partum Document:*
"Documentation I: Analyzed fecal stains and feeding charts", 1974.
Courtesy Mary Kelly Archive.

Additional text is located at the bottom of each nappy. In the left corner the date is repeated in abbreviated form. The lower-right corner contains a numeral, either 01, 02, 03, 04. These numbers correspond to the artist's classification of the child's faeces as constipated, normal, not homogenous, diarrhoeal.[15]

While the notion of classifying faeces may have seemed absurd to a contemporary and largely male art audience, for a new mother at that time this would have been familiar territory. Classic child-rearing books, such as the popular *Dr Spock's Baby and Child Care*, which Kelly owned and has a copy of in her archive, used faeces as an indicator of the child's normality and health. In Benjamin Spock's book science met popular culture as he proposed a hands-on approach to caring for the child. It was a huge success, with almost every mother owning a copy of his best-selling book.[16] While at a primary level the mother's insecurities about her child's health can be alleviated with this book, Spock's position was progressive. He opened up a generation of empowered parenting, by giving parents choices and encouraging them to use their own instincts in raising children.[17]

For Spock, and for the mother, the stains on the nappy liners are the visual and undisputable traces of the mother's care of the child. In Kelly's "Documentation I" she transforms the faeces stains into art. As the

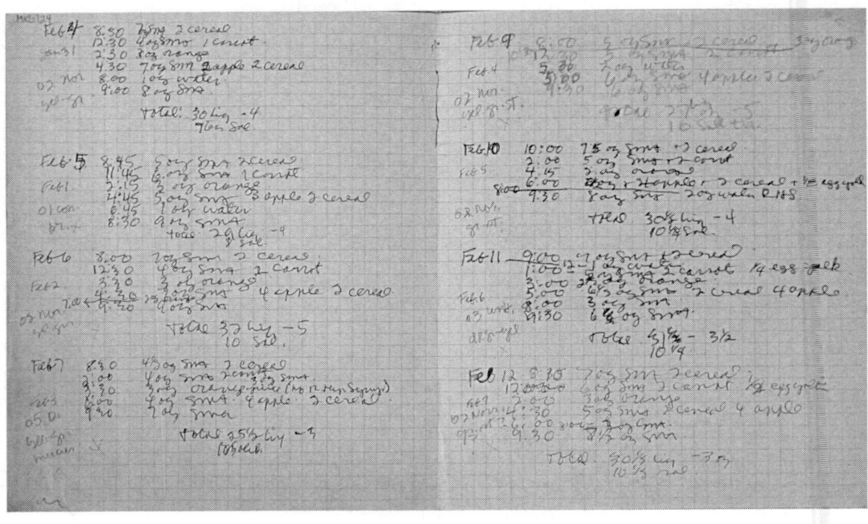

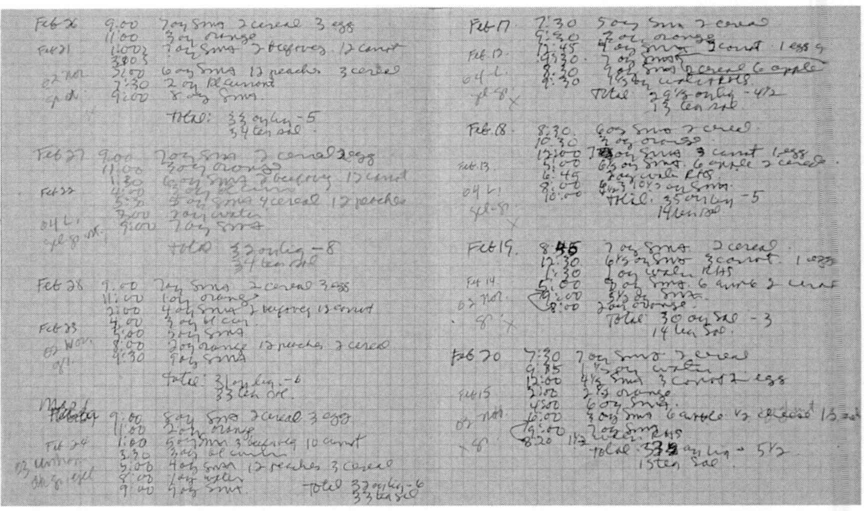

Figure 1.4
Original handwritten feeding charts, 1974.
Courtesy Mary Kelly Archive.

month of February progresses, and the child's intake increases, the stains increase in size. This correlates with the growth of the child. Kelly has mentioned that in creating *Post-Partum Document* she was illustrating the lopsided division of labor within the family structure, where typically it is the woman who is responsible for the care and upbringing of the child. Here she illustrates that labor by documenting the daily duties of the mother, without actually presenting an image of her body. The schedule of feedings, combined with the fecal results, is an index, and hence non-figurative depiction, of this effort.

Kelly spoke to Douglas Crimp about her reluctance to depict her own body in the work:

> Kelly: In the mid 1970s, a number of women used their own bodies or images to raise questions about gender, but it was not that effective, in part because this was what women in art were expected to do. Men were artists; women were performers. ... I wanted to question those essential places. ... For instance I decided to use the vests in the *Introduction* because I couldn't really "figure" the woman in a way that would get across what was going on, the level of fantasy that was involved, in an iconic way. I needed something that was more indexical, more like a trace.[18]

It was through Kelly's close friendship with Laura Mulvey and the understanding that they developed, through the study of psychoanalysis, of voyeurism and fetishism,[19] that the strategy of replacing her body with a trace in order to effect a critical distance emerged.[20]

DEPICTING EMOTIONAL AND PSYCHOLOGICAL STATES

"Documentation III" may also be considered here with regard to Kelly's strategy toward the body. This section contains one introductory diagram followed by ten units of sugar paper mounted on white card, and the concluding *Experimentum Mentis*. Each of the ten "visual" units represents a chart, which is roughly divided into three sections. Reading the work from left to right, the first box contains a condensed transcription of the child's conversation, recorded by the artist, and played back immediately following the session. The middle section contains a transcription of the mother's inner thoughts as related to the first section after Kelly played back the recording later in the same day. The final segment, on the far right side of each unit, represents a revision of the middle section, made one week later. This is handwritten as opposed to typed, as in the first two sections.

The artist selected recordings made at weekly intervals between 7 September and 26 November 1975, culminating when her child was adjusted to nursery school. This period of extra-familial socialization is a crucial time for child and mother, as it is here that the splitting of the dyadic mother-child unit is socially materialized.

The artist used her son's nursery drawings, which were daily presented to the parent as presents, as well as evidence of work done. This "visual diary" is then juxtaposed with Kelly's "narrative diary". Kelly places the diary entries over these drawings, utilizing a revised presentation of the traditional artificial perspective system devised by Leonardo da Vinci.

In this section the viewer begins to hear the mother's voice, although it is disembodied. While the mother's voice makes an appearance in "Documentation II", it is as a vehicle for the development of her son's language skills. In this case her voice is diaristic and one gets a better sense of her inner self. Without depicting herself in figurative terms, she paints a self-portrait of her psychological status as mother. She, as any other parent would, questions the child's behavior as well as her own. It is as if at the point of his separation from her, Kelly distinguishes herself from the child and in the process reveals a glimpse of her mental state. For example, on 20 September 1975 she writes:

> HE NOT VERY TIRED. (sic) I CAN'T DECIDE IF I SHOULD STOP HIS AFTERNOON NAPS.

> HIS PRONUNCIATION ISN'T VERY GOOD. I DON'T KNOW HOW PRECISE I SHOULD BE ABOUT IT.

As in the nappies section, Kelly's insecurities seem normal for a new mother, and one can imagine a chapter in Spock's book dedicated to such anxieties. What makes the piece extraordinary are the charts that are integrated into it. The narrative element of the work is far easier to digest than the diagrammatic infrastructure placed over it. There is tension between the scientific and rigorous versus the narrative and emotional. In the earlier sections the viewer analyzes the mother through her actions and obsessive processes. In this section the mother's voice enters, perhaps available now because the child, or phallus in psychoanalytic terms, has been separated from the mother, because of his entry into school. The viewer sees the mother struggling with her desire for her son's well being, as well as to keep making her work.

This effect is heightened in the third segment of each unit in "Documentation III", where the mother's voice becomes even more colloquial. In contrast to the R1 and R2 sections, which are typed and resemble institutional observation, the R3 section is handwritten. This gives the viewer the feeling of reading someone's journal, and reflects intimate emotions. For example, note the differing tones of the R2 and R3 sections from 4.10.75/11.10.75:

I WANT TO BE PATIENT BUT EVERY EVENT, ESPECIALLY BEDTIME,
IS A CONTEST, I FEEL TIRED (HE DOESN'T)

I was upset by his anxiety over going back to school (when he
finally got well) and I felt guilty about being away all this week
teaching. Wednesday he had a tantrum and freaked S.[21] out.

The combination of clinical diagrams and text is neither sentimental nor
scientific. Dan Graham writes on this aspect of Kelly's work: "what I liked
about *Post-Partum Document* was the 'do-it-yourself' science. My parents
were scientists, and I liked art being partly about education and partly
about increasing your own understanding of your subjective life situation.
Post-Partum Document was somewhere between two normally irreconcil-
able positions, it was totally scientific *and* subjective."[22] It demonstrates
the anxiety of the artist, as mother, who is aware of the theory, or how
she's supposed to act. This investigation of gendered domestic roles is a
theme that frequently was taken up by feminist artists, including Bobby
Baker, Kate Walker and Su Richardson, who will be discussed in the next
chapter.

In Kelly's work, the rearing of her child also becomes a real-time
performance documented through its traces, which are transformed
into art. But this task-oriented "performance,"[23] if one can term it as
such, happens outside of the scrutiny of an audience. It correlates with
the unseen aspect of women's work in the family. Women, like men,
have traditionally spent countless hours employed in the service of their
family; however, women's work typically takes place in the domestic
environment. In this section, Kelly brings into view the frequently invisible work of the mother with her presentation of methodical observation
and care. However, the visual embodiment of performer is lacking. While
the child, or arguably the mother, may be seen as the subject of the
work, neither appears in bodily form. It is instead the trace of the child—
in the form of faeces or sound—that becomes the sign for his presence.
This is in contrast to other feminist artists, for example Tina Keane, who
included her daughter into some performances

These traces—of faeces and of Kelly's speech (and handwriting)—are
important for their qualities as alternative media. At the time of the
production of *Post-Partum Document* in the 1970s, the mainstream art
world was still dominated by painting and sculpture, but conceptual
practice was beginning to occupy an important position as well. Curator
Clive Phillpot[24] remarked on the proliferation of new techniques in the
art world:

Well art metamorphosed, if not ruptured. It's an incredible
period. Basically the 1960s, but on into the 1970s. Most of the

> things had their seeds in the 1960s. To me, as I said in the *Live in Your Head* catalogue, this is a more important moment than Cubism I think. The only moment like that in the last century is Cubism, where suddenly different ways of looking and making came out.[25]

Phillpot's remark supports the argument that the traditional notions of fine arts were faltering. Kelly's use of domestic intimate objects—nappies—may have been unusual, as she was one of the first artists to use such materials in her work, yet it was part of a wider movement away from the traditional fine arts. Within just a few years, the domestic as a theme would become paramount for artists aligned with the women's movement. The nappies, and the traces of shit on them, as well as the recordings can be seen as domestic found objects that Kelly "archaeo-logically" retrieved from her own house and categorized systematically.[26] Celebrating the Duchampian tradition of taking a banal, everyday object and placing it in a gallery context, Kelly subversively inserted feminist politics into the ICA.

It was in fact these very same traces of the baby's faeces that were seized upon by the tabloid press in London.[27] Fixing upon this one aspect of the larger series of work, the tabloid press saw it as a subversive plot to dupe the unsuspecting masses. Reporters ignored the larger picture and concentrated almost entirely on the question of excrement being part of a work of art.[28] The headline of the *Evening Standard* read "On Show at ICA … dirty nappies!"[29] Yet, within the same paper, in a review of the exhibition by Richard Cork, then editor of the prestigious *Studio International*, heralded *Post-Partum Document* as an important artistic inquiry into the everyday: "Two[30] absorbing one-person shows in London now, one by a woman and the other by a man, try to analyze and provoke an enlarged awareness of the way society erects formidable structures around our everyday behaviour."[31] Cork criticizes *Post-Partum Document* for not making more explicit the psychoanalytic theory it employs, but concedes that "the show as a whole supplies impressive evidence of an intelligent desire to translate theory into an adequate visual form."[32] Cork's review illustrates how large the gap between the general public and the contemporary art viewing audience was in 1976. Today's contemporary artists, especially in the UK, garner widespread publicity with the increased radio and television programing. Even the Turner Prize is televised annually.

TRANSGRESSING TABOOS: BLOOD, SHIT AND SEMEN

Judy Clark's exhibition at Garage,[33] a gallery in Covent Garden, also presented an intensely personal, series-based project. *Issues*[34] was the second show ever presented at the gallery and focused solely on the work of Clark, then a recent art school graduate. The exhibition should be seen today as a landmark in feminist art, but is largely neglected in the history of this period. *Issues* consisted of a complete corpus of work based on the traces of the human body that were primarily made by the artist while she was a student at the Slade School of Art. Like others of her generation Clark was enrolled in the painting department, but didn't find much affinity with the genre. She began a relationship with a sculptor who was a research fellow at an architectural school, and "became quite interested in the boundaries between architecture and art."[35] Clark has spoken of the lack of formal teaching at the Slade in the early 1970s:

> JC: I went to the Slade with this very "anti"-attitude because we'd had such a lot of problems at Portsmouth.[36] It was just that I found the Slade very weird. And the first day I remember going there walking around the studios, and there was no one to say "hello" or "welcome to the Slade". There was nothing. And you were supposed to grab a space. I don't know what you were supposed to do.
>
> *KB: And there was no formal teaching?*
>
> JC: I don't remember anything, any formal introduction. It was just like you wandered in, you sat down, and you started to paint. I couldn't relate to it all.[37]

Clark increasingly spent less time at the Slade, and took on outside jobs, such as freelance work at the architectural firm Pentagram. Another job as assistant to her partner, who was a successful artist, allowed Clark to travel to the Continent and see the work of artists such as Daniel Spoerri, Dieter Roth and Joseph Beuys. It was in fact works such as Beuys' *Fat Chair* 1964, that encouraged Clark to look at bodily materials.

The artist claims she received only two useful bits of advice while a student at the Slade. The first came from William Townsend, who encouraged Clark to interact with the biology department because of her interests. The second was Bernard Cohen's advice to read Mary Douglas' *Purity and Danger*. Her interest in traces of the body, hygiene, and cycles came together to produce an outstanding degree show. Knowing she was under pressure to create an entire series of work, Clark risked everything and showed her forensic experiments with bodily fluids and traces. She produced large-scale slides mounted on structures that resembled music stands as they could be tilted backward of forward.[38] The slides contained traces of various bodily functions including hair lost during sleep, menstruation blood, semen, and other corporal detritus.[39]

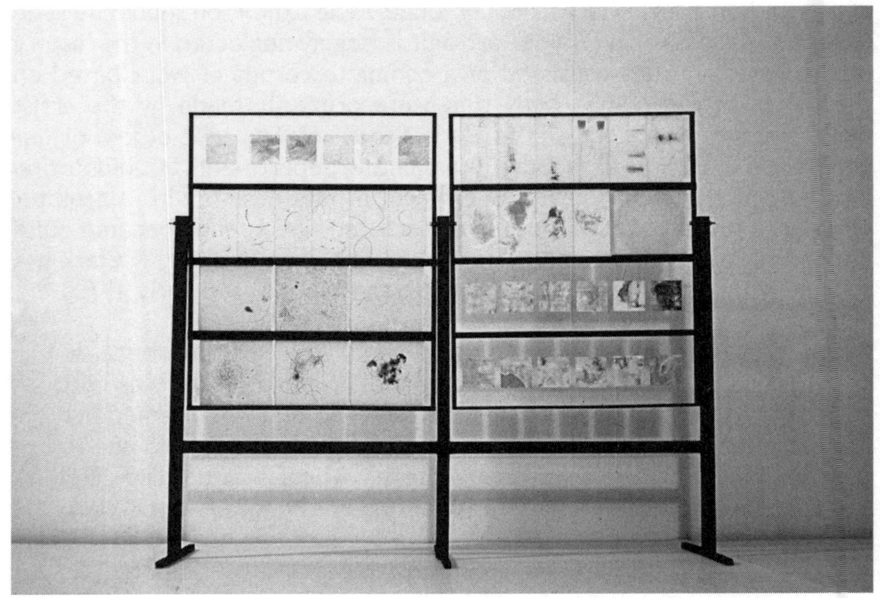

Figure 1.5
Frames, 1973. Judy Clark. Courtesy of the artist.

The Slade exhibition was a resounding success:

> [I] just put the work up and it just completely took off. ...
> Everybody was amazed by it and it sort of became famous over-
> night. And I was offered a show in a London gallery that evening.[40]

It was Anthony Stokes and Martin Attwood, the co-directors of Garage,
who saw Clark's degree show and offered her an exhibition on the spot.
While Clark's practice, like Kelly's, sparked a debate at the Slade over
whether or not it was art, she moved forward and prepared her first
professional exhibition.

Clark's work in the Garage show was presented in Perspex and wood
boxes, hung in series on the white gallery walls. The title of the exhibition, *Issues*, had a double meaning: the first was literal, meaning what
the body evacuates; the second was figurative, meaning issues relevant
to the artist's work, and to her status as a female artist. *Semen in Boxes*,
1973, shows dried semen-soaked tissues that correspond to twenty-eight
days of love-making with Clark's partner. The similarity between Clark's
and Kelly's work—series-based, created over time—illustrates a shared set
of concerns for feminist artists at the time. Kelly's work was concurrent

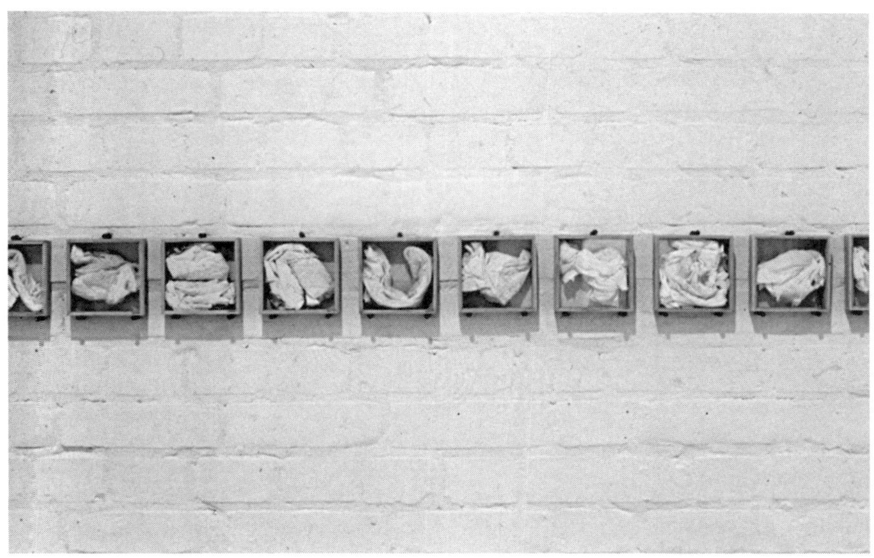

Figure 1.6
Semen in Boxes, 1973
Judy Clark. Courtesy of the artist.

to Clark's, as well as projects such as Judy Chicago's *Menstruation Bathroom* and *Womanhouse* (both 1972) in the United States.[41] This work in particular, with its collaborative nature, also shows a shared interest with Carolee Schneemann, whose groundbreaking film *Fuses* 1965, showed explicit scenes of lovemaking between her and her then partner.[42]

Clark's work, like Kelly's, relied upon traces from her body, as well as her partner's. It is interesting that both artists looked beyond themselves for traces of the body in domestic spaces. Clark's *Clipping* comprises a line drawing of nail clippers with the residue of fingernail clippings mounted below it. *Menstruation* includes the bloodstains left from a monthly cycle. Each work consisted of the most intimate bodily cast-offs, clearly material that was hitherto not conceived as artistic substances.

As in Kelly's work, these items of bodily waste were presented in a highly ordered fashion, due to Clark's awareness of propriety and taste, or better stated, transgressions of taboo. Clark said in an interview at that time: "one of the reasons it is put out in an ordered way is that it is so dangerous that if it was out of control it would be totally unacceptable. It would be obscene and revolting and nobody would look at it. But because it is laid out so carefully it creates a dualism between unacceptability and acceptability."[43] It is interesting to note that Carolee Schneemann made

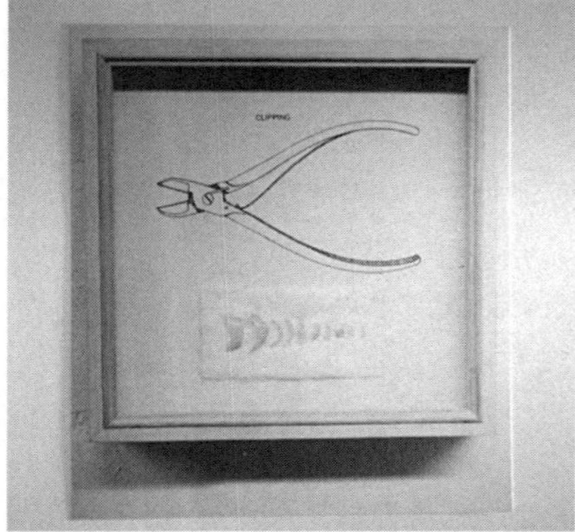

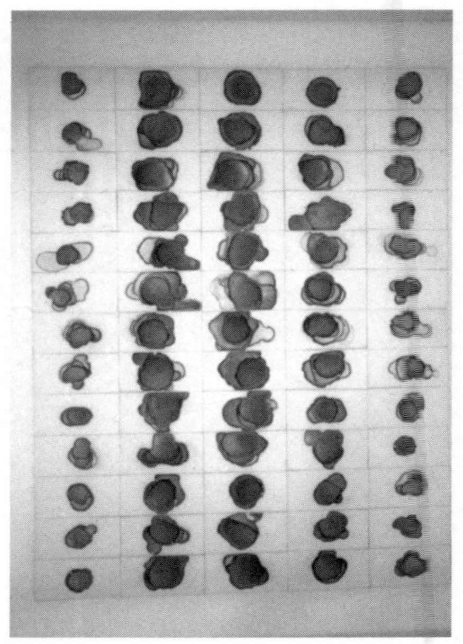

Figure 1.7
(Above) *Clipping*

Figure 1.8
(Right) *Menstruation* (detail), 1973.
Judy Clark. Courtesy of the artist.

similar work to Clark's; the artists were not acquainted with each other, but, they had similar impulses. Schneemann didn't exhibit her menstruation piece for fear of the taboo nature of it.

That *Issues* and *Post-Partum Document* consisted of series-based work is significant. In both of these cases, it is surely related to the then-current trend of conceptual time-based and systems-based art such as the work of Art & Language, Joseph Kosuth or Marcel Broodthaers, which Kelly was interested in and Clark would have seen on the Continent. Looking closer, we see that Kelly's and Clark's practices were both concerned with real time: in *Post-Partum Document* Kelly illustrates the child's development over time and in works such as *Menstruation* and *Semen in Boxes,* Clark investigates the natural cycles of the male and female bodies. Both the *Document* and *Issues* installations—consisting of individual units that render a narrative when viewed as a whole—resemble frames of a film unraveling in time. Specifically, the devices of editing and frame units of film can be compared to the units from *Post-Partum Document.* This is no accident as, in Kelly's case, she was deeply interested in avant-garde film[44] at the time of the work's production. In the early 1970s, film was beginning to emerge as a medium for artists, and increasingly was finding its way out of the cinema and into galleries. Kelly has remarked:

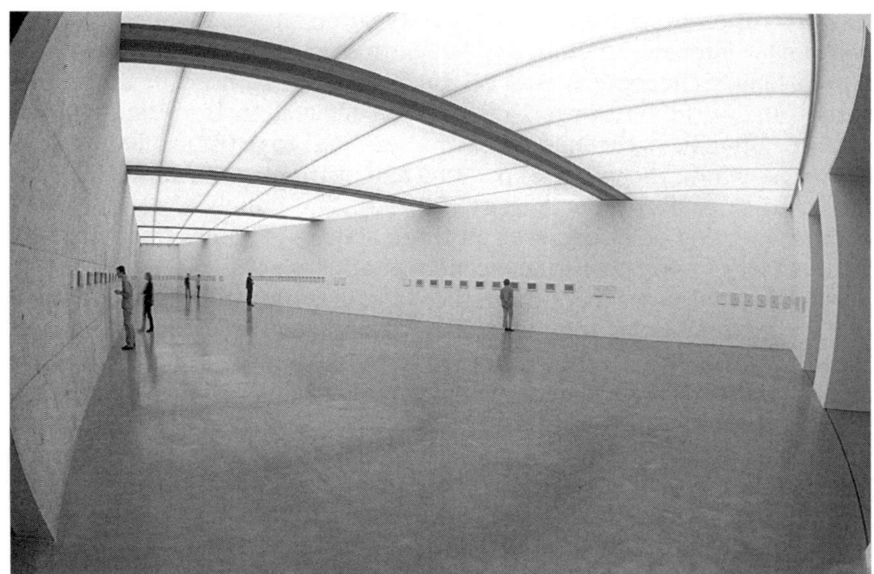

Figure 1.9
The Complete Post-Partum Document, installation view, 1998.
Mary Kelly. Photograph: Werner Kaligofsky. Courtesy Generali Foundation.

when I saw Straub and Huillet's *Orthon*, the long take going into
Rome—you know they run the whole reel, it's ten minutes—I was
knocked out, it just took my breath away, and I thought: why
should all the interesting work be in film? Why can't you do that
in an exhibition? Why couldn't I think about drawing the spectator into a *diegetic* space: the idea of real time or what you
might call the *picture* in the expanded field. And that's what I
eventually got back to in *Post-Partum Document*.[45]

Kelly's interest in time came directly out of her involvement with the
avant-garde film scene in London during the early 1970s. She made films
that relied on notions of real-time and serial activities.[46] Kelly also collab-
orated on the film *Nightcleaners*.[47] In 1973 she produced *Antepartum*,
a rarely seen[48] black and white 16mm film that lasts for about seven
minutes. The film is a straightforward, real-time representation of Kelly's
stomach, which is heavily swollen by pregnancy. The film is shot from
below, and the viewer sees the distinctive *linea negra* as well as the
bottom swell of the artist's breasts. In the first instance the film seems
to resemble a Warhol film such as *Sleep,* where nothing really happens.
However, occasionally the baby kicks or moves, and one can see the

tiny protrusion from the artist's belly. As noted above, Schneemann also had similar interests to Clark and Kelly, especially the latter in regard to film-making. Schneemann was celebrated and ensconced in the avant-garde film world.[49] However, rather than looking to the French struc-turalist film-makers, Schneemann was indebted to artists including Stan Brakhage, whose technique of painting and distressing the celluloid made for abstract painterly portions of the reel. The notion of seriality was another meeting point between all three artists—in Kelly's *Document*, as well as Clark's and Schneemann's menstruation pieces.

Clark has said above that she put the works in *Issues* into Perspex because of their material being too taboo; thus, containing it somehow distanced the viewer from the trace. In addition to her interest in Douglas's writing on taboo, Clark's work also derived from Douglas's view of the body as a system that could be substituted for any bounded system in life. Clark's work finds an uncannily similar incarnation in Carolee Schneemann's *Blood Work Diary*, which was made during one menstrual cycle in 1972.[50] The inspiration for Schneemann's work came from one of her lovers, a strong "football captain-type" who became faint while making love to the artist because of the sight of menstrual blood. Schneemann said, "The whole masculine trope is to blow up bodies and eviscerate them and pound them into the earth. The whole language of Vietnam was about pulverising bodies and then the contradiction of this modest amount of menstrual blood carrying this immense taboo."[51] She created the work on tissue paper using egg yolk to fix the blood, which was left to dry on the floor of the flat that she shared with her partner Anthony McCall.[52]

Indeed for a young woman to use fluids from the orifices of the human body in her first professional exhibition caused Clark her share of noto-riety. In the *Financial Times* Marina Vaizey wrote, "Her first ... exhibi-tion ... has made people react, sometimes with nauseated indignation. I found it complicated, deeply touching, and certainly disturbing."[53] Clark's knack for hitting a nerve was praised by critics such as Vaizey and Caroline Tisdall from the *Guardian*, who commented: "Dirt is seen as out of place, a threat to good order, yet with it she builds a form of neat and ordered minimation. There's a wryness to that that only a woman could hit upon, the vindications of accusations against myopic vision."[54] That a woman could seize upon what society ignores or hides is not unusual. Much of feminist art practice has been concerned with bringing issues into the light, and thinking about themes such as the excremental, the maternal or the political. Clark, however, did this in a subtle and insidious manner:

> Along with the rows of stained plasters and impregnated tissues the effect would grate horribly with everything good girls are taught about keeping the nest and body clean. Either that or it

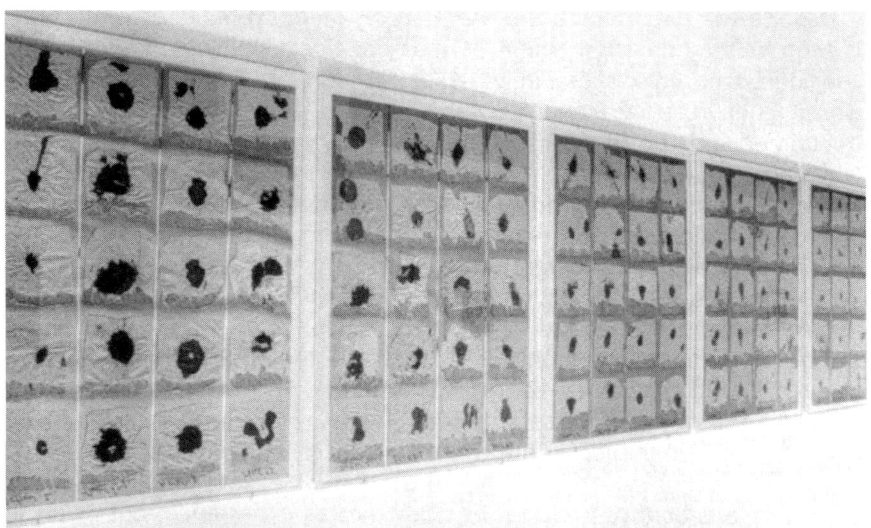

Figure 1.10
Blood Work Diary, 1972. Carolee Schneemann. Courtesy of the artist.

would provide them with a good old liberating laugh. Grooming, house dust, cleansing, menstruation ... Clark had summed it up and boxed it up and with this simple exposure of the minutiae of women's lives she led her less hardy audience to the edge of shock-horror.[55]

Clark's show undermined the post-war ideal of the perfect housewife. Where hygiene was a top priority in the idealized feminine world favored by advertisers, Clark opted instead to bring to light the detritus of the household.

Clark's work may have been forgotten in subsequent accounts of feminist art history because of her fleeting presence. [56] Soon after her show at Garage, Clark received a Beuys Travel Scholarship and went to India, where she remained for the rest of the decade. Soon after her return to London, *ca* 1980, she became pregnant and decided to become a single mother. Like others discussed in this book, such as Bobby Baker, Clark's career suffered from various obstructing circumstances and commitments. A few years ago she wrote in a letter: "My art practice has been sporadic over the years due to chunks of time spent travelling, early parenthood, work in architectural and fashion textile design, and, more recently full time employment."[57] Clark, however, would continue to make art and show in galleries.

Despite the patchy nature of her career, Clark's 1973 *Issues* exhibition is seen as a landmark moment by many of her colleagues, and must be considered in any discussion of 1970s feminist art in London. Not only was it concurrent to canonical work such as Mary Kelly's *Post-Partum Document* and the visceral performance work of both Catherine Elwes and Carolee Schneemann, it is also an important example of practices which touch vicariously on the body, but do not feature it as directly as the visual subject of the work. Kelly has commented on this recently, looking back at the *Document*:

> To return to the body/language question: at the time when I began my work, not only *PPD*, but also the *Nightcleaners* film (1975) and *Women & Work* installation (1975), I was also caught up in the critique of "essentialism", I mean, the idea of a predetermined femininity, or disposition that ascribed, say "theory" to the masculine and "the body" to the feminine. And that's why it seemed logical to exclude the body, not as experience, but as a figurative image, so that I could focus on the woman as speaking subject.[58]

It is clear that Kelly's methodology was actually closely aligned with Clark and Schneemann. Although seemingly disparate the work of these three feminist pioneers struggled with the same issue: how to communicate the physical experiences of womanhood without necessarily depicting the female form.

POST-PARTUM DOCUMENT, ISSUES AND CONCEPTUAL STRATEGIES

Post-Partum Document and *Issues* emerged at a time when conceptual art was dominant among contemporary artists. As noted above, Barker's exhibitions at the ICA were led by an international avant-garde that used conceptual strategies, including Dieter Roth, Dan Graham and Art & Language. While the style of Kelly's *Post-Partum Document* resembled the conceptual, there were various aspects of the work that were not typical of conceptual practice, specifically Kelly's interest in interrogating subjectivity.

Conceptual art was largely dominated by the examination of language and the visual form. In an attempt to eliminate the art critic from the equation, conceptual artists created works comprised primarily of text, instructions, numbers and indexes. As Charles Harrison said, "It's like if no one is sure any longer what kind of object a work of art is, you can go on making different kinds of objects or you can make philosophical inquiry into the nature and definition of an object."[59] Language and critical inquiry became equally important as visual form. Even with the most obtuse conceptual pieces, the artist makes formal decisions. For example, Art & Language's *Guaranteed Painting*, 1967–68, contains two panels, each 92 cm squared. One is painted monochrome, the other is a mounted photostat. This second panel reads: PAINTING CONTAINS A 6" x 6" BLACK SQUARE. It replaces figuration with a statement about how the work should look, in essence, a set of instructions. In this work the text and image are intended to bear critically on each other in such a manner that they compete for the same space.[60]

Kelly was very much aware of conceptual practice[61] and made reference to it throughout *Post-Partum Document*. In its "Introduction" she used baby vests with Lacanian diagrams. The vests were made in 1973, but are related to a work that Kelly experienced in 1972. During that year the Hayward Gallery and the Arts Council of Great Britain hosted an exhibition titled *The New Art*, which presented conceptual work of an all male line-up including Art & Language, Richard Long, Gilbert & George and Victor Burgin among others.[62] Kelly, who was just leaving St Martins School of Art, was familiar with and interested in the procedures of conceptual art, and many of the exhibitors at the Hayward had been her colleagues there. Charles Harrison, Richard Long, and Gilbert & George were graduates of St Martins School of Art. Art & Language (which Harrison would become aligned with) showed their index piece and in the accompanying catalogue, spoke of their version of intersubjectivity. For them, this entailed speaking to each other and documenting it systematically. For Kelly, their notion of intersubjectivity seemed "somewhat naïve and problematic."[63] Art & Language's idea of intersubjectivity was more of an imperative for work, which didn't allow for the unconscious. Kelly said, "the *Document*'s vests (with Lacan's L schema on them) just beautifully address this blind spot."[64]

Kelly's "Documentation II: Analyzed utterances and related speech events" is a section in *Post-Partum Document* that bears resemblance to conceptual art. There are 23 separate units in "Documentation II", each of which is divided into two sections. This is preceded by a graph, and concludes with a reworking of Lacan's Schema R and the *Experimentum Mentis*. In this section the baby is now between one and two years old, and beginning to enter language. It is the period in which the baby makes the transition from the use of independent signs (words) to their combination in syntactical form.[65] The artist recorded 12-minute sessions with her child, over the period from 26 January–29 June 1975, which were used as source material. A now iconic photograph of the artist and her child, which was used as an advertisement for the exhibition at the ICA, was taken by Kelly's partner Ray Barrie during the creation of this section of the *Document*, and shows the artist and her son during a recording session.[66] (It is interesting that a figurative image was used as the advertisement for a piece that so clearly avoided representing the artist's body.) The artist recorded these sessions in the communal household at Alderney Street in which she, Barrie and the child were living, and thus characters such as "R" for Ray, her husband, and "S" for Sally Alexander, the historian who owned the house, enter into the dialogue.[67]

"Documentation II," like the other sections of the work, begins with a chart that measures the age of the baby in months. The remaining units contain two sections each: a lower segment, which features index cards with typed snippets of conversation between the baby Kelly and his mother, father and others; an upper portion that includes two printed columns arranged right and left justified, and in reverse above, rubber-ized stamps used to create the printed text, which Kelly acknowledges as "a whole kind of mirror".[68]

Kelly tried to give "Documentation II" the same kind of materiality as "Documentation I", although it was focused on the entry into language. The cards registering what she calls "the speech events" are made to reflect or represent the traces of language. Kelly studied linguistic tech-niques[69] in order to make the investigation as accurate as possible.

If "Documentation I" recalls child-rearing instruction books, "Documentation II" satirizes the scientific nature of linguistic analysis. Juli Carson writes, "Kelly first mimics, through extensive documentation and empirical analysis, the 'scientificity' of this discourse."[70] Kelly asserted her interest in linguistics at the time, in particular the sexualised subject in language:

> Here I was, having the child and this was going to be a project, not so much about motherhood, which is how it can be read and has been read because of different kinds of work that are informed by feminism, but it was in the larger sense about the subject's sexed position in language. How you enter into language. If we're dealing with language then this actually has to be addressed.[71]

Kelly's interest in semiotics as well as the work of Julia Kristeva and other French theorists was based on their investigations of language. But in the *Post-Partum Document* Kelly tries to get beyond the kind of language used in other conceptual art. Take, for example, Art & Language's use of language in *Guaranteed Painting*. Kelly's use of text differs from their approach as it attempts to use narrative as opposed to language as description; here language and narrative are cleverly combined with quasi-scientific investigation into her son's utterances.

Several writers note how Kelly's work exposed the limitations of conceptual art. Helen Molesworth writes, "conceptual art's meta-discourse about the status of art can be seen as unwittingly continuing a modernist paradigm of art for art's sake."[72] Margaret Iverson has also discussed Kelly's work in relation to conceptual inquiry:

Her "style" evokes the precision and formal restraint of Minimalism and her use of language and diagrams which record and analyse the results of extended research projects links her to the strategies of Conceptualism. But what Conceptualist would have thought of inserting a mother and baby into that art discourse?[73]

Kelly has acknowledged her interest in conceptual art, in particular the stylistic traits of systems and series.[74] However, for Kelly, evolving into a practice had to go beyond conceptual strategies. She has said, "this unsolved question in terms of conceptual art ... The interrogation of interrogation, it had to include subjectivity."[75]

Retrospectively it is said that feminist and conceptual art overlapped insofar as both resisted conventional practices of representation. However, conceptual artists and feminist artists at the time stood on very different ground. Kelly has spoken about this, mentioning that while conceptual art investigated, as Molesworth correctly notes, "art for art's sake," any variable in the equation, such as politics, feminism, or similar ideology was seen to contaminate the conceptual project. She concludes:

> that kind of contamination with process or the readymade does already make a break from what a lot of historians consider to be conceptual art. Once the question of say, sexuality or class enters in, that's what I mean that it kind of contaminates the conceptual paradigm. And it's the mess of the stuff. I remember Benjamin [Buchloh] saying, "I like the theory, but why do you have to have that stuff?"[76]

One might as well add "the body" to the list of contaminations for artworks.

Juli Carson acknowledges Kelly's reliance on conceptual strategies but notes that "the *Document's* subject challenges the interiorised Cartesian subject that conceptual artists either wanted to keep out (Kosuth, Art & Language) or fetishistically engage (Douglas Heubler, Robert Barry, On Kawara)."[77] For Carson, Kelly's internal interrogation (which becomes more evident in "Documenation III") perfectly exposed the blind spot of conceptual art. Carson quite accurately articulates where the *Document* exceeds the limitations of conceptual art. This will become further apparent in the following sections of the work.

It was indeed this "extra" subject matter—the domestic, personal and corporeal content—of Kelly's work that led to a virulent tabloid response. The press reaction, although not considered in its analysis, was an indicator of the public hostility towards contemporary art at the time.[78] Unlike many of the so-called yBa[79] generation, young artists in 1970s London were underfunded, politically motivated and looking to break away from a gallery system that was not serving them.

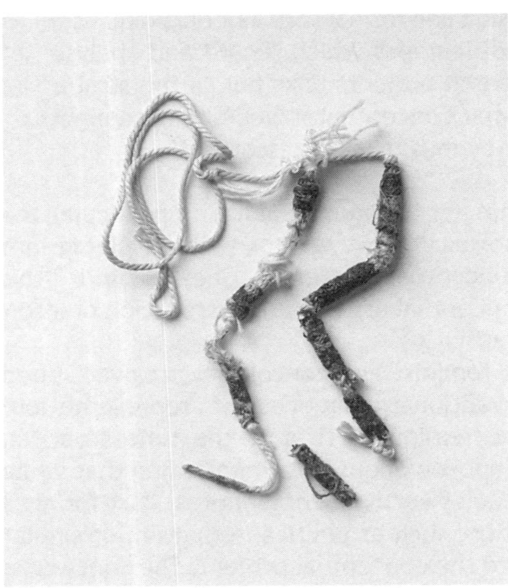

Figure 1.11
The Egg Timer, 19XX. Linder.
Courtesy of the artist.

The controversies generated by Kelly, Clark and others like Carl Andre centered on the breakdown of the traditional fine arts into a more conceptual and less directly representational practice. Another controversy that happened concurrently, also at the ICA, would bring into the fore a central debate of the decade: the body as material for feminist artists.

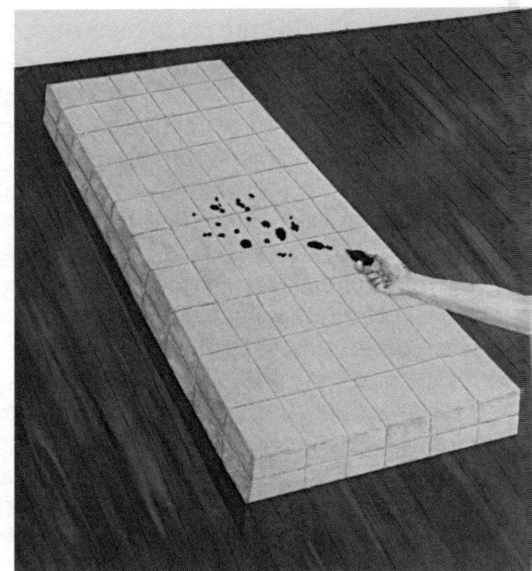

Figure 1.12
The Last Gesture, 1977.
Bobby Baker. Courtesy of the artist.

POST-PARTUM DOCUMENT, PROSTITUTION, AND THE BODY

For feminist artists during the women's movement in London and abroad, the body became an important site of debate. Reclaiming the female body from its traditional role as artist's model was an aspect of much of the work produced in Britain and America. For some, such as Renee Green and Adrian Piper in America, this meant depicting themselves in the work, as a political signifier of the—in these examples—African American artist. For others—such as Hannah Wilke, or Jo Spence in Britain—this meant the use of the nude female form as a subversive tactic. In Wilke's and Spence's cases they depicted themselves in various states of disease (in both cases cancer) to subvert the notion of the idealized female form. Another artist, Cosey Fanni Tutti, used her body in an intentionally subversive manner in works of art, which were shown by coincidence at the same time as Kelly's *Post-Partum Document* at the ICA.

Prostitution, held at the ICA, ran for only eight days: 19-26 October 1976. It was officially an exhibition by Coum Transmissions, a performance and music group led by Genesis P-Orridge and featuring, among others such as Chris Carter and Peter Christopherson, P-Orridge's girlfriend Cosey Fanni Tutti.[80] The exhibition consisted of four elements: framed pages from pornographic magazines featuring Tutti in erotic poses; props used by the group in past performances (including tampons, meat cleavers, anal syringes, chains and Vaseline); framed photographs of Coum performances; photocopied press cuttings on the group.[81] Simon Ford writes, "The exhibition according to Coum had three aims: first it was intended to comment on methods of survival for an artist; secondly it was meant to reveal how 'presentation' had become an end in itself; and thirdly it was meant to demonstrate the gap between representation and reality."[82] In an intentionally subversive move they served beer instead of wine at the opening, had a stripper instead of a speech by the ICA Director, and for entertainment there was a performance by a punk band.

Like the controversy over *Post-Partum Document*, the press picked up on this show, which inadvertently served to quell some of the debate around Kelly's exhibition. Hundreds of articles were written[83] and satirical cartoons appeared in the national press. Questions were asked in Parliament, and P-Orridge and Tutti became well known, reminiscent of Kelly and Clark. Much of the controversy over *Prostitution* focused on the content of the exhibition, as well as the fact that the group had been given British Council grants earlier that year.[84] Barker and Little had expected the controversy to develop around this show:

> I didn't expect Mary's thing to break, but I knew Genesis P-Orridge would. ... Because it was meant to. That was the whole idea.

> That's why they called the show "Prostitution". It was a reflec-
> tion on the press. And the response that they got is the response
> that they wanted. I didn't expect that of Mary's. It was a beau-
> tiful bit of program timing.[85]

The *Prostitution* show was also significant for providing an antidote to theoretically based feminist art. The pornographic depictions of Cosey Fanni Tutti[86] represented the depressingly small room to maneuver for a female artist in London at the time. Tutti, who was not aligned with the mainstream women's movement, nevertheless had artistic and subversive intentions. While she posed for the pictures to earn money for Coum's activities—in essence prostituting herself—she did see it as empowering. (However, her colleague P-Orridge forgets to mention this aspect when he writes in January 1976, "Cosey has been coumtinuing [sic] her Prostitution Actions to support our coum actions. … Now we are really underground again, finance is harder, we survive by prostitution in every form."[87])

Cosey made contacts in the nude modeling world through a friend at Space Studios,[88] where she and P-Orridge worked. For her the photo shoots were more than just a way to supplement her income. The images were used as part of their art practice, and were claimed by Cosey as her own, despite conventional publishing law, which sees the model relin-quish any claim of copyright of images. Posing herself on one extreme of the debate over pornography[89] Cosey attempted to reverse the power relations between artist and model. Simon Ford writes that "The model as artist was vocal and active and possessed a shifting identity that negated the usually passive, silent, objectified role of the model as erotic spectacle, object of the gaze of the male artist and audience."[90] One might ask how such a photograph in a girlie magazine could be claimed as art. For the Coum Transmissions group Tutti's compromising photographs took on the status of art when described as part of their strategy for "subliminal performance art".[91] Their idea was to infiltrate popular culture in order to make art more accessible. Artists such as Dan Graham and Robert Smithson in the 1960s had been making conceptual works of art in magazines as a reaction against the commodified gallery system. However, their pieces were read and received in the context of art. One wonders how Coum Transmissions or Tutti ever thought the general public buying girlie magazines would become aware that it was actually a work of art?

Installing Tutti's photographs in the *Prostitution* show at the ICA further served to legitimize their role as works of art. However, when the scandal broke Tutti was the member of the group who suffered the most. While the other members of Coum Transmissions received the notoriety they sought, for Tutti the attention would prove fatal to the continuation of this body of work: she was blacklisted from the pornographic industry because photographers and photo editors were rightfully upset that she used their work without credit in the exhibition, and duped them in the process.

Tutti, like Kelly and Clark, was not accepted by all viewers. She was reviled by feminist artists, making her in a sense an outcast from those with whom she could have created a discourse. Lisa Tickner wrote "those who claim an art form out of being 'intentionally' exploited like Cosey Fanni Tutti of the Coum Group ... shift the meaning of the work, however serious its original or possible intentions, from parody to titillation".[92] Tutti's tenuous position was significant, especially for performance artists who would continue to question whether to use their own body as subject matter in feminist work. Only the previous year Laura Mulvey's article, "Visual Pleasure and Narrative Cinema"[93] was published, drawing attention to the problematic nature of the male gaze and female subject.

The *Prostitution* show, and particularly Cosey Fanni Tutti's contribution to it, occupied an important position within what may be loosely seen as a feminist binary. Mary Kelly represents those artists who took great pains to avoid using their own body in their practice. Tutti represents another position, where female artists reclaimed their bodies for use in their work, rejecting the notion that women were only useful as models by creating a situation where the model is the artist as well.[94] It is significant that Kelly's work has become an icon of feminist art whereas Tutti's has been largely ignored by the art establishment until recent years,[95] and when shown, has been placed in more "radical" non-feminist contexts. However, even if Tutti's practice was anathema to certain schools of feminist art, her contribution should be discussed as a reference point, as occupying an opposing position to a certain type of analytical, theoretically based work.

Prostitution, along with Kelly's and Clark's exhibitions earlier in that year, highlighted several elements of the public's engagement with artists in London during the 1970s. Why the vociferous distrust of contemporary art? Why were experimental forms so opposed? In Kelly's and Tutti's case the public suspicion of feminism enters the debate. Who has the right to judge what is or is not a work of art? These are questions that are still being asked today, for example in relation to Damien Hirst's animals preserved in formaldehyde from the late 1990s, Tracey Emin's *Bed* shown in the Turner Prize exhibition in 1999, and Bob and Roberta Smith's *Stop it Write Now!* in the *Intelligence* show.[96] Reactionary and conservative attitudes toward contemporary art are still common press fodder. However, now they are effectively used by host institutions to garner larger audiences, high profile funders and to enhance their image as contemporary cultural purveyors.[97] It is notable that 1976 is a key moment in the history of debate over contemporary art. If anything, these scandals succeeded in opening up a discourse, however populist or ill informed it might have been, about the state of contemporary visual arts. As Barker says:

And I think we were pioneers in that way because we broke through into that general public arena. ... through a barrier of people seeing that the visual arts is important, even if it's just to say it's a waste of money.[98]

POST-PARTUM DOCUMENT:
THEORETICAL ENQUIRY AND THE WOMEN'S MOVEMENT

Subsequent to the body debate was that regarding the use of psycho-analytic texts in the women's movement. Kelly's interest in psychoanalysis grew out of friendships with like-minded colleagues including Laura Mulvey, Peter Wollen and Parveen Adams who were reading Freud and translating Lacan at the time. Topics such as the castration complex, the Oedipus complex and penis envy were being debated during this period, and *Post-Partum Document* reflects Kelly's interest in these topics.

The "Introduction" section consists of a series of four units, each containing a child's vest mounted on card in a Perspex box. On the vests[99] are printed diagrams with "Intersubjectivity Axis I–IV" and a date corresponding to four months in 1973, the year Kelly's child was born. The months—September, October, November and December—correlate to the first four months of the baby's life.[100] The fragility and vulnerability of the child—something that has been commented on by Kelly's critics who question the use of her child as subject matter—is emphasized by the diminutive size of the vests.[101] The juxtaposition of the Lacanian diagrams break with the traditional or idealized image of motherhood depicted throughout the history of art.

(T)hey were very aesthetically appealing so there's a combination of that sentiment as far as the baby and the feel of the material when you fold it up that just probably made it the right one.[102]

It is the folding action that attracted Kelly to using the vests as found objects in the piece, and what connects them to the Lacanian diagrams printed upon them. "You can see I was just folding on the diagram, unfolding on the axis of intersubjectivity. It's just an irony."[103] Kelly received hostile criticism from those who saw her work as too laden with theory, and therefore, not supportive of the "sisterhood" ideology of women's movement. However, one sees that even in the first stages of the project the artist is parodying the male theory, mixing it with the mother's unconscious desire, which is presented through the fetishized objects, the vests.

A viewer familiar with the work of Lacan would recognize that Kelly's diagram is a bastardization of the analyst's "Schema L" diagram (*The Schema of the Intersubjective Dialectic*), originally published in the French *Écrits* (Chapter One). Lacan's diagram can be interpreted on various levels: most simply as a chronological or developmental account of the child from birth to the resolution of the Oedipus complex. It can also be read as an outline of the "decentered subject", or a structural schema of the various psychical agencies that function in the subject. Finally, Lacan's Schema L can be read as a plan for the structure of the transferential relationship between the analyst and the analysand. Therefore, Lacan's Schema L can be read in relation to temporal, psychical or interpersonal space, or as a combination of the three.[104] The temporal reading seems most significant in Kelly's diagram, where each additional line contains a month of the year in ascending order from September to December 1973.

Kelly's diagrams work on several levels: because they are imposed on to the vests, there is the combination of the sentimentality of the baby clothes, and the more rigorous theoretical aspects of the original Lacanian diagram. Even for a viewer unfamiliar with Lacanian analysis or writing, the diagrams would signal that this series, and *Post-Partum Document* on the whole, is concerned with psychoanalysis and semiotic theory.[105]

Discussions of Kelly's work often center solely on her use of psycho-analytic theory, which has been duly documented by several writers.[106] While Kelly's circle was interested in working through this theory, other women in the liberation movement were not enthusiastic. Craig Owens wrote about feminist artists and the debate over the use of theory in an essay entitled "Feminists and Postmodernism". He situates the axis of the debate precisely in the overlap between theory and practice. Owens recounts Martha Rosler's and Laura Mulvey's alliance with theory and writes:

> the kind of simultaneous activity on multiple fronts that charac-terises many feminist practices is a post-modern phenomenon. And one of the things it challenges is modernism's rigid opposi-tion of artistic practice and theory.[107]

Owens articulates precisely the juxtaposition that Kelly created in *Post-Partum Document*. Her theoretical inquiry is combined with prac-tice, although some viewers felt that the theory occluded the practical elements. The artist Catherine Elwes recalls that:

> although, as you say, people tended to focus on the shit aspects of it … what you came away with was a lot of theory actually. There were all these diagrams that nobody understood. It was very dense. What she was presenting was her brain. What she was presenting was her mastery, and I use that word for a reason, of male theory.[108]

Elwes—who recognized the need for contradictory stances within the women's movement—was a supporter of Kelly's work, and had been instrumental in inviting the artist to speak to students at the Slade in the late 1970s. However, the younger artist acknowledged that Kelly's work incited dissent among those in the women's movement who were not invested in a psychoanalytic approach.

Such disagreement among various groups of feminists was not uncommon, and a typical example is the Patriarchy Conference that was held at the Architectural Association in 1976, the same year as Kelly's exhibition. This provided an important opportunity for feminists to exchange their research. The conference[109] included differing viewpoints on the problem of women's oppression. Ros Coward, Sue Lipshitz and Elizabeth Cowie gave a paper called "Psychoanalysis and Patriarchal Structures", which relied on heavily on Althusser, and Susan Himmelweit, Margaret McKenzie and Allison Tomlin gave the paper "Why Theory?". These papers used political ideology to discuss familial structure and the oppression of women. Meanwhile, this kind of work was opposed by The Dalston Study Group, a neighborhood-based consciousness raising group. In their contribution to the post-conference publication—"Was the Patriarchy Conference Patriarchal?"—they wrote:

> It felt ironical, then, to arrive at a women's conference and feel defined negatively in relation to it; to listen to papers being read about women's silence and women having no social language. which itself made us passive and silent.[110]

In fact, the only thing that the speakers agreed upon was that the predominant problem was how disparate and unconnected the various strands of feminism were. This may be seen as typical regarding the role of theory in the women's movement: while some, such as Kelly and her colleagues, were immersed in it, others felt estranged and silenced by it.

While Kelly was producing *Post-Partum Document* she was engaged in myriad pursuits: besides being a mother and partner and member of a communal household, Kelly was also teaching, making films, writing on film and psychoanalytic theory as well as working collaboratively with other artists. Concurrently she was shooting and editing *Nightcleaners*, teaching at the London College of Furniture and creating *Women & Work* with Margaret Harrison and Kay Hunt. Each of these in a sense is a catalyst for what one finds in the *Document*. The resulting work that she produced, therefore, cannot be easily placed into any category such as conceptual, feminist, film or time-based media, because it is a conglomeration of each and all of them, and must be read in that way.

Nor can *Post-Partum Document* be reduced to a question of dirty nappies as if it was simply a "breakthrough" work. To simplify it in this way is to underestimate and under-evaluate the work, which now occupies a central role in the discourse of contemporary art in London during the 1970s. It is tempting to look back and mythologize an artist's participation in a movement or a piece of work's creation. However, it does seem incredibly important to stress, as the artist herself does, that Kelly was working through the debates over conceptualism, avant-garde film theory, psychoanalytic writing and feminism, but was not always consciously situating herself within them.

An example of how Kelly was finding her own way is her film, *Antepartum*, which is very different in feel from other work made at that time, such as *Post-Partum Document* and the film *Nightcleaners*. As mentioned previously, it features the nude body of the artist and the protrusion of the child. Curiously, this work has been much forgotten in the study of Kelly's practice and was only shown once in thirty years.[111] Is this a result of the artist editing it from her oeuvre? It is not discussed in books dedicated to this period of her practice. It certainly adds a layer of complexity to Kelly's rejection of the use of the body in the work of art and demonstrates how the pro- and anti-camps which developed around this subject were often more rigid in theory than in practice. Nonetheless, the combination of such diverse investigations into one body of work and one artist is also testimony to the decline of the previously hegemonic fine arts practice, and the gestation of alternative and experimental means of producing artwork.

This chapter introduces many of the key debates relating to the women's movement and visual arts in London during the 1970s. First, its relationship to conceptual art is important; many of the other artists discussed in further chapters adopted or reacted against conceptual strategies. What Kelly's work illustrates is that feminist art practice, although borrowing from conceptual art strategies, imbued added elements into the work, such as politics, familial structure, gender relations and traces of the body.

Finally Kelly's *Post-Partum Document* as well as Judy Clark's *Issues* and *Prostitution* represent the beginning of a trajectory for this book. The artist's concern with trace, memory and documentation is echoed in work found throughout the following chapters. Kelly's interest in documenting her everyday life is part of a larger feminist oppositional practice as it attempts to illustrate the invisible role of women in the division of labor in the family. Other feminist artists such as Judy Clark and Bobby Baker would take up this theme over the course of the decade. This idea of the invisible becoming visible, and the embodiment of memory, is crucial to my project. It is, as a whole, an attempt to make visible work by women artists engaged with the women's movement during the 1970s in London.

Chapter 2

THE BODY AND PERFORMANCE ART

Concurrent with the rise of the women's movement, performance art became central to contemporary art practice. Tracing its path back from early Dada events, through futurism and happenings, one observes the increasing importance of time-based and live events using the body as material, quite often associated with a polemic, or a particular political position. These type of events, based around the body in a live situation, become an important element of the development of a feminist art practice in 1970s London. From a negation of the commodified gallery system, to a return of the domestic, British feminists, although largely trained in traditional media such as painting and sculpture, relied on performance as an alternative medium, and on their bodies as (some artists would claim) newly emancipated source material.

For artists involved with women's liberation, performance provided outlets for several of their concerns: it was an opportunity to reclaim the female body from what was seen as its muse-like status, as female artists transcended objectivity by taking the active role of creator in addition to, or instead of, the model. Performance also provided a means of breaking down what many female (and male for that matter) artists saw as a patriarchal gallery system based on the traffic of objects. Performance also accommodated a celebration of previously taboo subjects related to women, such as menstruation, sexual desire and the boundaries of the female body. Most importantly, live events often allowed women to reach an audience beyond the traditional gallery and patronage system. As Amelia Jones writes, "Works that involve the artist's enactment of her or his body in all of its sexual, racial, and other particularities and overtly solicit spectatorial desires unhinge the very deep structures and assumptions embedded in the formalist model of art evaluation."[1]

For feminists, there was division regarding the role of the body in performance. Some were fiercely opposed to conventional representations of women as sexual objects, and avoided showing their nude bodies. Artists such as Rose Finn-Kelcey, Silvia Ziranek and Bobby Baker are discussed in this chapter for their reluctance to portray their bodies as nude or sexualized objects. Another camp of women attempted to express their autonomy through their bodies. Artists such as Catherine Elwes and Carolee Schneemann aimed to reclaim the female body and liberate feminine sexuality in their performances.

Despite the centrality of performance for a feminist practice, it would be inaccurate to conclude that event-based work was solely female terrain.[2] Performance was equally heralded by men as an alternative form of expression, and as a strategy to bypass the traditional means of making art. For example, Paul McCarthy[3] and Stuart Brisley[4] created performances in every way as visceral as the female artists who focused on menstrual bleeding, sex and abuse. However, in the case of women artists, performance becomes charged with an added sexual tension. For the female performance artist is always acting under the weight of her historical status as art object. It is for this reason that some female artists who chose to perform nude were criticized by their female colleagues, while other artists were chastised for not doing so. This debate is still current in art practice today, as is illustrated in this dissertation.

Performance became an increasing trend in artworks of the late 1960s and early 1970s. From Jackson Pollock's gestural canvases, to Alan Kaprow's early happenings, and John Latham's subversive protest against the theories of Clement Greenberg,[5] the body in action became an important part of the new artistic processes, heralding a new practice that combined bodies and traditional artistic material to create an alternative to the art object. However, as Guy Brett notes, "in the very gesture of negating the art object and affirming life, these artists exaggerated the myth of the artist as master and unique author."[6] The resulting objects were often exhibited, and usually documented. This documentation, mostly photographic, and sometimes in the form of film or video, becomes an integral part of the process, and is a necessary means of the work entering the art market and the institutions.[7] However, as we have discussed, it is in some cases the lack of documentation that adds to the marginalization of 1970s feminist practice.

RoseLee Goldberg, an authority on performance art,[8] writes:

> Performance in the last two years of the sixties and of the early seventies reflected conceptual art's rejection of traditional materials of canvas, brush, or chisel, with performers turning to their own bodies as art material, just as Klein and Manzoni had done some years previously. For conceptual art implied the *experience* of time, space and material rather than their representation in the form of objects, and the body became the most direct medium of expression. Performance was therefore an

ideal means to materialize art concepts and such was the practice corresponding many of those theories.[9]

Goldberg's concept of performance corresponding to theories is especially relevant for feminist practice, which will become evident in the sections below. For feminist artists performance became a way of expressing issues central to the women's movement, for example, domestic labor, sexuality and reproduction as well as the role of the female nude in the history of art.

Often the performance artist occupied a left-wing stance, critical of the prevailing cultural or political circumstances, especially in the case of feminist artists. For example, the American artist Martha Rosler has had an abiding interest in third-world politics as well as a concern with the rights of women.[10] Her stateside colleague Adrian Piper similarly addressed the issues of race and class.[11] Kristine Stiles, an American writer whose work centers on performance, writes:

> In both theory and practice, artists who developed the performance medium conveyed the substance of the indeterminate social and political experiences of late modernism, and they augured a new and indefinite cultural condition prematurely announced by postmodernism. Often uncommodifiable, difficult to preserve and exhibit, and defiant of social mores and morals while upholding the highest ethical principles, performance art rendered palpable the anxious corporeal, psychic, and social conditions of global culture in the radically changing electronic and nuclear age.[12]

Amelia Jones sees a similar link to the economic and political situation of the time:

> The emergence of the artist's body in the radicalizing 1960s is linked to the problems of subjectivity and socially endemic to late or "pan" capitalism, characterized by a single "globally dominant political economy" that demands individuals submit their bodies so that they can function more efficiently under its "obsessively rational imperatives ... (production, consumption, and order)".[13]

Like Stiles, Jones links the use of the artist's body to increasing globalization. She goes on to write, "The emergence of the artist's body addresses this voracious commodification, and, in particular, the marketing of the artist (via the artist's body) as commodity fetish."[14] If the artist's body becomes fetishized, it still resists commodification. However, seen from the perspective of the twenty-first century, documentation and props

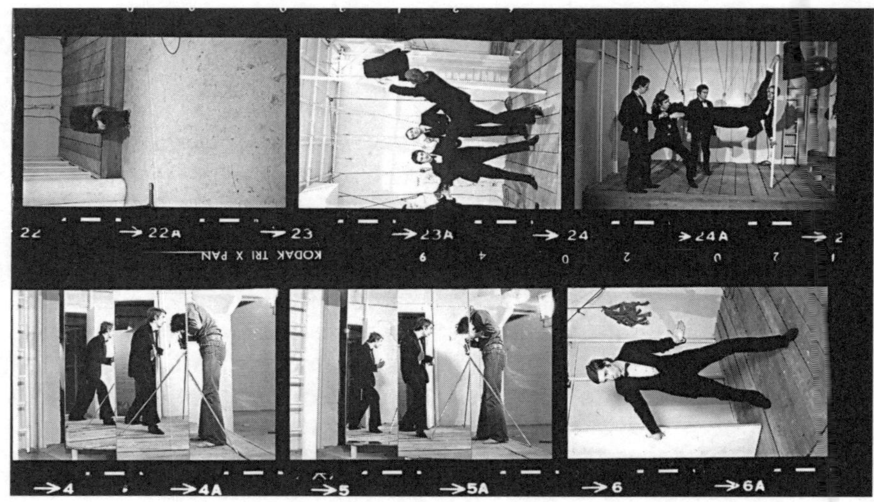

Figure 2.1
Nice Style, promotion shots. Courtesy Anthony Stokes.

from these early performances have now entered the art market.[15] Ours is arguably an age of commodified performance.[16]

Although Jones and Stiles write from a North American perspective, similar analyses apply to Britain. Many artists, both female and male, used performance as an alternative to the established salon or patronage system.[17] This chapter examines a range of performance by women artists during the 1970s in London, from the humorous work of Bobby Baker and Silvia Ziranek to more agitprop performances by Catherine Elwes and Carolee Schneemann.

THE BODY IN ACTION:
WOMEN AND PERFORMANCE IN 1970S BRITAIN

As the women's liberation movement grew, feminist artists sought new means of expression beyond painting or sculpture. For these artists performance became a method of rejecting the permanence of the art object. It also necessarily resisted any one type of "feminist aesthetic". Like Kelly or Clark, these artists worked with traces, but traces of their activity that were left largely unrecorded. In an age where exhibition catalogues were not obligatory and documentation was scant, the immediacy of performance became an all-important factor. Silvia Ziranek, an artist whose work has been performance-based since she was at art school in the early 1970s said, "I never practice. I never rehearse. ... I have it all prepared, and I'll have a rudimentary walk through, but I will never rehearse it properly because for me that takes away the edge of performance."[18] Rose Finn-Kelcey said, "We were much more concerned with it being live and with it being there and then not there. We liked the ephemeral. But again you see we could do that because we felt confident enough."[19] Catherine Elwes, another artist discussed below, felt similarly to Finn-Kelcey: "Performance art offers women a unique vehicle for making that direct unmediated address. ... She is author, subject, activator, director and designer. ... She is both signifier and that which is signified. Nothing stands between spectator and performer."[20] These artists believed that the one-off experience could provide a powerful alternative to traditional media. However, one might pose the question: Can any experience be unmediated?

As performance gained momentum as an alternative form during the 1970s in Britain and women increasingly made work based on personal experiences, performance grew popular as a feminist art form. By the end of the decade there would be performances by feminist artists in major institutions,[21] and even an exhibition dedicated to women's performance art in Britain.[22] It would be impossible to depict a comprehensive history of this practice in the decade, especially as it was inherent in the nature of the work that documentation of it was even less meticulous than that of traditionally made art.[23] Instead, I will illustrate the dominant themes found in women's performance and how it relates to the other work presented here. I begin by discussing the work of Rose Finn-Kelcey, who over time incorporated her body into performances as a sculptural feature. I proceed to discuss the theme of the domestic body in performance, looking at the work of Bobby Baker and Silvia Ziranek. This leads into the work of artists such as Catherine Elwes and Carolee Schneemann, whose graphic utilizations of their bodies caused viewers to question the notions of propriety and taboo. Finally I will turn my attention to alternative sites for performance, looking at the work of Silvia Ziranek, Sally Potter and Rose English.

THE EMPOWERED FEMALE BODY: ROSE FINN-KELCEY AND CAROLEE SCHNEEMANN

Rose Finn-Kelcey's performances were, according to some writers,[24] among the most memorable live events of the 1970s. Although her work was neither shocking, nor explicit, nor did it focus on extreme experiences, it nevertheless captured the attention of critics and historians.[25] When Finn-Kelcey left art school in the late 1960s,[26] she became part of the British avant-garde and was featured in several international shows.[27] Finn-Kelcey's remarks show that the stakes for young artists emerging from art school at that time were not as high as they currently are today, as few would become wealthy or celebrated:[28]

> The aspirations weren't there for being on television or being courted by the media. … It wasn't available. Making art has subsequently become sexy. At that time artists in the UK were generally considered to be outcasts from the rest of the culture, people were deeply suspicious of us, we appeared indulgent. We were conscious of being outsiders and made use of that position.[29]

With these lower stakes, artists could experiment with any medium, as well as feel free to reject the traditional route to success via a commercial gallery. Originally working with photography and installation pieces[30] Finn-Kelcey turned to performance after meeting artist Tina Keane[31] in the Women Artists Collective, one of the many consciousness-raising groups that women artists attended.[32]

Finn-Kelcey began to see performance as a more unexplored territory than the traditional media of painting and sculpture. She says, "Particularly in painting, the weight of tradition had seemed so male dominated. For women it was liberating to have access to open territory that was fresh, that we could explore, or use in an autobiographical way."[33] Artist Sally Potter mentioned a similar mindset in an interview in the mid-1970s:

> Work in performance is often hard to define in terms of existing art categories. It has evolved essentially as an anti-specialist area. Some women may have gravitated towards it because traditionally they haven't had much access to highly specialised areas of work; … But this has paradoxically become a strength—women don't have such a vested interest in upholding specialist traditions and so they can be freer to challenge the mystique that surrounds them.[34]

With less precedent, women artists could use performance to create a practice that commented on issues relevant to their lives; simultaneously, they avoided some of the pitfalls and iconology associated with traditional media such as figurative painting and sculpture.

In 1976 Finn-Kelcey staged a performance in the window of the Acme Gallery during the "London Calling"[35] series. *One For Sorrow, Two For Joy* featured the artist in the front window with two live magpies. The artist—as well as the birds—made sounds, which were relayed to the audience in the street outside the gallery.[36] Finn-Kelcey identified with the birds, which by legend are attracted to shiny objects. The artist noted that magpies are traditionally associated with women, and conducted research in a folklore library where she found the phonetic translations of the birdcalls. The translations sparked Finn-Kelcey's interest in language, and how each person's experience of it could be different.[37] She says,

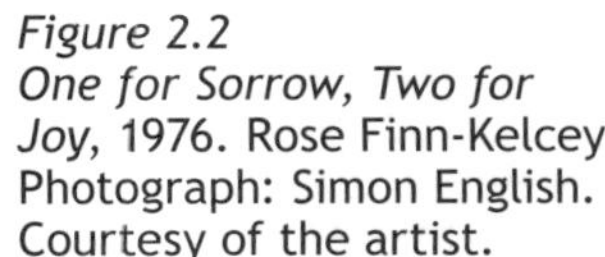

Figure 2.2
One for Sorrow, Two for Joy, 1976. Rose Finn-Kelcey. Photograph: Simon English. Courtesy of the artist.

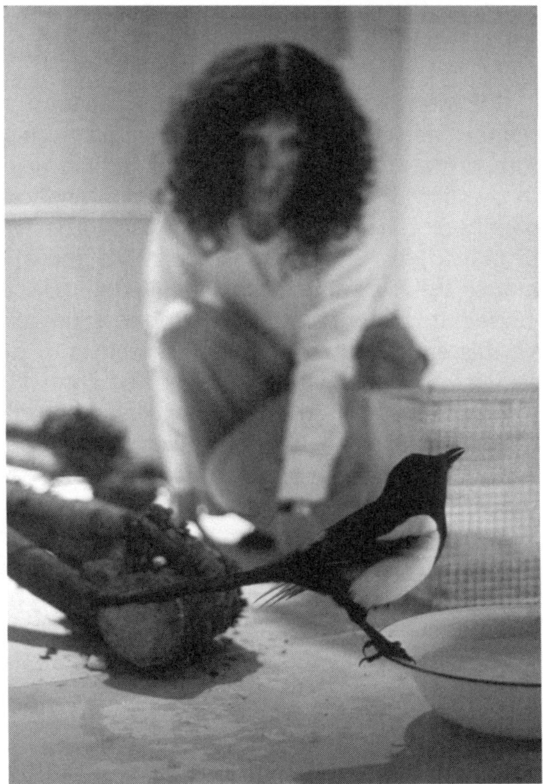

"Through the magpie sounds I wanted to talk about the potential for another language, apart from the existing one that we tend to feel is the only one ... and through that talk about a potential for women having a voice."[38] With this intention Finn-Kelcey cornered a major debate of the women's movement, that is, their ability to form their own voices of expression and critical language and practice, and to challenge the authoritative "male voice" that dominated throughout history.

It is notable that while Finn-Kelcey used her body as material, she did not perform in the nude. She commented on the feminist debate over this topic:

> I don't think I was a good feminist in that respect. I also wore makeup! And I didn't take my clothes off when performing! They were two cardinal sins. ... It was assumed that part of your job as a performance artist was to reposition the body in relation to culture. To raise the audience awareness so they would take on

board a more enlightened attitude toward the body, which on
some level, de-sexualized it.[39]

It is interesting that Finn-Kelcey believed that using her body in performances de-sexualized it, as this was opposed to other important feminist
interpretations. Mulvey's seminal article discussed female performances
in classic Hollywood films in order to analyze what she terms "the male
gaze", or the fantasy projected onto the woman, who is exhibited and
displayed, by the male viewer.[40] At the time of Finn-Kelcey's performance Mulvey's article was being widely discussed in feminist and artistic
circles. It is important to remember again here that artistic intention may
be misread in retrospective discussions of historical work, and that the
reception of such work can never be controlled by the artist.

Finn-Kelcey relied on language and sound to carry the performances.
In *One for Sorrow, Two for Joy* and more especially *Her Mistress's Voice*,
1977, the sound becomes abstract, with the audience left to discern
the meaning of each cry. The attempt to replace body imagery with
language[41]—albeit a bird's language—is a tactic that can be compared
to Mary Kelly's *Post-Partum Document* in Chapter One. While Kelly was
critiqued by some feminists[42] for her use of psychoanalysis and the structures of language, Finn-Kelcey's similar interests were not commented
upon, possibly because her use of such theories was not so visually
evident in the work.

Two years later[43] Finn-Kelcey performed *The Boilermaker's Assistant*.
The audience was invited to the artist's first-floor studio on Shaftesbury
Avenue, in central London. "Following a white tape up the stairs and
along a dingy corridor, visitors found themselves in the shadowy decaying
grandeur of a panelled boardroom,"[44] where there was installed a park
bench, upon which the artist sat on the far end, neatly dressed and
brightly lit. The bench—"the seat of the five senses"—was lettered with
silver studs, and perched on it was a motionless magpie that stared with
an attentive eye. A whispering voice passed between four loudspeakers in
the corners of the room. Throughout the evening the artist continuously
read, at whisper level[45] into a hand-held microphone, from an instruction
manual, a "recondite work of Victorian origin."[46] The banal text became
something like a meditation for visitors:

> where T is the thickness of the plate in mm and C is a co-efficient
> whose values are given, both for lapped joints and for double-
> butt strapped joints ...[47]

The book was the only part of the performance that was left to
chance.[48] Finn-Kelcey purchased the manual only moments before
the performance, in an attempt to locate the most incomprehensible

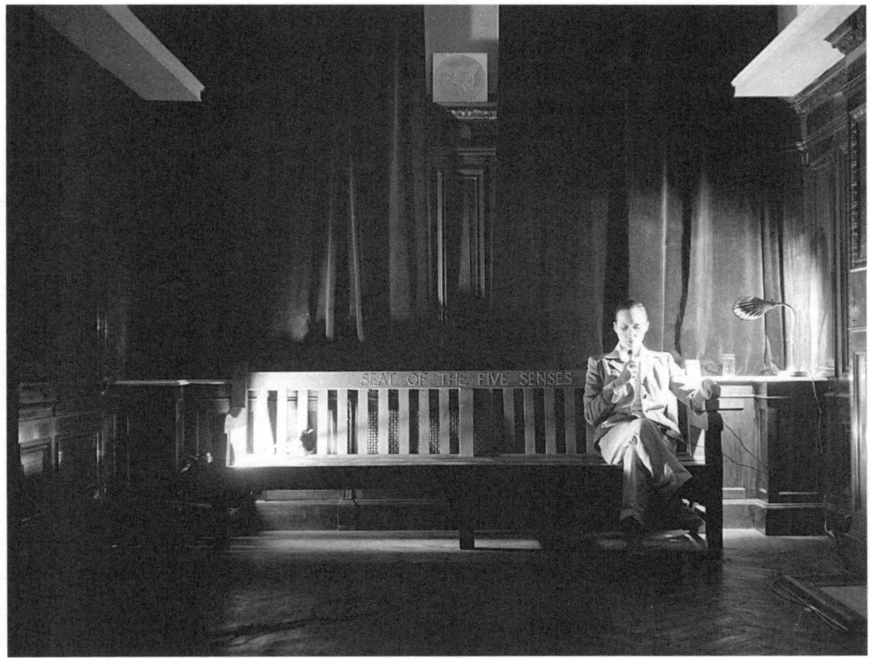

Figure 2.3
The Boilermaker's Assistant, 1978. Rose Finn-Kelcey. Photograph: H. Watton.
Courtesy of the artist.

technical book that could be found. This meant that she drew attention to the aural quality of her reading, rather than the material itself. This again exhibits her interest in language:

> I could also draw attention to … other implications. For instance, the *absurdity* of the existing language, when it's put together in a particular way it can be apparently nonsensical. The importance attached to specialisation, and for women how much we might feel outside of that. Boilermaking being very much a male vocation![49]

The microphone,[50] which may be read as a phallic symbol, was for the artist indicative of men and their assertive speeches; obviously Finn-Kelcey's performance subversively undermines this authoritative use of language.

One writer calls the use of sound in this piece, "an aural backdrop to the visual action."[51] I would argue, however, that the sound actually becomes the dematerialized subject of the piece, rather than the performer. The sound takes equal billing to the visual, as it would have surrounded the audience, who actually became part of the piece when they entered the room. Instead of a group seated in front of the performer, Finn-Kelcey chose to create the action around the audience.

Catherine Elwes, who attended the event, commented:

> She remained perfectly poised and controlled throughout, and I remember feeling both enthralled at the beauty of the spectacle and disturbed by the thought that she might be parodying the then feminist emphasis on autobiography, on the personal as political. But although Rose's work is often predicated on the ironic use of cultural icons, her work has addressed the tricky issue of how a woman might find a voice within the male culture and take up a masculine position of visible skill and mastery without renouncing her gender.[52]

Likewise, writer Guy Brett eloquently describes Finn-Kelcey's practice as one in which "the doubts are given equal substance as the certainties in the realization of the piece."[53]

In her 1980 performance *Mind the Gap*[54] Finn-Kelcey never actually performed, except for two brief appearances after a female voice had apologized for her absence. This performance further explored her interest in language and resulted in a virtually disembodied performer. In the exhibition catalogue Finn-Kelcey used a sixteenth-century French painting of two nude women, one tweaking the nipple of the other, by an unknown artist and titled *Gabrielle d'Estrées et une de ses soeurs*. Underneath this was written MIND THE GAP. Using an image of feminine fecundity, Finn-Kelcey undermines this in her performance, which features the *absence* of a female subject. The audience sat in the darkened gallery of the ICA, which included a spotlit treadmill and a block of ice glowing under a blue light, while muzak was pumped in. The notes to the performance read, "One blithe tune matched another, and still there was no action; until a female voice-over formally announced Rose Finn-Kelcey's apologies for failing to appear, and explained that 'finally, she didn't know what she wanted to say.'"[55] While the audience remained stalwart, sensing a bluff, the voice intermittently read a selection of working notes towards the unfulfilled event. Suddenly the artist appeared carrying two dumbbells attached by a fine wire. She placed the wire across the ice block and let the two weights hang in the gap between two plinths. Then she disappeared and the muzak continued to play. The artist returned at the end and mounted the treadmill, running against her own stamina until she reached her limit.

By removing herself (for the most part) from the performance, Finn-Kelcey inadvertently suggested the difficulty in finding an accurate method of expression. With the female body so loaded with meaning and the weight of history, how does an artist find her way out? The answer is she doesn't. It would be unreasonable for the artist to assume that an audience can cast off the tradition of female imagery in the same way that one cannot remove desire from the gaze. Finn-Kelcey attempts to negotiate a way forward, which may necessarily include the enacted absence of the feminist artist.

Guy Brett has written of the dialectic between performing and not performing as an abiding characteristic of performance art at the time. On the subject of Finn-Kelcey's use of this tension he wrote that she "took this a step further: her absence, her deflection of attention to object, action, sound, space, time, paradoxically accentuated her dialogue with the audience."[56] It is the absence that makes the most impact on the viewer. It is also the absence of a voice that may be read as paradigmatic of many feminist artists responses to a patriarchal societal order.

If Finn-Kelcey offers a strategy for acquiring a new language, or a new voice for women, it is a subtle and as Elwes eloquently puts it, ironic, one. What about women who chose to make a more overt strike at what they saw as the masculine order? Carolee Schneemann also questioned such issues in her *Naked Action Lecture*, performed at the Institute of Contemporary Arts in London in 1968. This performance asked, according to the original script: "Can an artist be an art historian? Can an art historian be a naked woman? Does a woman have intellectual authority? Can she have authority while naked and speaking? Was the content of the lecture less appreciable when she was naked? What multiple levels of uneasiness, pleasure, curiosity, erotic fascination, acceptance or rejection were activated in an audience?"[57] While closely aligned with Finn-Kelcey's interrogations of the voice, Schneemann's performance took a very different approach.

The performance was a lecture on the artist's visual works and their relationship to the history of painting. This lecture was conducted as she dressed and undressed. Accompanying the lecture were three slide carousels: one which projected slides of Schneemann's paintings and constructions; one with slides of her kinetic theater works; and one with slides of collages, and performances. The artist entered through the audience, who were seated, describing the sets of images to be shown. She wore a string undershirt and oversized overalls from which she extracted oranges that she distributed among the audience. The lights were then dimmed, the artist began to conduct her lecture at the front of the room. During the thirty-minute lecture, Schneemann continued to undress and dress again, using a pointer to discuss the slides.

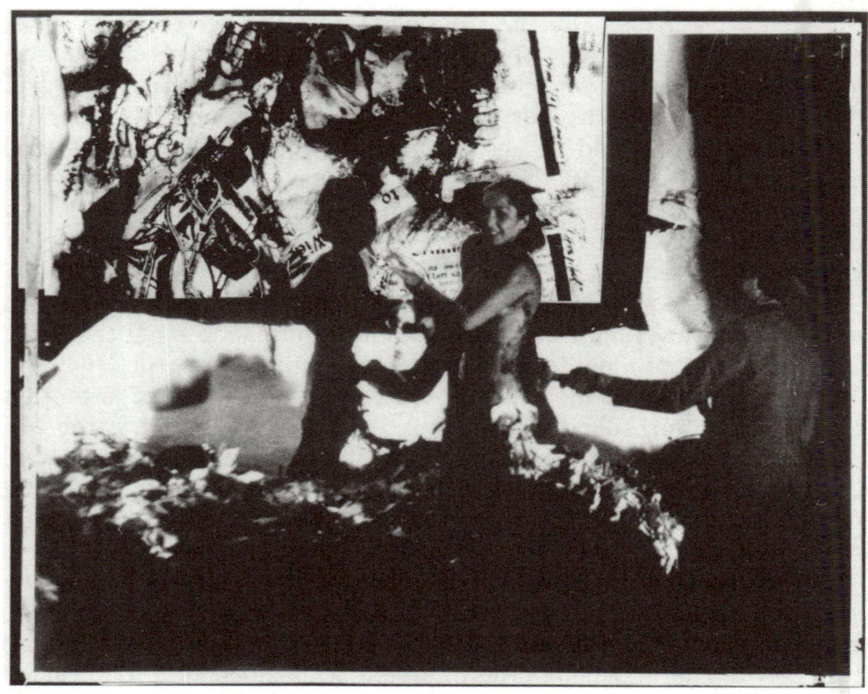

Figure 2.4
Naked Action Lecture, 1968. Carolee Schneemann. Courtesy of the artist.

Once the slides presentation concluded Schneemann asked for volunteers from the audience in order to demonstrate the principle of collage. Two young men—strangers to the artists—volunteered. In the light of the projector, they undressed each other, covered themselves with liquid glue and leapt from the stage into mounds of shredded paper, twisting and writhing so as to cover their bodies like a collage. The performance concluded when the artist returned to the stage and finished the lecture with points about the collage process and the gestalt patterns in the three human examples. At this point the performers exited and her film *Fuses*, 1965, began screening. *Fuses*, a film that shows graphic detail of Schneemann and her boyfriend making love, is in itself like a collage, with its burned out and painted on celluloid, *à la* Stan Brakhage. A review from the time quotes the artists as saying "After it was all over one man came up to me says, 'Madam, you've abused my sexuality' and quoted Wordsworth to me."[58]

The performance touches upon many of the themes discussed here. First, the notion of the female artist reclaiming their authority through the use of the voice in performance. In addition, Schneemann uses her nudity to make a point about the female in traditional art history; normally a muse, the nude woman has been objectified for centuries. Claiming back female sexuality, a motif that runs across Schneemann's body of work, would require a radical assault on the senses. This represents one strand of feminist thought regarding the body. The next section of this chapter deals with women who chose not to use their bodies as sexual objects in performances, but to use them to focus on their gendered role in the domestic order and the unequal division of labor within the home.

PORTRAIT OF THE ARTIST AS A HOUSEWIFE:[59] PERFORMANCE AND THE DOMESTIC

In Chapter One I have illustrated that concerns with the domestic were paramount for feminist artists in the 1970s. From the outing of women's work, normally hidden from view, to the investigation of the space of the family, domestic themes were seen in a range of work made by women artists. The concern with the domestic has its roots in the feminist literature that emerged in the United States and Britain in the late 1960s and early 1970s, such as Betty Friedan's book *The Feminine Mystique*. Examining artifacts from contemporary culture such as women's magazine advertisements, Friedan illustrated how even educated working women were debased by their representation.[60] Similarly Sheila Rowbotham's *Hidden From History* took as its primary concern the inability for women to be given the credit they deserved because of the patriarchal social structure. Increasingly feminist views became widespread in the public domain, and issues such as the division of labor in the family came to the forefront. The feminist slogan "The Personal is Political" also became a battle cry for feminism.

Feminist artists explored this territory, drawing on their personal experiences to inspire a feminist practice. In Britain Helen Chadwick, Bobby Baker, Alexis Hunter, Mary Kelly, Kate Walker, Su Richardson, Tina Keane, Hannah O'Shea, Silvia Ziranek and many others made work around domestic themes. In America artists such as Martha Rosler[61] (with her now well-known work *Semiotics of the Kitchen*), Judy Chicago and Miriam Schapiro (especially in their *Womanhouse* project) used domestic themes and sites in their practice. For artists here and abroad the investigation into the domestic represented a wide range of women's issues. Women's hidden labor as valid subject matter, a refusal of the commodification present in a gallery system that normally excludes women, and the idea of the domestic craft as "low" culture brought into the sphere of "high" culture were predominant among these issues. The economic and political considerations of women's work also factored in here.

In this section I present work made by feminist artists in Britain in the 1970s to illustrate the importance of the domestic as a theme in

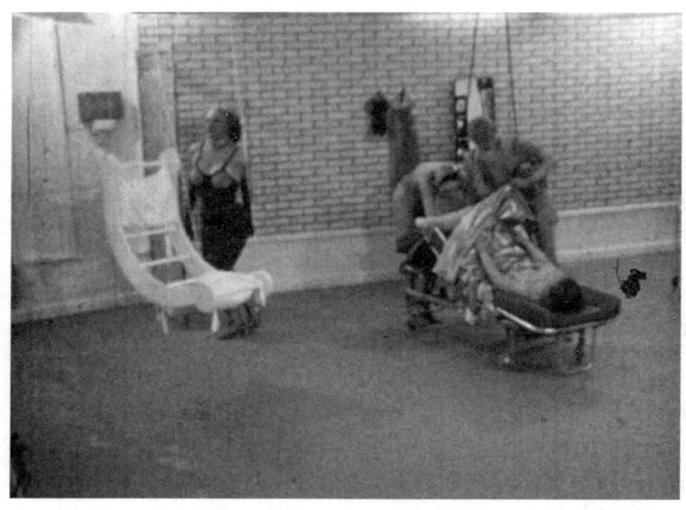

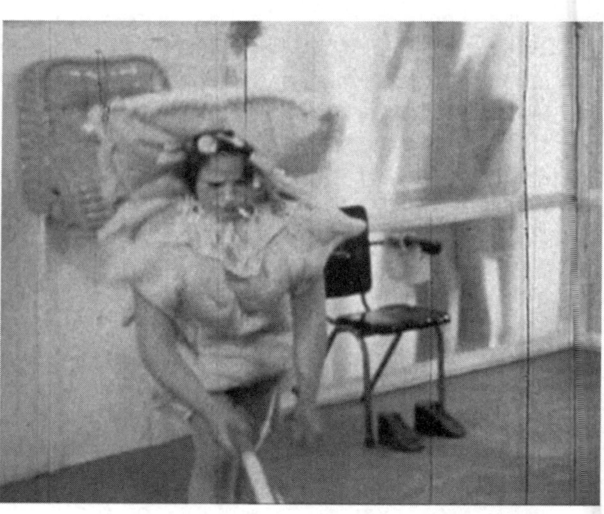

Figure 2.5
(Top and bottom)
*Domestic Sanitation/
The Latex Rodeo,*
1976. Helen
Chadwick. Courtesy
of Leeds Museums
and Galleries (Henry
Moore Institute
Archive). Estate of
Helen Chadwick.

performance. While some feminists in Britain focused on the theoretical issues relevant to the women's movement, resulting in exhibitions such as *Post-Partum Document,*[62] the publication *m/f* and films such as *Nightcleaners,* other women strove to make work on a more accessible level, concentrating on the quotidian experiences of being daughters, mothers, workers and wives. Common motifs running through their work included the domestic division of labor and the patriarchal ordering of the family, as well as the lack of a space outside the home for women to make work in.

Helen Chadwick's[63] *Domestic Sanitation/The Latex Rodeo* is an intriguing example of early feminist performance in Britain. Made in 1976 the work may be read as a predecessor to artists such as Matthew Barney or Daria Martin, who use sculptural props and costumes to create holistic artworks. Chadwick's early work while at art school involved creating skin-colored casts of latex that were painted directly onto women's bodies to suggest clothing. These "erotic artefacts"[64] were used in performances such as *Domestic Sanitation/The Latex Rodeo*, staged as a performance during her student days in Brighton, and unlike most early feminist performance in Britain, recorded by video for posterity.

Latex Rodeo begins with a group of four women (one of them Chadwick herself) that are engaged in a satirical activity of cleaning and grooming. In the opening of the performance three latex clad women submit one of their cohorts to a strange grooming process. Played out to a "Studio Girl" cosmetics voiceover with a strong American accent, the women wear parodic merkins and seem suggestive of an antiquated and grotesque concept of femininity. The object of their attention lies back on a table as if experiencing some gynaecological procedure. The obvious comparison between the painful and sometimes extreme lengths women go to to look good is enacted here. Little could Chadwick have known the craze for plastic surgery that would ensue in forthcoming decades, where women and men alike submit themselves to extreme surgical processes to look younger and/or more beautiful.

The second part of Chadwick's *Latex Rodeo* takes the form of women dressed like pieces of bedding who perform dull, mundane household duties. The repetitive[65] and perhaps nonsensical nature of housework is seen here with one woman vacuuming, another woman bouncing off a strange latex object and yet another bouncing off what appears to be a mattress mounted to the wall. The woman vacuuming is smoking a cigarette, a wry nod to the frustrated housewife, a far cry from the idealized notion of the happy homemaker so often seen in post-war advertising. While this performance is at times humorous, which seems to be a common characteristic of British performance art, it is a harsh depiction of the housewife and so-called womanly duties.

Another artist who used humor to explore the domestic was Bobby Baker,[66] who emerged from St Martins School of Art having studied painting, like most women artists of her generation.[67] It was at St Martins that Baker saw performances by Gilbert & George as well as that of Bruce McLean and his group Nice Style. However, the dominant influence at the art school at that time (*ca* 1970) was the New Generation[68] sculptors, led by Anthony Caro. For Baker and other female colleagues at that time, the New Generation sculptors represented the masculine-centered forces of the art market and all of its biases. While at St Martins, Baker wanted to write her thesis on the technique of making chocolate mousse, clearly a pun on conceptual instruction/strategy pieces by the likes of Art & Language and Joseph Kosuth. She says, "I got very excited about the processes involved in cooking."[69] Baker began making cakes out of boredom, rather than as a polemical art practice. Eventually she saw them as works of art, exhibiting them as sculptures:

> I started making these little armchairs out of cake, and icing them. They were quite rudimentary, very badly made, but I loved them. I didn't know exactly what I was making them for. They were really sort of exercises for myself. Then one night I made this baseball boot because I was dyeing boots and selling them by mail order, so I made this baseball boot out of cake and I just had … one of the most wonderful moments of my life, when I looked at this very badly made cake and I realized that it was a work of art. … This was a sculpture and … it was of equivalent stature to the pieces of work that were going on in the British school of sculpture that was represented by St Martins School of Art. These huge pieces that were by Anthony Caro. My work could be compared to that. And it was so liberating and so funny and so subversive.[70]

This conceptual leap also provided a way into performance for Baker because she wanted the work to be consumed. In the beginning she hosted tea parties where invited guests would eat elaborate edible sculptures of naked women.[71] Then she met a group of performance artists and became involved with staging live events. Her first performance, however, did not involve food. It took place at St Martin's School of Art on the wedding day of Princess Anne, who is the same age as the artist. Baker took the part of the princess, and became convinced of incorporating herself into the event as a work of art, combining this and her love of baking. "It was just fantastic. Like the scales fell off my eyes. From then on I incorporated my edible pieces in the performances."[72] In her earliest events with food, Baker would schedule an installation in a gallery, working days in advance so that the cake would be fresh and could be eaten on the day of the event.

One such performance took place a few years later at the ICA, from 25 May–22 June 1978.[73] For this installation and performance Baker created an art supermarket in the gallery, replicating the setting of a grocery store. Baker's supermarket was made up of 3,000 objects that the artist had constructed by her own hand in the lead up to the show over the course of nine months. Each object was decorated in sugar, and resembled a food product, which could be purchased by visitors to the exhibition. The objects were lined neatly on shelves, giving the effect at a distance of an authentic supermarket. Banners on the wall proclaimed

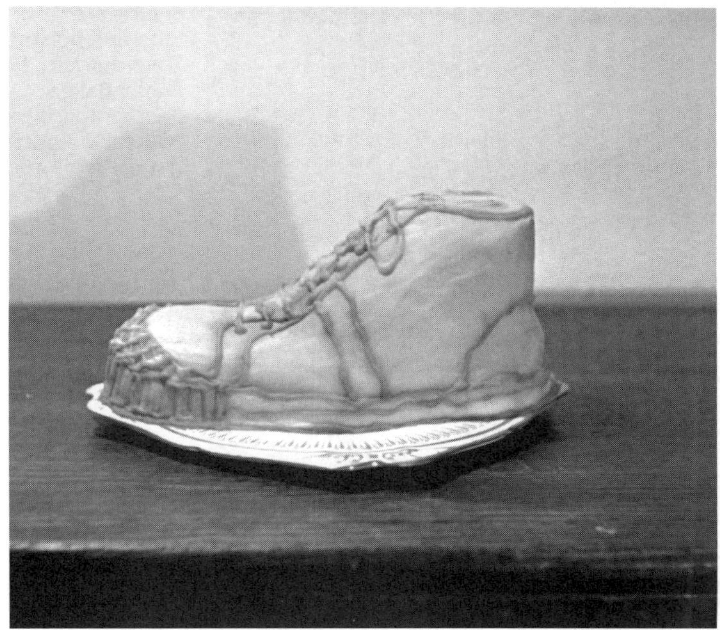

Figure 2.6
Baseball Boot Cake, 1972. Bobby Baker.
Photograph: Andrew Whittuck. Courtesy of the artists.

"art bargains galore" and the artist wore a smock with a badge that read "art sella" and a paper cap, emulating the traditional uniform of the women who work in normal supermarkets and institutional kitchens. Baker herself manned a cash register that was set up in the gallery.

Baker's idea for *Art Supermarket* represented a commentary on capitalism, which would be destroyed by the consumers who acquired the objects.[74] Her primary interest was art's transformation over time, which relates to the time-based pieces by artists such as Kelly, Clark and Schneemann. She said, "It was open for two weeks and by the end the image was destroyed,[75] but it wasn't obvious at the opening or on the early days."[76] Later in her career, Baker would rectify her frustration by making the transformative quality of the work apparent over a shorter period of time, for example, an hour or the length of a film. The *Art Supermarket,* though, represents the "outing" of domestic labor that was prevalent among feminist work of the 1970s. Baker, through this piece, takes the invisible and unrecognized work of women to the extreme and presents it with a sense of humor. The incorporation of her body into

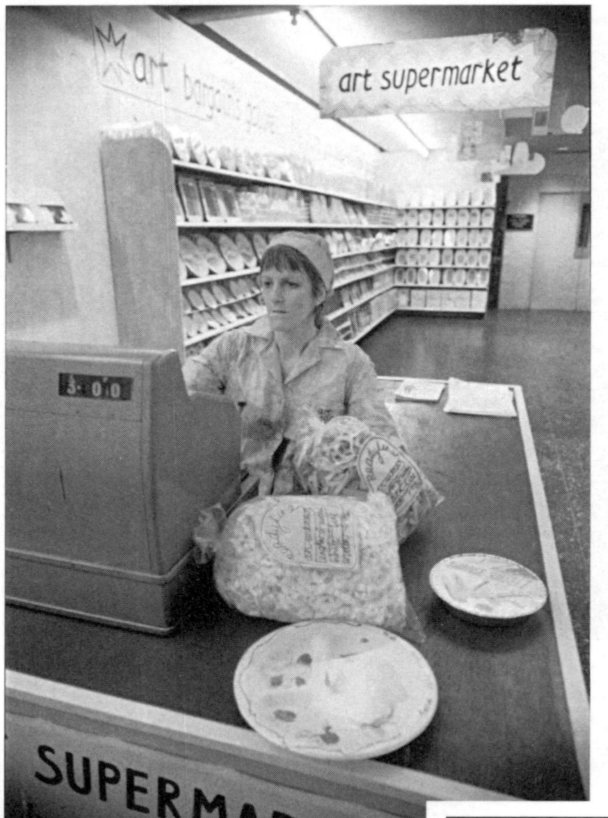

Figure 2.7
(Top and bottom) *Art Supermarket*, 1978. Bobby Baker. Photograph: Andrew Whittuck. Courtesy of the artist.

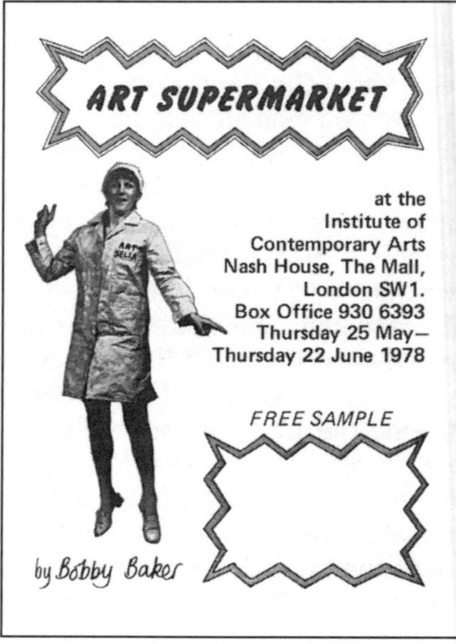

the work adds to the humorous element as Baker satirizes the desirable female object by depicting herself as a "lunch lady" type, with uniform, cap and badge. Underneath Baker's humorous subversive performance, the message conveyed to the viewer is that the woman is responsible for selecting and preparing food for the family, and thus, the unequal division of labor in the family structure is invoked. This can be compared to Kelly's investigations into the division of labor in Chapter One.

Baker has commented on the presence of her own body in the work:

> It's very much an integral part of my work. I made that decision early on that I would necessarily be present in every single piece, and the work would be based on my own personal experience of life. That it would be from my own mind out. That implied that I would be physically present.[77]

For Baker, the work would not function without the presence of her in it. The importance of being present in the work is often mentioned by feminist artists of Baker's generation who worked with performance. The notion of the art object as the certified work of a genius, appreciated by a civilized connoisseur (in other words, the elite), is rejected. For a feminist project, it also subverts the status of female as object by drawing attention to the author's own position and appearance. Baker says, "I acknowledge with every performance that I do that I'm a woman. I draw attention to that. I draw attention to my weight, my imperfections, I make fun of it. ... It reclaims that sort of territory for myself."[78] Marina Warner writes of this exorcism of the female self in relation to Baker's performance: "These private sketches strip away the comic play-acting which Bobby Baker uses to present herself in performance, and they reveal the work's roots in profound and painful self-exposure."[79]

Is Baker exposing herself, or playing a part? Baker repeats in a public forum the daily activities of the housewife and mother. Judith Butler writes on the idea of gender as a cultural performance:

> In what senses, then is gender an act? As anthropologist Victor Turner suggests in his studies of ritual social drama, social action requires a performance which is *repeated*. This repetition is at once a reenactment and reexperiencing of a set of meanings already socially established; it is the mundane and ritualized form of their legitimation.[80]

Baker's re-enactment of the banal aspects of shopping, and in other performances, preparing food, encompasses Butler's points about woman as a gendered construction. Baker is in fact playing out the traditional female role as carer and nurturer for the family.

A review of Baker's project at the ICA pointed out another important aspect of the time-based *Art Supermarket* installation and performance: its ability to engage a wide audience. It reads:

> The best thing about Bobby Baker's work is that it is so accessible. Anyone, even philistines, can understand and enjoy it. Her performances are visually enthralling, very funny, very brave. Food is her medium. That, and words. She talks as she performs, stomping about in her pink nylon overall, setting up situations, making statements, questioning and explaining.[81]

The wide accessibility of the work is a goal that many feminists strove for in a reaction against elitism and connoisseurship.

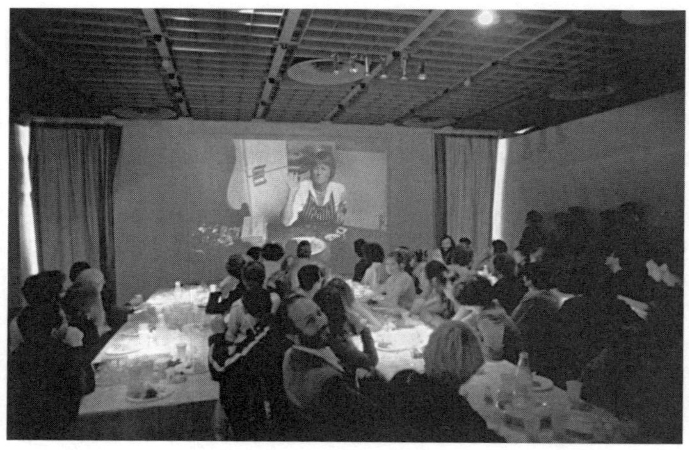

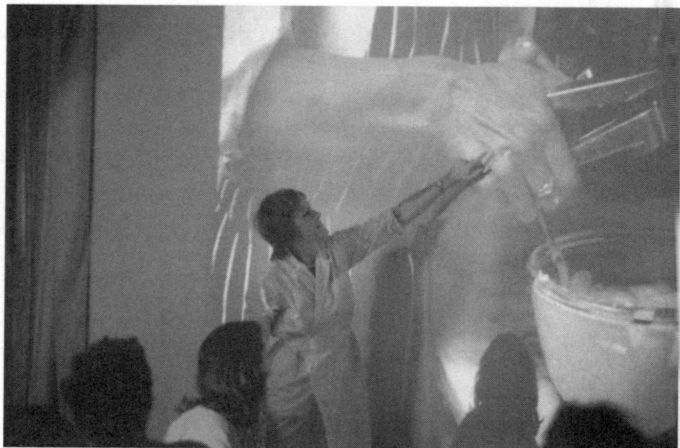

Figure 2.8
Tasting the Mayonnaise (top), *The Fine Sinews* (bottom), 1979. Bobby Baker. Photograph: Andrew Whittuck. Courtesy of the artist.

In 1979 Baker took part in the Hayward Annual, a yearly exhibition of art that had normally centered on successful, and hence, male artists.[82] In 1979 the exhibition was programed by Helen Chadwick, and featured four performance artists, including Silvia Ziranek,[83] Cosey Fanni Tutti[84] and Anne Bean. Baker performed *Packed Lunch*, in which she created a packed lunch for each visitor to the performance. Her partner, Andrew Whittuck, photographed Baker preparing for the performance, meticulously creating homemade bread rolls, hard-boiled eggs, and other snacks. These bits were assembled and labeled and were later eaten by the audience while Baker performed. Her performance consisted of a parodic lecture on the work that had gone into making the lunch, illustrated with 80 slides of the preparation, delivered with deadpan humor.

Domesticity and efficiency play the central roles in this performance. The domestic, and therefore invisible, work of the woman is made evident to the audience. Baker's irony and deadpan delivery subvert any signs of subversiveness. The ease with which the audience is able to digest the work (figuratively as well as literally) has to do with its subject matter. Underneath the humor is the matter of division of labor within families, which typically takes the form as the woman as carer and nurturer, performing most of the food preparation for the family, and taking care of her children and husband.

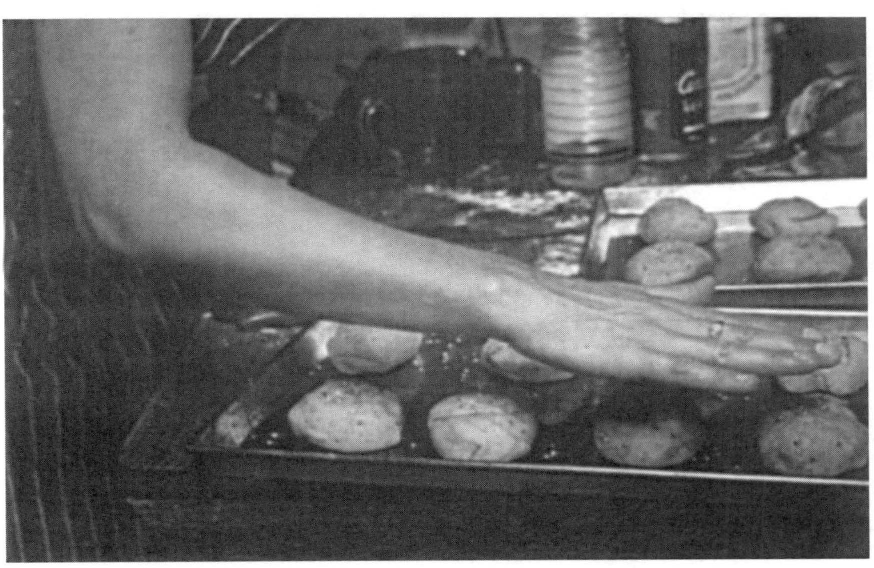

Figure 2.9
Preparing the Rolls, 1979. Bobby Baker.
Photograph Andrew Whittuck. Courtesy of the artist.

In the same performance series Silvia Ziranek also took a humorous view of domesticity in her work, *Chili Con Cardboard: A Contemporary Triptych*. In Ziranek's typical style, which was a form of social commentary cloaked in humor, she presented her recipe for Chili Con Cardboard. In a presentation similar to Baker's, Ziranek gave a three-part performance where she would undress to reveal different outfits. The first, was a rubber and plastic ensemble (as Ziranek was opposed to wearing leather because she was a strict vegetarian), which complemented a piece on the political mayhem wrought in South Africa. Next she donned a pink voluminous ballooning outfit constructed from kiting fabric, and finished in a Pierrot costume. Ziranek would undress, but never reveal her body. While she notes that this was not a specifically feminist tactic, her performances did derive from a critical social commentary. Ziranek spoke of her early work:

> I suppose my work ... used to be about social commentary. I did rather bemused and stylish verbal visualizations of lifestyles ... and rather genteel. It wasn't mocking, but there were so many things that I remembered in such detail about my upbringing about how people live, how people react to one another, ... what they say, what they do, what they wear, the way that they live, their grasp of politics, of reality, of fashion, geography, food.[85]

Her interest in food grew out of working in her kitchen, and a genuine love of cooking. Recipes from dinner parties became a journalistic device for her, a record of personal events.[86]

Like Baker, Ziranek's use of the domestic subject matter was more related to humor than to a feminist ideology, which, Ziranek asserts, was not her primary agenda at the time:

> I don't really call myself a feminist. ... when I traveled the bows in my hair were far too large and far too pink. But in Australia it was great. Just by being a woman you were part of the movement, whatever the movement was. ... Being gay wasn't an added bonus. You could be gay if you wanted to.[87]

Ziranek touches upon the difficulty inherent to feminism in England, which included constraints placed on women from various factions of the movement. In retrospect it is clear that Ziranek was concerned with women's issues and liberation; however, her interest in fashion and makeup and light-hearted approach to art-making meant that she was not subject to criticism in the way that for example, Kelly or Clark, were. In the case of Ziranek and Baker, their engagement with feminist ideas remained cloaked in humor and dressing up, but more radical

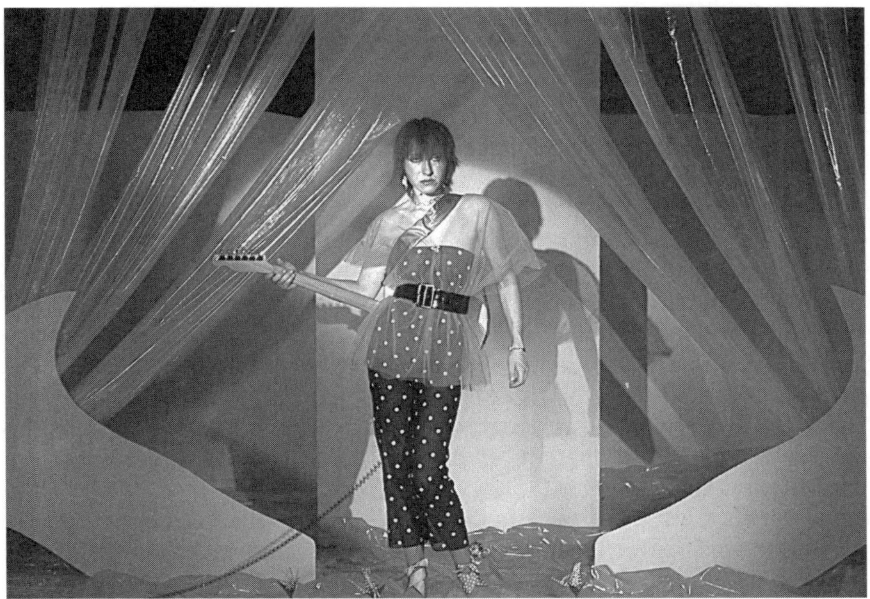

Figure 2.10
I Lost my Sole to Rock 'n' Roles. Silvia Ziranek. Courtesy of the artist.

feminists might have opposed such a whimsical approach to making art. This is one of the key problems with the women's liberation movement: the contradictory stances on issues meant that there was little unity among feminists at that time. The lack of agreement among feminists seems to support Butler's ideas on the impossibility of a cohesive idea of "woman".

THE EXTREME BODY: CAROLEE SCHNEEMANN, CATHERINE ELWES AND TABOO SUBJECT MATTER

Because she made her body the literal site of so much of her art, and because she underscored her sexuality as a creative force in her work, Schneemann was often dismissed as self-indulgent and narcissistic by the art establishment. But she was not alone. Other women, many influenced by Schneemann, had begun to make similar work confronting the sacrosanct boundaries separating female sexuality and artistic authority. The roots of feminist performance art, which would flourish in the 1970s, took obstinate hold and many boundaries, closely linked to the socially demarcated margins separating artist/woman, high/low, subject/

object, began to leak and bleed together under the banner of political purpose.[88]

In the quote above Rebecca Schneider touches on one of the central debates in women's performance art: the exposure of taboo subjects, which usually involved exposing one's body. While this type of action would provide feminist artists with a powerful agenda, it also garnered a great deal of malice and critical contempt. For the female artist coming out of art school in the 1960s a woman's body in performance usually took on the status of an object: one need only think of Klein's paintings, Manzoni's actions or Pollock's artist-wife Krasner captured for posterity looking on submissively at her husband's wild gesticulations on to the canvas. The next generation of women artists would begin to question the role of the woman as spectacle in artworks, and seek to shift the emphasis away from that of submissive participant to a more active, confrontational role.

American artist Carolee Schneemann,[89] whose *Blood Work Diary* was examined in Chapter One, was one of the earliest avant-garde female performers. One of her early live events was as a participant in male artists' work, for example when she was seen as the "Olympia" figure in Robert Morris' 1964 action *Site*. Here she is seen as a passive, silent, female nude (from Manet's painting *Olympia*) watching the activity that centers on her.[90] Schneemann, however, was already creating her own performances, which existed on the boundaries between art and pornography, and used visceral imagery to confront audiences. Catherine Elwes commented on Scheemann's changing role, "She becomes active as opposed to being an object in some male fantasy of a performance with the same status as any other object in the piece."[91]

Schneemann lived in London for the first part of the 1970s, and had performed one of her best known works there earlier in the 1960s. Arguably Schneemann's most recognized work, *Meat Joy,* was staged in London in 1964.[92] It is a performance of about 70 minutes that begins with participants seated at a long table and evolves into a Dionysian orgiastic frenzy of men and women, who wear tiny fur bikinis and writhe around the floor in paint, with carcasses of dead chickens and fish thrown on them as well as at the audience. Schneemann's words give some indication of the essence of the performance:

> *Meat Joy* has the character of an erotic rite: excessive, indulgent, a celebration of flesh as material: raw fish, chickens, sausages, wet paint, transparent plastic, rope, brushes, paper scrap. Its propulsion is toward the ecstatic—shifting and turning between tenderness, wildness, precision, abandon: qualities which could at any moment be sensual, comic, joyous, repellent.[93]

During the performance, a group of men and women begin by eating and drinking, then perform actions such as "body falling" and take part in choreographed sequences. The animateur, or person who keeps time and directs the performance, proceeds to cover the chorus with chicken carcasses, dead mackerels, paint and newspapers. The performance has become infamous for its visceral materials as much as for its celebration of eroticism and sexuality.

Schneemann's inspiration for the unusual materials in the performance came from urban and pastoral experiences. She had spent time working on farms in the countryside. She said:

> I would be a summer labourer and assist with the artificial insemination of the cows. And then all this work with chickens. I would slaughter something like twenty chickens every Friday for a camp where I worked. And it was old-fashioned style with a little hatchet and a wood block and steaming and plucking them. Different buckets for this and different buckets for dipping the bodies, so chickens are very intimate for me.[94]

While the visceral aspects of *Meat Joy* have secured its notoriety in art and performance history, it is actually a carefully choreographed and structured piece. Schneemann was interested in the "leg choreography" of Busby Berkeley's synchronized swimmers.[95] She made drawings and carefully worked out details of the performance, which is synchronized to a soundtrack of 1950s and 1960s dance hits.

While in Paris it was easy to get participants to rehearse the project and show up for the final performance, London proved much more difficult. When the intended participants never arrived, Schneemann was forced to recruit strangers on the street on the day of the performance. Schneemann recounts the nightmare of organizing *Meat Joy* in London:

> Norman Toynton ... was so drunk at the time of the performance he didn't know which way he was walking, backwards or forwards. I was pushing him around and the women that were supposed to participate had disappeared. It was the beginning of learning the nightmare of performance principles. Somebody brought back four girls with hockey sticks who were on their way home from high school ...[96]

Once the performance was under way, there was a flood in the church hall because a performer forgot to turn the water off. Hence, blood and feathers were scattered throughout the hallway. When the minister in charge of the hall tried in vain to stop the performance, he called the police. Sirens signaled the end of the performance, with Schneemann and her group escaping from the police in the back of a taxi.[97]

The explicitness of Schneemann's performance occupied a tenuous position, even for feminists. Catherine Elwes, whose work is discussed below, noted the fine line between woman as powerful performer and as sex object. Although crediting Schneemann as an important figure for her she also "had significant and important reservations about her work".[98] For Schneemann, appearing naked was a celebration of female sexuality, and in essence, a political act. Dan Cameron, curator of Schneemann's mini-retrospective at the New Museum of Contemporary Art in New York wrote of her nudity, "The transgressive aspect of Schneemann's nudity was a key element in the way these issues transcended sculpture and become political acts, charged by the public spectacle of a woman dictating the terms by which her body could be viewed, and in so doing ensuring that her work would be misconstrued."[99] Indeed, her work has been celebrated as much as it has been reviled by future generations of feminists.

Amelia Jones writes, "Thus, putting the artist's body—as female body—in movement radicalizes the painterly female nude, denying that it is necessarily only the object of a 'male gaze'."[100] While I agree that it was important for women to be able to use their bodies as material, it cannot be forgotten that there is a history of depictions of female nudes whose ideology cannot be cast off so easily. As Sally Potter wrote at the beginning of the 1980s, the female who makes herself the center of the performance is always risking objectification:

> Women performance artists, who use their own bodies as the instrument of their work, constantly hover on the knife edge of the possibility of joining this spectacle of woman. The female body, nude or clothed, is arguably so overdetermined that it cannot be used without being, by implication, abused. But of course it is unthinkable that the only constructive strategy for women performers would be their absence.[101]

Potter's alternative strategies include building imagery based on the female body, including menstruation, reproduction and sexuality; or for others it is getting "the female nude and muse to speak." While arguably Schneemann has taken these steps, there is always a fine line between provocative and fetishistic use of the female nude. It is difficult to obtain reviews of *Meat Joy* in London to gauge the British reaction to it. Schneemann writes of the British temperament in a letter to her parents from London: "most English men (women) are reserved, recalcitrant ... 'uptight' ... most of the time I feel like I'm in a sweet mad-house, or an army or nunnery."[102] Would this society that stymied Schneemann have understood her attempt to reclaim female sexuality? Or would they have simply found it titillating or morally retrograde? Certainly to expect a viewer at the time to understand the full implications of the performance is naïve. Once again the gap between artist intention and repetition remains a continual dialectic in performance art of this period.

Many feminists and writers were opposed to artists such as Schneemann who used their bodies, which happened to be quite attractive, in explicit actions.[103] Schneemann insists her work was about freeing women's sexuality, and casting off the image that women were oppressed and victimized. Her reference to herself and her colleagues at the time as "activists"[104] suggests the political dimension of the work, which for her reached far beyond the explicit images that she created. Critics said Schneemann and others exploited their own beauty to create provocative performances. The use of the explicit female nude creates a volatile subject. For a writer such as Andrea Dworkin in the United States, this was tantamount to a crime against humanity. Her argument is that pornographic images of women are harmful to the sex on the whole because they emphasize their "carnality" and prove that women like to be whores.[105] Dworkin ignores socioeconomic factors, such as the fact that some women were forced into prostitution and pornography in order to make a living. However, she does make the point that while Schneemann says she is liberating her sexuality, this does not mean the viewer is similarly liberated, and can determine the difference between performance art and pornography—or wanted to. And, it does seem that some of these artists did enjoy getting nude in public.

Mulvey's writings on scopophilia are applicable here, for she notes that it is not only the viewer who receives pleasure, but also the object of the gaze. In the case of Schneemann, and Elwes below, there is an ecstatic, celebratory pleasure involved with being looked at. Here the erotics of spectatorship are somewhat reversed. The artists assert that their performances were concerned with liberating their sexuality, but there was also the sheer enjoyment of that liberation, the desire to be seen and acknowledged. This becomes more than just the use of the body as material and moves toward an investigation of the workings of desire, on both the part of the viewer and the viewed.

Catherine Elwes, coming from a younger generation than Schneemann, also concerned herself with performance-based imagery that was previously taboo.[106] Her *Menstruation* performances are among the most memorable pieces in radical[107] British feminist art. As a student at the Slade School of Art she studied under Stuart Brisley, who was well-known at the time for his outrageous performances, which often included visceral materials such as bodily fluids, including vomit, blood and spit. Elwes gravitated toward the studio that he taught at the Slade because, although male-oriented, there "you could do all things experimental, performance and video."[108] While at the Slade Elwes made a book that was an inside joke about the male-dominated area of performance called *A Plain Woman's Guide to Her First Performance.*[109] Her most striking works of this period, though, were done on successive occasions at the Slade.

Menstruation I 1979 saw the artist dressed in a white dress on top of a circular white sheet upon which she bled, drew and wrote. Elwes spoke about the piece as a logical step in the development of a feminist performance art:

> Well, as I said before, the ground had been laid by Stuart [Brisley]. He was permanently throwing up, so to evacuate your body as part of a work of art was not a very original thing to do. But nobody had used menstrual blood as far as I knew, in this country anyway.[110]

In *Menstruation II*, also at the Slade, Elwes used the same principle, this time enclosing herself in a small makeshift room, with a glass partition between the artist and the audience, which consisted of people passing by at any time of the day. People would write questions on the walls, which would be answered by the artist writing on the glass. By the end of the three-day performance the glass was covered in writing.

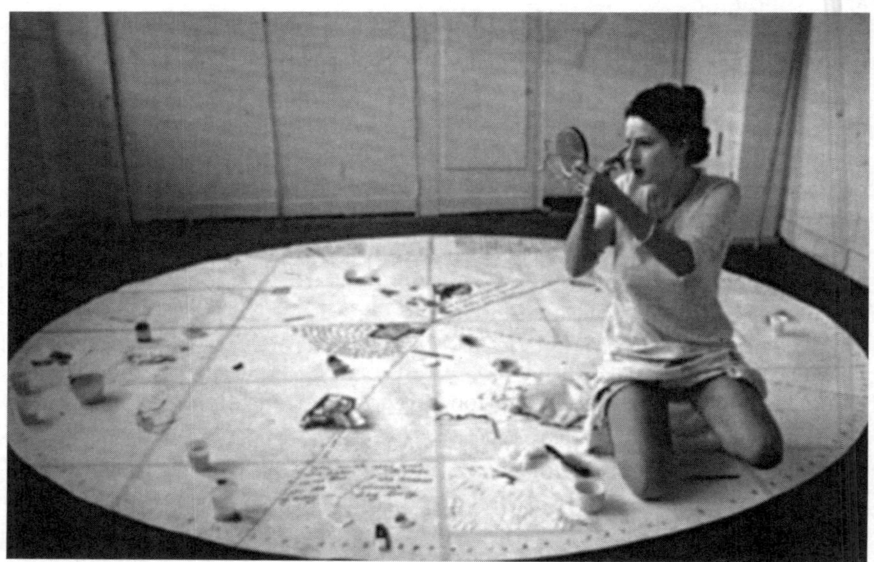

Figure 2.11
Menstruation I, 1979. Catherine Elwes. Courtesy of the artist.

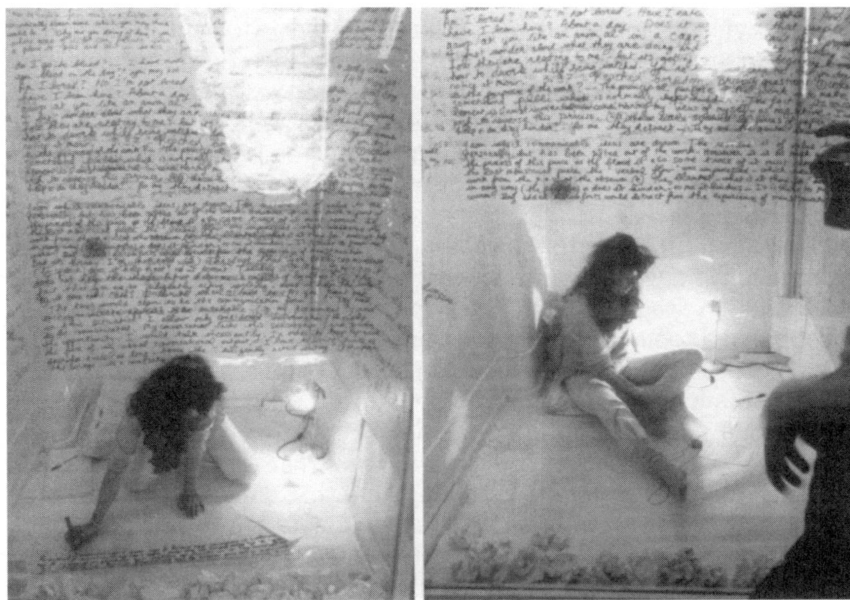

Figure 2.12
Menstruation II, 1979. Catherine Elwes. Courtesy of the artist.

Alexis Hunter was a fellow feminist who saw the point of the work, which is that there is an absence of cultural recognition of menstruation:

> Catherine Elwes is reversing this cultural void, and has to work against taboos that she has experienced in her own conditioning. She feels that the "material" of women's culture/experience does not work within a masculine structure, and that painting and sculpture, because of what they have been used to express in the past, are too loaded for illicit imagery.[111]

The absence of images of menstruation throughout the history of art is testimony to its status as taboo, or unsuitable subject matter. For some feminist artists menstruation provided an outlet for exposing this "cultural void", as Hunter describes it above. Orifices of the female body, traditionally only shown in religious paintings whose subjects' mouths are often represented open in spiritual ecstasy, equally became subject matter for feminist artists in the 1970s. Intimate borders of the body were exploited by artists including Judy Chicago, who, like Elwes, presented menstruation in an aesthetic language. Lucy Lippard wrote, "A good deal of this current work by women, from psychological makeup pieces to the more violent images, is not so much masochistic as it is concerned with exorcism, with dispelling taboos, exposing and thereby diffusing the painful aspects of women's history."[112] Chicago's *Red Flag* 1971 depicts a close-up of the artist's torso, truncated from the pubic area to her thighs, while removing a bloody tampon.[113] In its aggressive attack on notions of traditional feminine propriety, it also attacks notions of artistic and cultural taboo.

Chicago's *Menstruation Bathroom* was exhibited in 1972 at *Womanhouse*, an artist-run initiative in which a house was remodeled and used as studio and exhibition space, in California. What appears to be an immaculately scrubbed bathroom has been contaminated by used sanitary napkins and tampons with additional feminine products featured on the shelves. Chicago's blatant display of female detritus provokes viewers in a direct transgression of acceptable artistic subject matter. Chicago, however, exhibited the *Menstruation Bathroom* in a site that was a domestic space transformed into a gallery. It is quite likely that viewers who would be willing to visit such an alternative site would necessarily be sympathetic to the work.

While in the United States artists such as Judy Chicago and her circle made vaginal imagery and menstruation a focus for their work, in Britain it seems less prevalent, although this may be because of the lack of documentation or interest in the work.[114] Judith Higginbottom[115] made works on the menstrual cycle at the same time as Elwes. For example, her piece *Water Into Wine* recorded details of the menstrual cycles of 27 women, examining the relationship between menstruation and the lunar cycles as well as dreaming and creativity. On a related topic, Susan Hiller, an American artist living in London, also made a work about her pregnancy entitled *Ten Months*.[116]

The focus on menstruation in Elwes' work was criticized. Some viewers accused her of reinforcing essentialist ideas based on physiology of men and women. Elwes says:

> Maybe I was being naïve, but I was trying to point to the value that was attached to menstruation. Biology should only be biology, not destiny. I wanted to dislodge the negative value associated with biological feminity. ... The bleeding isn't the problem. It's the negative value attached to the bleeding that causes us the problem.[117]

While she admittedly focuses on the differences between men and women, Elwes attempts to undo essentialist arguments on the basis of cultural value, or lack of value. That Judy Chicago's static imagery could be viewed and reacted to by the visitor is clear. Elwes, though, allowed people to watch her bleed in a public location, and one that was certainly male-dominated. Their reactions were directed, at least in some cases, at the artist, who responded on the glass wall.

Elwes,[118] Chicago, Higginbottom and Schneemann each made attempts to deal with unspeakable subject matter relating to women's sexuality. Painting or sculpture might not have been as effective in dealing with this subject matter as performance (or installation-based work such as Chicago's) that provides a confrontational impact on the viewer. Surely part of the excitement of *Meat Joy* and *Menstruation I & II* is that the public is allowed into very intimate and sexually charged events. Incorporating her body in extremity, the female artist creates a plat-form for dialogue on topics that could not easily be conveyed other-wise. Here, the difference between documentation and the performance itself is crucial. While photographs of *Meat Joy* and Elwes' menstruation performances are how we encounter the work today, there is never the possibility to recreate the atmosphere of a particular location and audi-ence. While these things provided the charge of feminist performance, it is their ephemeral nature which has resulted in the lack of witness of these events in histories of post-war British art.

A ROOM OF ONE'S OWN: PERFORMANCE IN ALTERNATE SITES

The move toward performance occurred alongside some artists' exclusion from and desire to avoid the gallery system. In fact, it is difficult to say which came first as they are inextricably linked. London in the 1970s had many alternative galleries that focused on performance, conceptual and

```
BERLIN

by Rose English and Sally Potter

Part One : The Pre-Conditions (in the house)
Part Two : The Spectacle (on ice)
Part Three : Remembering the spectacle (in the water)
Part Four : The arguments (at home)

Part One is at 41 Mornington Terrace, N.W.1. on Fri 26th
and Sat 27th March, 8 - 10 pm. Camden Town Tube.

Details of Parts two to Four in Time Out etc.
```

Figure 2.13
Original *Berlin* invitation, 1976. Rose English and Sally Potter.
Courtesy Rose English

installation work. A selection of these will be discussed in the following chapter. However, in this section I will look at the specific relationship between performance and the alternative site. Using the example of a work in four parts, I will show how live activity could be enhanced by the use of non-traditional settings, and how working outside traditional sites allowed women artists a greater freedom than the white cube.

Berlin was a performance created by Rose English and Sally Potter[119] in 1976. It was divided into four sections that took place at three different locations: Part One took as its setting the large squatted Regency house where the artists lived, 41 Mornington Terrace, Camden Town; Part Two was at the Sobell Center Ice Rink; Part Three was staged in the Olympic swimming pool at Swiss Cottage Baths; Part Four took place back in the house. English had been involved with political activities in the 1970s, mostly concerned with housing, as well as the practical and theoretical aspects of feminism. She had met Potter while working on a piece called *The Boy Baby*.[120] Needing dancers for the piece she went to a performance that Potter and Jackie Lansley had done, and they became acquainted. They eventually combined their efforts in a live piece called *Park Cafeteria*, which took place at the Serpentine Gallery, and used the park as an additional setting to the gallery.

Berlin came at a time when the artists were questioning the gallery system, and considering if the theatrical world could accommodate their needs. English spoke about her boredom with contemporary theater:

> It was an incredibly dreary moment theatrically at that time. Unfortunately it was entirely dominated by a style of theater at that time that was very well rewarded, which was a form of agit prop theater.[121]

English's lack of interest in the theater and gallery spaces led her to find new settings for her live work, which included a horse-racing arena. English was drawn to the settings of *Berlin* because "of the sheer beauty of the spaces that we decided to place the work in."[122]

English and Potter did not script *Berlin*, but they did spend time writing in preparation. They also made paintings, drawings and photographs, had discussions and played music in rehearsals for the piece. In the place of a written script, they created a scenario that would be acted out by the participants, who included a chorus of men and boys in addition to the artists. The artists sent invitations to their friends and colleagues. The invite directed the audience to arrive for Part One, and to find further information in *TimeOut*.

Each section of the *Berlin* series exploited the aspects of the existing architecture of its setting. Part One (The Pre-Conditions)[123] took place in the house at Mornington Terrace, with Potter appearing bare breasted, dressed from the waist down in a skirt covered in magnolia leaves and carrying a fur muff, clearly a pun on the female anatomy.[124] Potter and her colleagues incorporated various aspects of the infrastructure of the house, from hanging light bulbs to the staircases, into the performance. The next installment, Part Two (The Spectacle) happened one week later at an ice rink on the other side of London. Potter exploited the possibilities of such an unusual setting, appearing on ice skates and parodying follies spectacles with a male chorus.

In Part Three (Remembering the Spectacle), which took place on the night following Part Two, the audience assembled in an Olympic swimming pool at Swiss Cottage, where the performers read pieces on the diving board, the area around the pool and in the water. The concluding section, Part Four (The Arguments), took place one week later back at Mornington Terrace, where once again the artists utilized aspects such as the mantelpiece and the bare floors of the house in the performance.

Berlin typifies feminist artists choosing to circumvent gallery or theater spaces. What is the significance of performing outside of a gallery, art school or space normally dedicated to the arts? One answer to this question lies in the absence of history. Like Finn-Kelcey, who chose to make

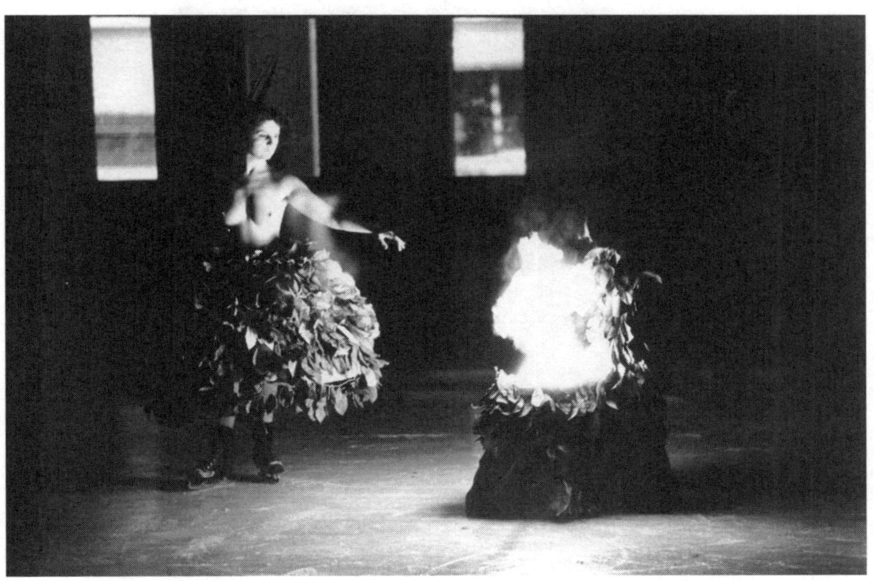

Figure 2.14
Berlin, from Part Two: The Spectacle (on ice), 1976. Rose English and Sally Potter. Courtesy of the artist

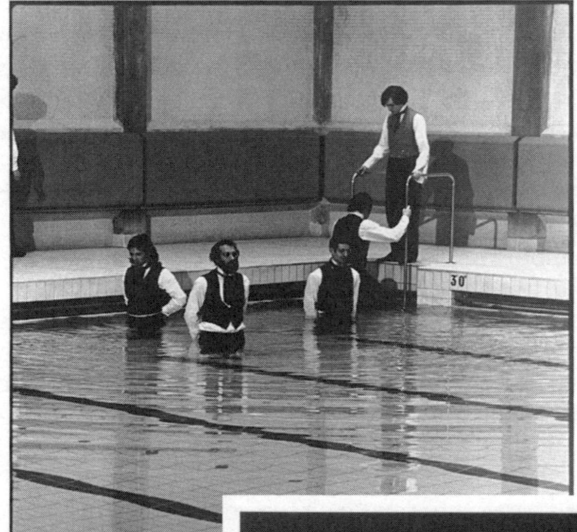

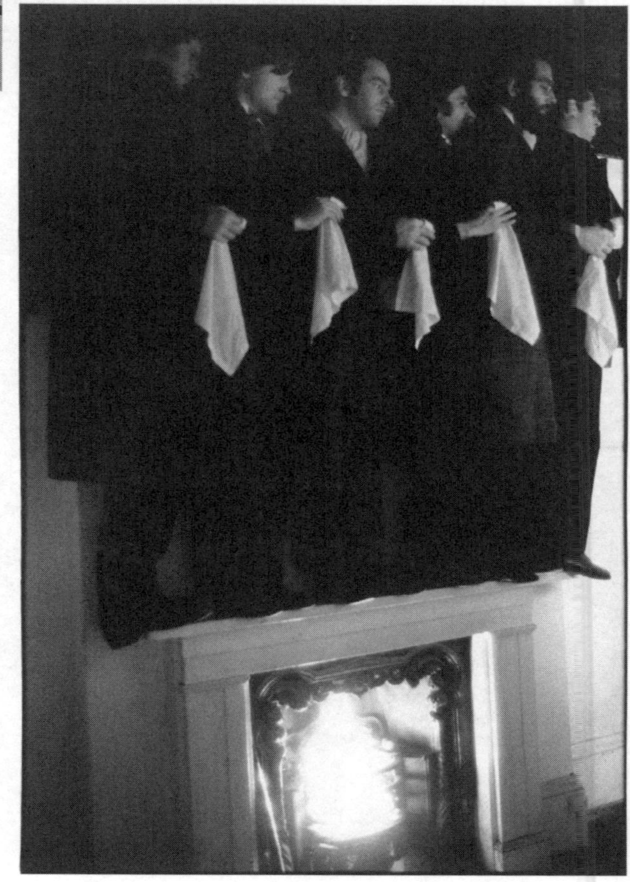

Figure 2.15
Berlin, Part Three: Remembering the Spectacle (in the water) (left), *Berlin*, from Part Four: The Arguments (at home) (bottom), 1976. Rose English and Sally Potter. Courtesy of the artist.

performance because she felt it was not loaded with the precedents that painting or sculpture were, or Baker who resisted the hard materiality of male-dominated New Generation sculpture, English and Potter were able to cast off elitist associations with galleries or similar artist spaces. They also could avoid the pitfalls of theater, which relied so often on spectacle and again, on women as objects. In the pool, ice rink, or their home the audience could become part of the performance, moving through the space with the artists. English and Potter, in their discussions of the representation of women that were part of the performance, bring attention to the difficulty in using the female body in any kind of work. By removing the female performer from a gallery or theater space, the artists attempted to reconfigure the female form without the loaded associations of such sites.

The notion of being outside of the conventional art site also leads to a bacchanalian sense of being outside of the laws of that culture. English and Potter did not have to adhere to any principles but their own, and could freely perform what they wanted to the invited public. They could also play with the audience in a way that would have been virtually impossible to fund in a gallery situation. For example, Part Three's location of a pool makes it seem like the ice rink from Part Two has melted overnight.[125] The humor in these performances is subtle, and the locations lend themselves to a sense of irony quite easily. English spoke about the importance of keeping a sense of humor at that time, when political debates (including feminist) were dominating the avant-garde of the cultural industries, including film, theater and art:

> what was terribly important through it all was to maintain a very sharp ironic eye and a great sense of humour because it was such a worthy time as well. There were elements of it that were verging on the Maoist really. You just needed to retain a sense of yourself and a sense of humour through it all whilst there were things that were really transforming as well. Like any moment in history, the fallout is sometimes formidable but the core is really interesting.[126]

CONCLUSION

It is important to remember what London-based artist Marc Camille Chaimowicz recently commented on a panel about art in the 1970s. He reminded the audience that terms like performance and event are retrospective categories, devised afterward to try to make a historical account of the work. Artists at the time of these activities were avoiding categories rather than trying to include themselves in them.[127] It is a futile activity now to try to put a hermetic structure around any of this work.

At least it is easier to understand the crossovers and exchanges between themes of the body, the domestic and alternative sites in performance at the time.

I have suggested before, and feel that it is worth reiterating, that this information only cracks the surface, and much more may be said about the performance works of the above artists; likewise, there are many more artists—Rose Garrard, Shirley Cameron, Hannah O'Shea, Anne Bean, Nan Hoover, Carlyle Reedy, Monica Ross, Tina Keane[128]—whose performance work has not been given the attention that it deserves in this account. A quote from artist Catherine Elwes, sums up the essence of performance art in the 1970s:

> Some people used to say that it was the only time that they felt truly alive, the moment when they were performing, and that everything in between was somehow mediated, constructed, unreal at some level. It was only in those "live" moments that they were absolutely in control, of themselves and the audience. You are in control, you call the shots. We were all megalomaniacs, I suppose.[129]

Her words describe the feeling that performance provided for the artists—one of elation and absolute control over the work and their bodies. It is a complex topic as there are several bodies at stake. There is the body of the performance artist who chooses to perform naked or to focus on biological themes and then there is the body of artists who elected not to undress at all for an audience. Yet, in both cases, the pleasure of being looked at seems to outweigh the fear of a "male gaze" exploiting the artist's sexuality; in fact, they saw themselves as exploiting it for themselves. For some of the artists, for example, Schneemann or Elwes, using their body was a liberating factor in the work. For others, such as Finn-Kelcey or Baker, it was simply the tool by which to perform. In all cases, it is concerned with de-idealizing the body, which in the western canon has always been about idealized women. For example the Vitruvian man is an ideal of the male body, which has always had a privileged relationship to the divine image, and is manifest in ratios and proportions of the body. In 1970s London, it is not simply the counter-assertion of women's bodies, but it is about the body as the negation of idealization; hence the corporeal elements like shit, menses, piss and spit.

It is not merely the body as object that is at stake in the work discussed in this chapter. In many cases, it is the body as instrument. That is why I refer to the work as performance art rather than performative practice. Whatever the value of that label, it is certainly the case that in some sense the prostheses of art (the paintbrush, the hammer and chisel) are abandoned in favor of the body as an instrument. Without seeking to resolve these questions of genre, they embody a move from an "object" to an "event". This could be understood in a number of ways. First is the belief that an event exercises a powerful effect upon the audience and indicates a new way of experiencing art for the viewer. The move from object to event also enables the avoidance of the increasing commodification of the art object in the retail space of the gallery. Of course, in retrospect sales of documentation from these performances have sometimes provided income to the artists; in the case of feminist artists, however, this trace is less an economic concern and more of a form of memory. Traces from performances such as Schneemann's *Meat Joy*, English and Potter's *Berlin* and Rose Finn-Kelcey's *Mind the Gap* are necessary for this work to find its way into a history of the period or an institutional context.

Lastly, the nature of the event as opposed to the object opened itself up directly to the incorporation and representation of political issues and positions. The body event found a new route into the political. In the case of the artists discussed in this chapter this concerned the liberation of their bodies as well as the larger ideology of feminism.

Chapter 3

ALTERNATIVE SPACES FOR FEMINIST ART

The rise of new forms of art practice was inextricably entwined with the reaction against the commercial gallery system.[1] Artists were increasingly unable to adhere to the conventional system of patronage as their work did not conform to traditional categories such as painting or sculpture. In addition, the economic recession in England at the time meant that there was virtually no market for contemporary art.[2] For women artists, especially those making work influenced by the women's liberation movement, galleries were unavailable spaces. Discrimination due to the subject matter of the art, personal demands such as family life, and what has in general been called a "patriarchal system"[3] led to feminist artists' isolation from the commercial system.

Artists were open about their animosity toward the mainstream system. Rose Finn-Kelcey says:

> The idea of belonging to a gallery and aiming to sell work was completely out of the question. If you look at the economics of the situation, we were all post-war babies who came along during the optimism of the late 1940s and 1950s and who in the 1960s were experiencing a buoyant economy and the most amazing optimism.[4]

Finn-Kelcey, like many of her generation including Anne Bean and Carolee Schneemann, presented shows in alternative gallery spaces as well as public sites in the city. This exploration of new venues grew out of uneasiness with market-driven tactics.

The artists that emerged from art school in the early 1970s had fewer traditional skills than in previous generations. Fundamental changes to art education made in the late 1960s meant that basic skills such as life-drawing and figurative painting were no longer necessary to graduate, substituted by alternative techniques such as photography and silkscreening.[5] Another crucial alteration in the educational system was the rejection of Greenbergian art history in favor of a more theoretical approach. All of these factors coincided with a rise in the number of people going into higher education; suddenly, one way of surviving without a job was to enroll in art school and live off a grant. As Finn-Kelcey and Rose English have pointed out, London in the 1970s was a different place and one far easier and cheaper to live in than today. Alternative living situations and grants for students made surviving as an unemployed artist possible. When Finn-Kelcey describes the "enormous possibility" of this situation, one can see that the need for commercial representation might have been less important to this generation of politically motivated and activist artists.

Changing policies in education and the harsh economic climate drove artists to seek out alternative conditions for showing work and hosting performances. Out of this necessity came the fashion for showing in non-commercial, or independent, spaces. As performance artist Rose English put it:

> A certain rigidity of expectation seemed to attach itself in either a gallery or a theater context, and somehow this rather arcane notion of a salon presented itself as an attractive thing, where one was in charge of the ambience and the terms under which the work was presented.[6]

As demonstrated in the previous chapter, English and her collaborator Sally Potter used unlikely locations for their performances in order to keep them accessible and evade the restrictions placed upon them by commercial galleries. In the case of English, Potter and many of their contemporaries, the non-traditional forms their work took would have been as unwelcome in a mainstream gallery as their feminist politics.

Art historian Lisa Tickner recently looked back on the feminist aversion to the commercial gallery system in the 1970s:

> I think there was a feeling in the 1970s, in certain quarters, and this is just a memory of the flavour and temperature of the times, that there was something called selling out, ... and to do this was absolutely unacceptable. And certain things would be considered without reflection as *ipso facto* selling out. So having a show, working other than in a group ... or being an individual but having an exhibition in a gallery ...[7]

While Tickner's remarks are poignant, it is difficult today to understand the intensity of these women's reaction against the commercial system. The contemporary art world celebrates artists who work with themes such as sexuality, identity and trauma—content which would have seen them ostracized in the 1970s. Can we say that we currently live in a less politicized age?

Works made by women artists during this period were shown in various types of spaces that were often in opposition to a commercial system.[8] In this chapter I examine alternative sites for showing work in London (and in some instances, locations outside of the city) during the 1970s. These sites fall most clearly into the following categories. First, public sites, where artists such as Rose Finn-Kelcey, Anne Bean, Silvia Ziranek, Carolee Schneemann, and Bobby Baker exhibited their work in unexpected locations where it was visible to the general population of the city. Second are domestic spaces, or situations in which feminist artists were obliged to harness their creativity in the home due to financial and familial constraints. This category is also inextricably connected with the domestic as a theme in the work produced. Third are alternative galleries born out of 1960s/1970s conceptual practices where women artists were encouraged to exhibit, in some cases alongside male colleagues.

The feminist exhibitions in 1970s London explored in this section were enabled and made possible by the pioneering exploration of alternative spaces and the feminist journals and publications such as *Red Rag*, *Shrew*, *WIRES* and *Spare Rib*. These publications formed in themselves an alternative forum for the members of the women's movement to network and exchange ideas, a new discursive space for feminist art outside the mainstream, male-dominated market.

In exploring the new and alternative kinds of spaces that female artists found to exhibit their art, I attempt to assess the positive and negative aspects of this artistic exodus and its cultural impact. What did working outside of the art market offer a feminist practice? Did opting out of the traditional system contribute to a ghettoization of women's art, resulting in the erasure of the female artists of the 1970s through cultural amnesia? How have the activities in these spaces informed contemporary practice?

GOING PUBLIC:
FEMINIST ARTISTS AND THE CITY

I left art school in the late 1960s, a period when many young artists were saying "We don't want to show in white cube spaces. We don't want to have anything to do with the commercial galleries." It was almost as if belonging to a commercial gallery was akin to a form of prostitution and was really frowned upon. Many thought, "well the older generation can do that, but it's not right for us." Some artists looked outside the gallery system for alternative sites, and made work for those locations. Of course now site-specific work is commonplace, but it's highly organized or curated. When I first left college I wanted to install twenty flags made from a variety of materials alongside the railway track. I liked the idea that passengers would come across the work and that commuters would see the flags daily, creating a change of experience depending upon the weather conditions. They didn't have to think in terms of whether it was art, or even going to a gallery. They would be brought to the work and past the work in a train.[9]

During the 1970s Finn-Kelcey's work, as discussed in the previous chapter, predominantly took the form of performances where either the artist or props of her devising would elicit activity. Her earlier work, however, relied upon the placement of objects in public sites to provoke response. In one of her first pieces after art school she devised an intervention on top of a historical building in London. In response to an invited contribution to Art Spectrum London[10] Finn-Kelcey placed a large flag with a text message on the top of Alexandra Palace. Any Londoner would find Ally Pally, as it is colloquially termed, a peculiarly apt site for any "message", as it is one of the highest sites in London, commanding the landscape around it, and the location for the first public broadcast of radio. The message—HERE IS A GALE WARNING—was an ironic tautological statement by the artist, referring simply to the movement of the object itself. Like earlier pieces of conceptual art by artists such as Joseph Kosuth and Art & Language, Finn-Kelcey was playing with the everyday object and its quotidian use, as well as the "instructional" text. Where Kosuth played with *ipso facto* information such as the definition of a chair juxtaposed with the object itself, Finn-Kelcey stated the obvious in this public work.

Within a short time of Finn-Kelcey's flag being raised the BBC was flooded with telephone calls from people asking "Are we going to have a gale? Is it true?"[11] The artist hadn't expected the viewing public to take the flag as a literal statement. She was pleased that the statements had credibility, but never anticipated that it would be so well connected with the function of the building.[12]

Perhaps the most provocative intervention in this series were the flags installed at Battersea Power Station in 1972. This self-generated project began when Finn-Kelcey thought that a building located directly on the Thames River and containing large flagpoles could provide the perfect site for her work. She began campaigning for permission to exhibit from the owners of the buildings—including MI5, the Church Commissioners, and the Central Electricity Generating Board—and supplied them with information on her project. Eventually the Central Electricity Generating Board allowed use of their building, and provided some money toward materials. The fact that Finn-Kelcey's text, which was a play on a political slogan, included an implicit advertisement for what they did, probably helped secure the site. However, when the flags were raised they read POWER FOR THE PEOPLE, a pun on the slogan "Power to the People", which played on the use of the building, the public were outraged. The company was inundated with telephone calls from people in Chelsea, the district directly across the river, who were incensed that the Electricity Board had put political slogans on their façade. In the end, the flags were removed because the Board found it too politically problematic to keep them in place.[13]

Finn-Kelcey's use of the phrase POWER FOR THE PEOPLE is also reminiscent of conceptual tactics of some of her predecessors, such as Kosuth's *One and Three Chairs*, 1965–67, where a chair is displayed as a definition of the word "chair" in text on the wall, a photograph of a chair to scale, and that same chair as a found object.[14] Finn-Kelcey similarly used words and language in a subversive way, asking the viewer to read between the lines. There was also the inherent political content of the

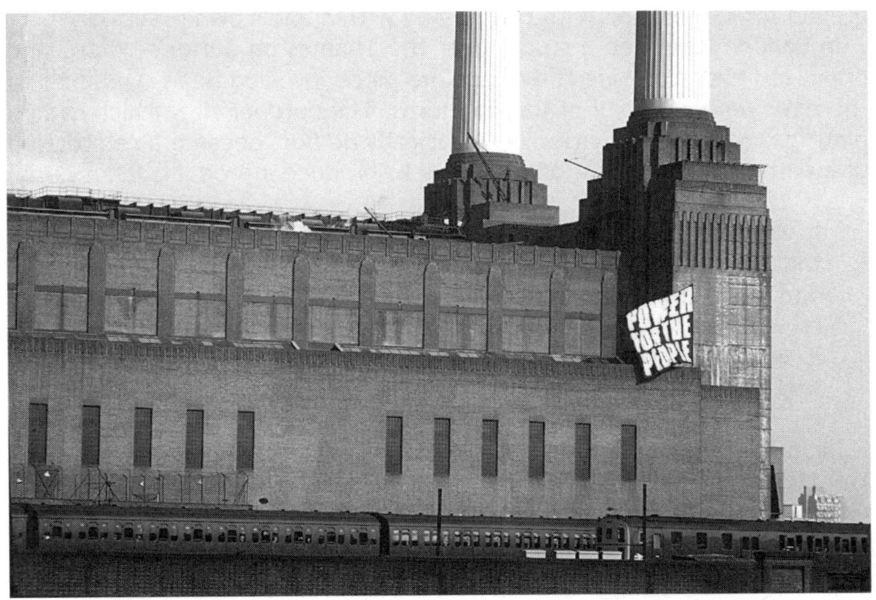

Figure 3.1
Flag, 1972. Rose Finn-Kelcey. Photograph: Rose Finn-Kelcey.
Courtesy of the artists.

work. Finn-Kelcey, who was adamant about showing her work in alternative spaces, and resisting the traditional trajectory of a working artist, was a political artist. She was aligned with the feminist movement, which utilized slogans and banners in agitprop activities. Finn-Kelcey's flags can be considered feminist interventions in the same way as agitprop posters or banners. In this way her work can be viewed in the context of others of her generation, such as Stuart Brisley and John Latham, who took political issues[15] as themes in their work at the time.

While Finn-Kelcey used *plein air* sites for her work, impromptu performances and happenings were also staged out of doors. For example, the Bernsteins—a group that consisted of fine art graduates from Reading including Anne Bean, Peter Davey, Malcolm Jones, Jonathan Harvey, Chris Miller, Brian Routh and Martin von Haselberg—staged impromptu performances with few invited guests.[16] Casual passersby would be witness to pieces such as *Taking Measurements of Yourself as an Artist*, which was staged in the woods nearby Hastings.[17] This type of event had parallels in the United States with artists such as Joan Jonas and Adrian Piper using the city as site for performance work.

Anne Bean,[18] a member of the Bernsteins, created events in locations in central London. At Reading she had been part of a group of students taught by Rita Donagh, where performative actions grew out of a life-drawing class. Donagh was supportive and provided "an incredibly fertile ground for exploration with people and within one's own practice".[19]

In London Bean had a studio near the Thames on Butler's Wharf, and organized events beside the river. One piece involved Bean swimming in the river wearing a pair of flaming horns. The outdoor site, which had no restrictions as the activities were basically *ad hoc*, became a celebration of creativity and a rejection of having to produce a product. Bean said:

> It was almost like the whole thing was a work in progress rather than individual pieces and the whole thing was about energy and interaction. I don't remember articulating where I was going or what I was doing. It was really about getting on with stuff. It was, in a sense, anti-academic, in that way, anti-product, anti-material.[20]

Bean had already done work in galleries with the groups the Moodies and Moodier. The opportunity to work outside of an organized facility fostered an alternative network or community, with Bean inviting fellow performance artists and friends, and news of the event traveling by word of mouth.

Silvia Ziranek fondly remembers one of Bean's performances by the river:

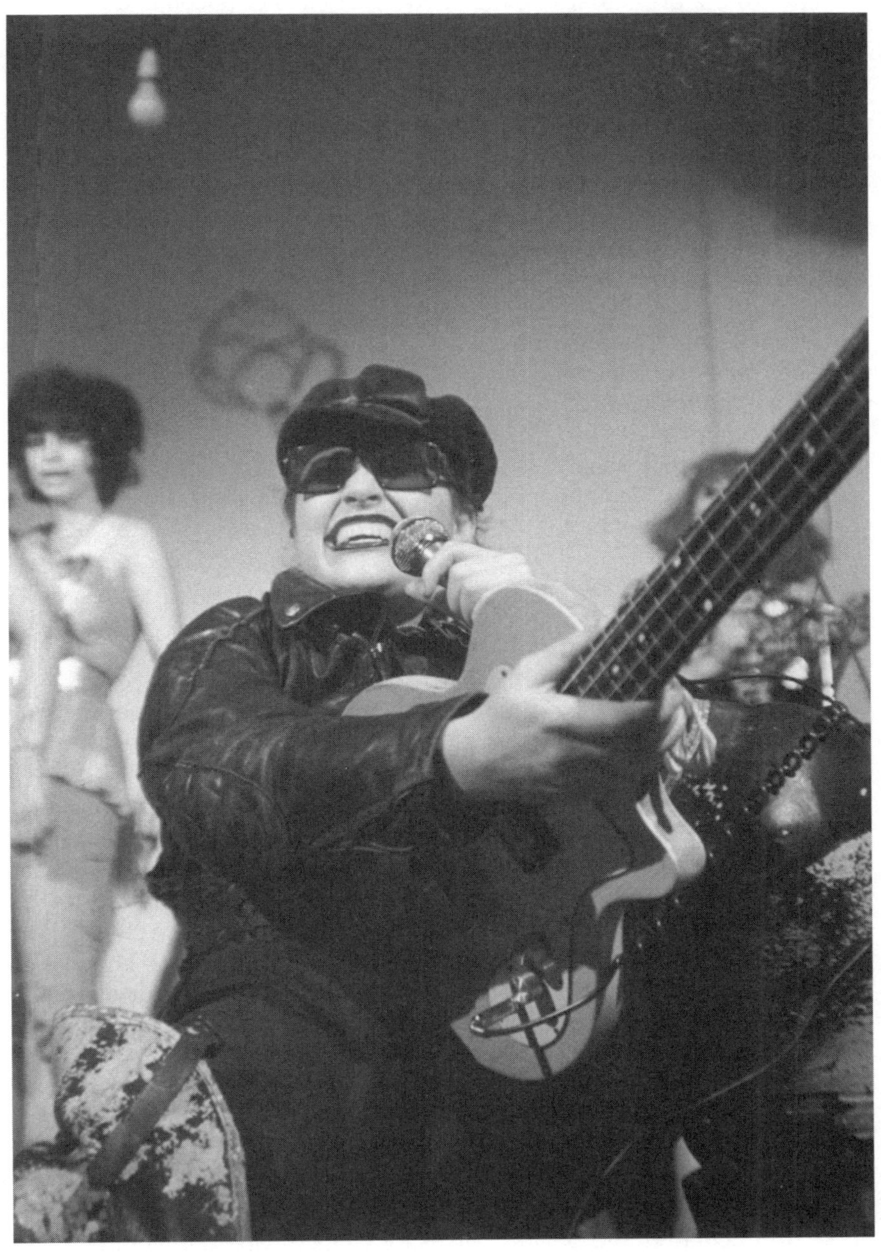

Figure 3.2
Moodies, *ca* 1975. Anne Bean. Courtesy Anne Bean.

> She wore a dress that was made out of rashers of bacon and then
> she stood in front of an electric fire as she twirled around. As
> she did ... the fat melted and presumably she was fairly edible.[21]

Bean's performances often took their resonance from notions of fear or danger[22] combined with playful actions. Her whimsical tone was reflected in pieces such as the following dialog, performed in one of Bean's riverside series. Ziranek, with two men accompanying her, entered the site. The men carried a telephone table, rug and glass handkerchief vase. The dialogue was as follows:

> Ziranek said "that charming vase".
> They said "tiddlypom".
> "That charming vase".
> "Tiddlypom".
> "That charming vase".
> "Tiddlypom". "Tiddlypom". "Tiddlypom". "Tiddlypom".
> "That charming vase".
> "Tiddlypom"
> "That charming vase".
> "Tiddlypom".
> "That charming vase".
> "Tiddlypom". "Tiddlypom".
> "Shall we go now?" and then they all said "Tiddlypom" together.
> Then they picked the bits up and all walked off.[23]

In her signature style, Ziranek's contribution was short,[24] humorous and a pithy form of social satire. The objects that were placed around her— the rug, the telephone, the table—suggest bourgeois tastes. The juxtaposition of these with the incongruous site near the river made for an eccentric approach. Artist such as Ziranek and Bean, as well as their male colleagues in London, were not paid for these events. They were self-funded and self-motivated. However, these small happenings, often overlooked in the history of this period, provide an important glimpse into the *zeitgeist* of the 1970s.

Without the restrictions of a traditional setting, artists were freer to experiment and take risks. However, as in the case of Bean and Kate Walker (discussed below), taking chances also meant risking physical harm. Perhaps the most important feature of the events at Bean's studio and Butler's Wharf, though, was the opportunity for members of the public to encounter the performances by chance. One can compare the work of Bean and Ziranek to Ana Mendiata's performances in the United States during the mid-1970s. These often took place in the landscape, where Mendiata's body became integrated into nature, at times covered

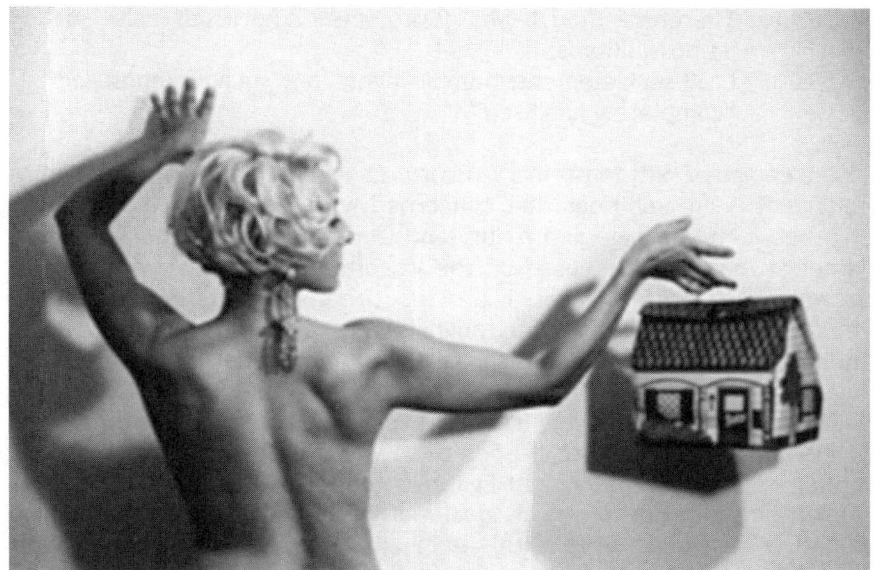

Figure 3.3
ICI VILLA MOI, 1989. Silvia Ziranek. Courtesy of the artist.

in twigs or earth.[25] Although Mendiata's work took a more somber tone than her British colleagues discussed above, both bodies of work prioritized the integration of performance into the landscape.

A few years earlier, Carolee Schneemann's *Ices Trip Train* 1972, which was also known as *Isis Strip* 1972, was completely integrated into a public environment. A program of films, videos, performance, and other events called Ices-72 started at the Roundhouse and took place in various alternative venues including on board a Channel ferry and an airplane traversing the Atlantic, as well as in swimming pools, fields, parks and various other sites. Schneemann's performance took place on a British Rail train traveling between London and Edinburgh during the annual festival in August. Tickets were sold for this journey, which also included ten live concerts.

Ices Trip Train 72 involved Schneemann undressing and redressing on a dining car table in preparation to roller skate the length of the train, as it moved between the two cities. During the act of disrobing and redressing the artist read paragraphs from Wittgenstein's *Tractatus Logico-Philosophicus* that were sequenced with rail time, for example: 3:11, 3:13, etc. For example:

> 3:13   Therefore, though what is projected is not itself included, its possibility is.
>
> 3:20   I call such elements "simple signs", and such a proposition "completely analysed".

The choice of Wittgenstein's *Tractatus Logico-Philosophicus* was significant as it is an ambitious text concerned with identifying the relationship between language and reality and to define the limits of science.[26] Although many have focused on the visceral and provocative nature of Schneemann's performances, it is evident that she was steeped in theoretical and historical discourse, aligning her work with that of others in the feminist movement, such as Finn-Kelcey and Ziranek, who were interrogating issues around language at the time.

This play with language carries over into the title of the work. Schneemann liked to keep it open as to whether it was "Ices" or "Isis", a phonetic play on the Ancient Egyptian goddess worshipped into Greco-Roman times for her role as an ideal mother and wife, and as the matron of nature and magic. Despite this ambiguity as to the title, Schneemann's notes for the performance read, "Isis takes you for a ride."[27] The integration of ancient mythology and religion centered on matriarchal figures was a common theme in feminist art, for example Judy Chicago's *The Dinner Party* 1976. As in Schneemann's earlier performance at the ICA (the *Naked Action Lecture*) here she conflates language, a typically male-dominated societal structure, with female power. How evident this was to an audience on a British Rail train en route to the Edinburgh festival, it is difficult to surmise; however, it is important to note that Schneemann was a forerunner for feminist artists in the UK and their quest to bring their art into the urban fabric of the city.

Another project located directly within London's urban fabric was Bobby Baker's *An Edible Family in a Mobile Home*. At the time the artist's studio was in a prefabricated mobile home in the East End of London, which was part of the Acme[28] trust for artists. She decided to turn her studio into a gallery for the course of one installation, in the hope that she could garner a more local, and perhaps less elitist, audience than would have been possible in an art gallery. It was also a touch of rebellion that spurred her on. She says, "I think it was quite subversive. ... It was the fingers up to the gallery system, which I still have great problems with."[29] Baker, like other women artists of her generation, spoke of the urge to resist the mainstream gallery system, which initially was not sympathetic to feminist agendas.[30] In the first instance this was not a conscious reaction to the fact that galleries were usually run by powerful men, but rather an instinctual urge to connect with a wider audience:

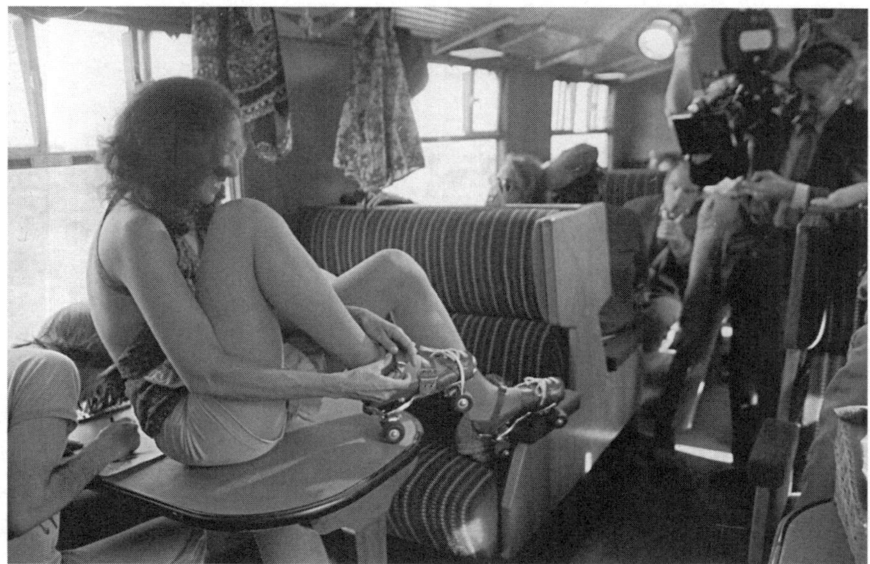

Figure 3.4
Ices Trip Train, 1972. Carolee Schneemann. Photograph: Anthony McCall.
Courtesy of the artist.

> When I look back on it clearly it was in response to the gallery
> system, the chauvinism, the fact that at art school I quite
> consciously felt excluded. I was a white middle-class girl who
> came from the suburbs of London and they didn't take me seri-
> ously and weren't interested.[31]

Whether acknowledged or not, Baker was the victim of institutional
sexism at the time, in which many art school tutors (and commercial
dealers for that matter) viewed women artists as hobbyists or young girls
trying to find husbands.[32]

Baker's resentment of her unwanted feminized role found its outlet in
An Edible Family in a Mobile Home 1977. The installation was constructed
on site, where the artist constructed a family out of cake. For three
months Baker prepared the exhibition, which eventually encompassed
every inch of the space, while she lived in the studio. First she baked
the multitude of sponge cakes necessary to sculpt the life-sized family
members, and froze them.[33] During this time she covered every surface
of each room with newsprint, including floors, ceilings, walls and furniture, and then iced it over, resulting in a glazed, sugar-coated surface.

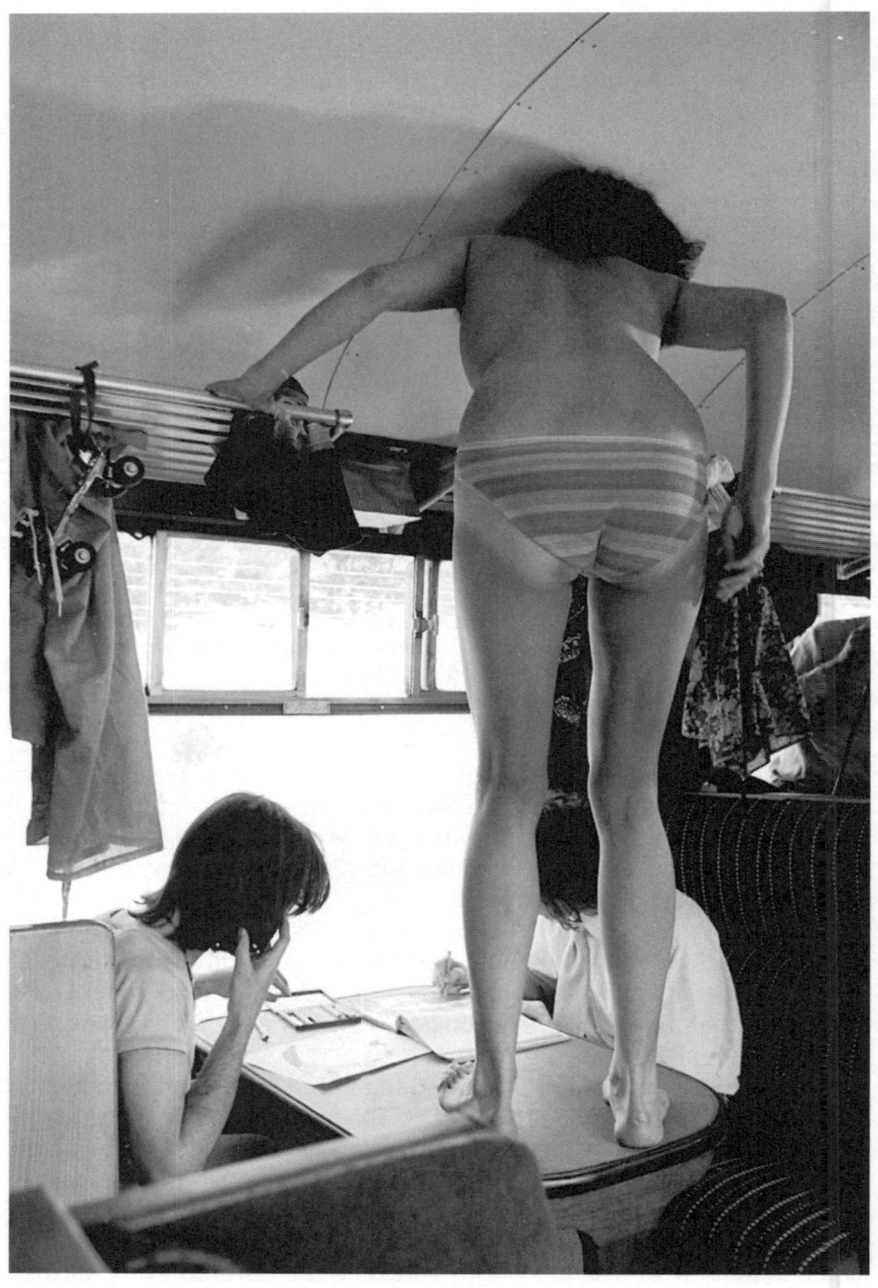

Figure 3.5
Ices Trip Train, 1972. Carolee Schneemann. Photograph: Anthony McCall
Courtesy of the artist.

Obviously, this kind of labor-intensive work over a three-month period would not have been possible in a traditional gallery space. Working outside of the mainstream system for showing contemporary art was not only apt but necessary for Baker's project.

Three days before the exhibition began, Baker defrosted the cakes, and sculpted the human figures. The group consisted of a mother, a father seated upright in his chair, a son in the bathtub, and a baby in a crib. The figures were made with the sponge cake placed on top of a structure of chicken wire to create a framework. With the exception of the "mother" figure, which was constructed from a dressmaker's dummy with a teapot forming the head, it was Baker's intention that the figures should all be consumed. Visitors were invited to eat the figures, and hence took part in the destruction of the work of art. A rather ominous documentary photograph taken during the installation shows Baker, standing beside the father with a knife, ready to begin serving the figure to visitors. As in Baker's *Art Supermarket*, discussed in Chapter Three, transformation was key to this work. By the end of the week's installation, what remained of the figures had gone rancid and stank. These remnants presented shocking images of a cannibalistic fantasy.[34]

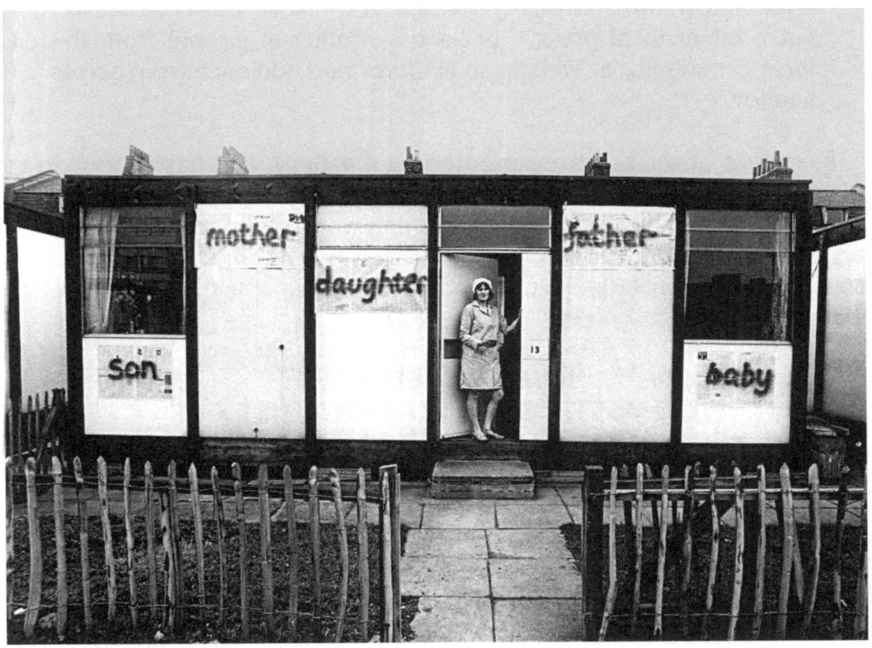

Figure 3.6
Edible Family in a Mobile Home, 1977. Bobby Baker.
Photograph: Andrew Whittuck. Courtesy of the artist.

The humor implicit in the project covers a darker theme. The dysfunctional family is displayed and destroyed in the process of experiencing the exhibition in a symbolic cannibalistic act. This presents an oppositional version of the traditional role of the female as care-giver, nurturer and provider. Instead the artist presents a horrific version of the woman as enabler to the destruction of her own family. Baker's congenial presence in the piece—serving tea from the head of the mother and dressed in a pink "dinner lady" smock—adds to the subversive quality of the work. The strength of the installation lies in its casual humor, which avoids any directly confrontational political slogan and was accessible to a wide audience.

For Baker, working outside of the gallery proved more satisfying than her previous efforts at the ICA and elsewhere. She was able to produce an installation that challenged viewers' notions and one in which an immediate transformation was more evident. She considers the success of this project:

> One thing I was particularly passionate about with *An Edible Family in a Mobile Home* was that it was on a council estate in Stepney. I wanted it to be very accessible to a non-art audience and it was extremely successful in those terms because I got a lot of local press. I got a huge influx of people from the local community as well as an art informed audience from across London.[35]

Baker has never been represented by a gallery, and has continued to place work in such unlikely places as church halls, a swimming pool filled with wine and in her own kitchen. Baker's work, rife with wry comments on domesticity and the familial home, was not an isolated case. Others of her generation relied on the home as studio space, inspiration and gallery.

HOME SWEET HOME: DOMESTIC SITES AND FEMINIST ART

The domestic role of women was a predominant theme in feminist art as well as the wider culture in Britain during the 1970s. Women were the main subject and target of advertising campaigns that peddled everything from Hoovers to dish soap. A happy home was a clean home, with a table full of healthy food. The kitchen became an especially loaded site, as it was often the locus of domestic labor. For Manchester-based performance artist Linder, the kitchen became a source of inspiration for collages that critiqued the notion of the housewife, transforming her into an eroticized, machine-like entity. Conflating soft-core pornography, cakes and sweets, as well as mechanical appliances, Linder's work

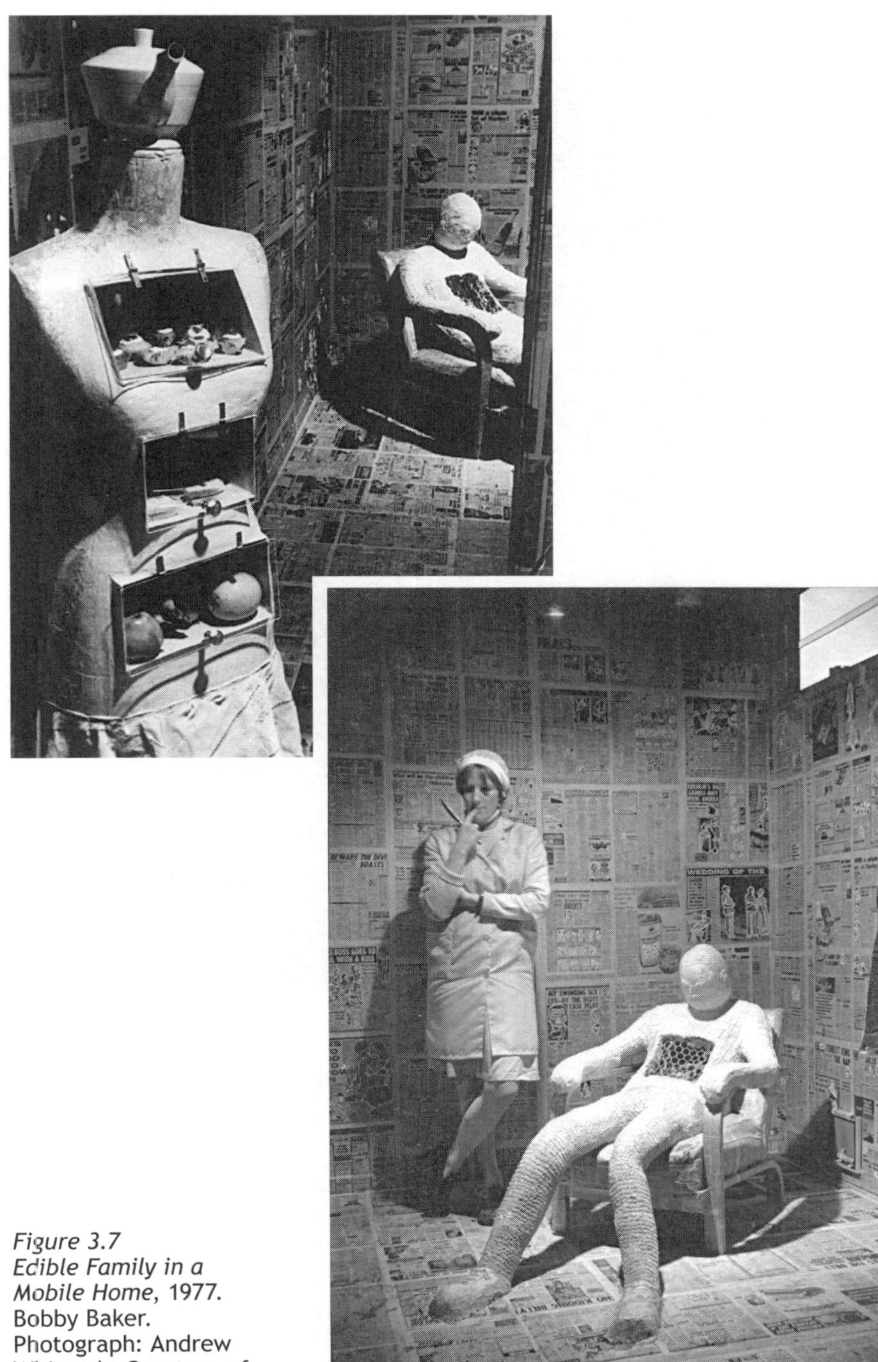

Figure 3.7
Edible Family in a Mobile Home, 1977.
Bobby Baker.
Photograph: Andrew Whittuck. Courtesy of the artist.

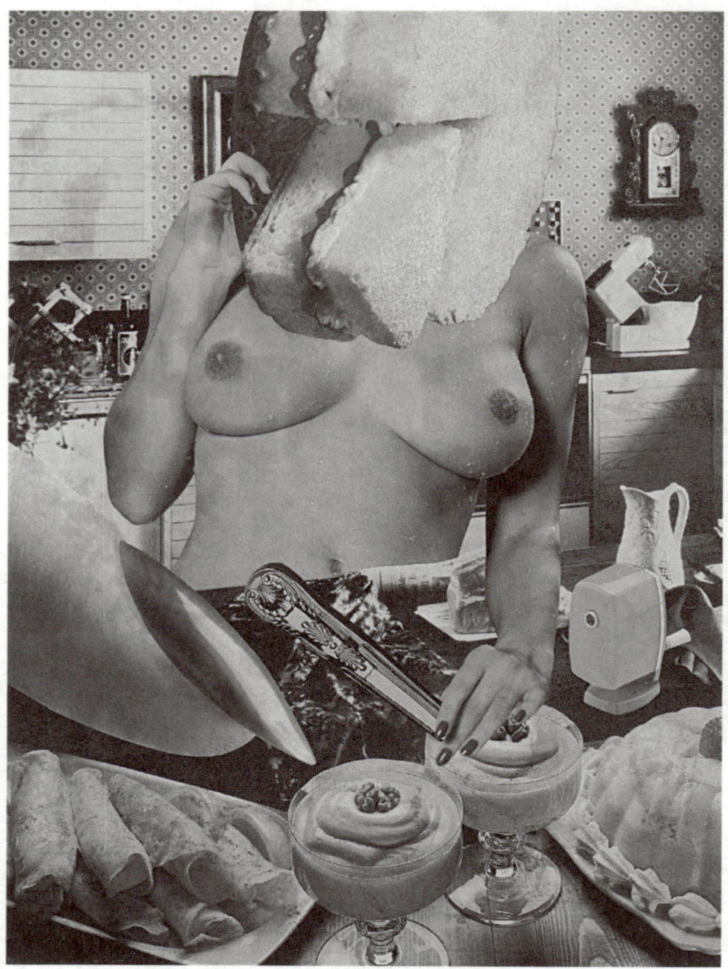

Figure 3.8
Untitled, 1978. Linder.
Courtesy of Stuart Shave/Modern Art.

from that period, striking in its graphic quality, represents an oppositional stance to the woman as both a consumer of commodities as well
as a commodity in herself. In this series Linder's women become another
object for consumption, as they transmogrify into blenders, toasters or
irons. Linder's work may be seen as emblematic of a generation of artists
who used the domestic to critique the notion of woman's role in the
household as well as their larger role in society.

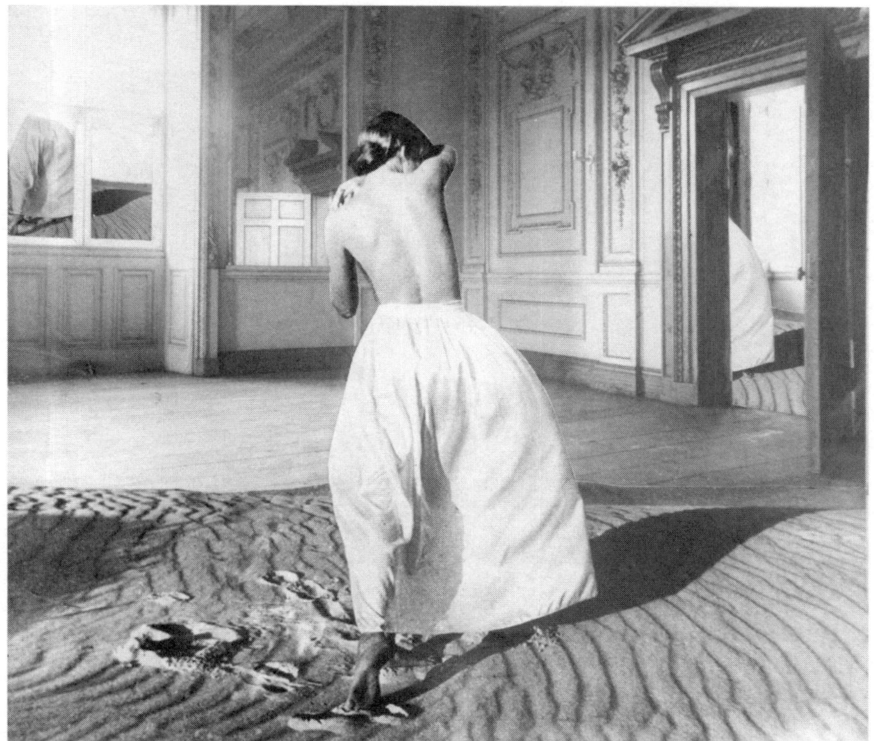

Figure 3.9
Who Turns Her Back, 1977. Collage mounted on board.
Courtesy of Broadway 1601 and the artist.

Linder acknowledges a debt to Penny Slinger, an artist known for her work in collage and performance. Slinger's handmade publications including *An Exorcism* were important contributions to the genre of artists' books. Her use of collage is seen in the work *Who Turns Her Back* from 1977. Here a surreal interior suggests a claustrophobic world of mirrors and empty space. The sand may be suggestive of escape but also the quicksand effect of domestic life.

For women who were largely confined to the home because of child-care or housewife duties, the domestic environment became both locus and subject of their artistic work. Many artists have spoken about their experiences showing work on the kitchen table,[36] which in fact was where much of that work had been constructed. Monica Ross captured the spirit of art as domestic activity in her presentation-cum-performance about women's art during the 1970s:

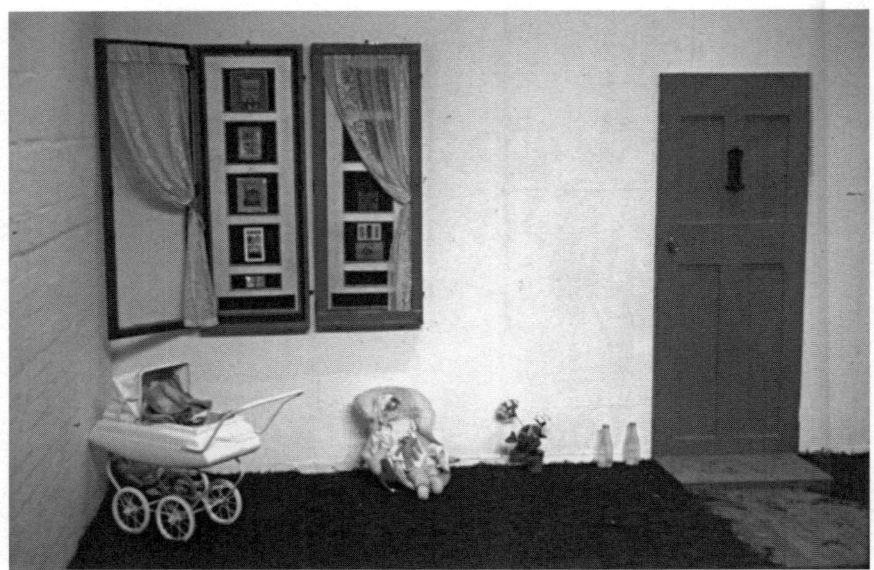

Figure 3.10
Entrance to gallery 1 "a portrait of the artist as a housewife", ICA London,
1977. Kate Walker/Feministo. Courtesy of the artist and the Women's Art
Library/make, Goldsmiths University of London.

> ...and we went out in the streets with buckets and flyposted
> the posters we'd silkscreened during the night on Phil Goodall's
> kitchen table and pegged up to dry next to the socks and the
> nappies.[37]

Ross also participated in the collaborative project *Feministo,* which
began in the middle of the decade as a correspondence between friends
who were unable to see each other on a frequent basis. By the end of the
decade it had evolved into a major touring exhibition that occupied various
public spaces around Great Britain, most notably the ICA in London.[38]

Feministo began as a casual venture by Kate Walker,[39] who initiated the
postal exchange with her friend Sally Gallop after the latter had moved
to a coastguard cottage on the Isle of Wight. Walker had also made
contact with women at the first women's art conference[40] in London,
June 1975, and began exchanging small artworks through the post as a
correspondence. Eventually the network expanded to 25 women, whose
ages varied from 19 to 60. These women shared many characteristics,
but were primarily and paradoxically brought together by their exclusion
from artistic and urban circles:

What we all had in common was our isolation. Either as young
mothers, or by location. Some of us lived in isolated country
areas, or just where there were no other artists to talk to. Some
of us were trained artists, but not all. Most of us were living out
the answer to that art college lecturer's famous question: "2/3
of all art students are women, but where do they go to when
they leave?"[41]

Walker was not as constrained in her domestic situation (as her children were already entering secondary school by that time) as many
of her younger colleagues and friends who were at an earlier stage in
their lives with young children and therefore restricted to the home. A
creative outlet was vital for these correspondents who otherwise had
little stimulation in their lives. The exchange of ideas, experience and
artworks between these women had a value beyond the purely aesthetic,
as Walker recounts:

It was important to me because working in a school and ... struggling financially, it was almost akin to a social life. ... One gained
friends through that. The object of it was for us to communicate.
For me it was a visual representation of the old consciousness-
raising groups. You discussed what it meant to earn your living in
such a circumstance and how to deal with conflicts in your life.[42]

Thus, as the women's network gained strength, the participants could
reflect on its concerns and express themselves by creating these small
works to be exchanged with others. In this case the gallery was not a
source of support for such artistic practice, and certainly not an option
for such artists to site their work.

The work produced during this exchange reflected the sharing of
conflicts; themes such as identity, sexuality and domesticity are prevalent. For example, Kate Walker's *Self Portrait* consists of a tiny pass-
port photo mounted on a diary of her daily schedule. Entries such as
"Housework until 5.30 and then SLEEP until children's breakfast at 7.30
ouch!" and "Rosie came to quarrel about the money she owes" are
juxtaposed with her passport-sized photo, which is dated "6 February at
Brixton". In a similar fashion to Mary Kelly's diary-style accounts of her
son's feedings, Walker illustrates how much of her existence is made up of
routine activities such as caring for the children and cleaning the house.
Su Richardson's *Nappy Sandwich* also reflects Kelly's earlier comments on
the unequal balance of domestic labor afforded to the female gender. (It
also relates to the excremental theme found in so much of women's work,
in such diverse practices as Kelly's and Baker's.) Similarly, Richardson's
Crochet Breakfast and *Crochet Table* pick up on this theme. Here she uses

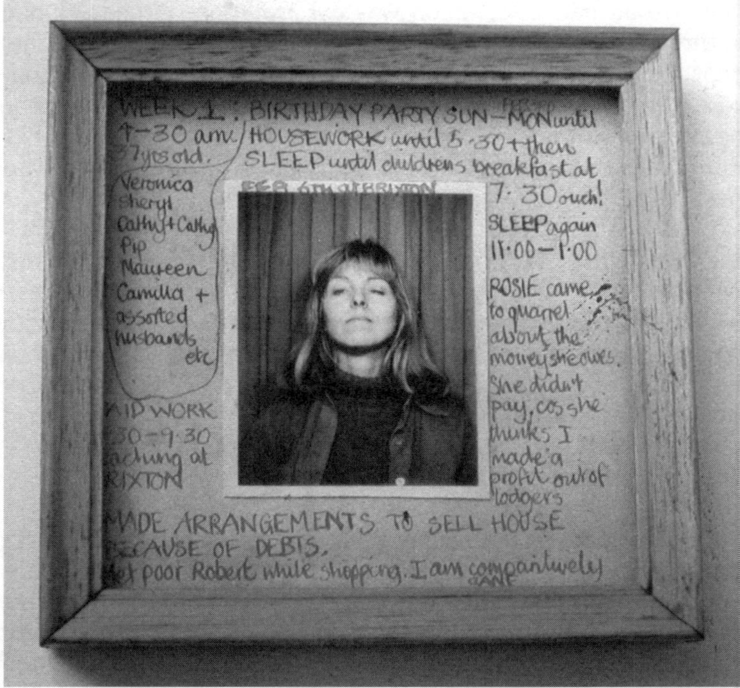

Figure 3.11
Self Portrait, 1976. Kate Walker. Courtesy of Women's Art Library.

practices normally ascribed to women—crochet and knitting—to illustrate women's primary concerns, which include feeding the family. The theme of food is also picked up in Walker's *Keep Smiling*, a box of homemade chocolates whose appearance oscillates between lips and vaginal forms.

An important characteristic of the *Feministo* work was its scale. It had to be small enough and light enough to post without incurring too many costs. One participant, Phil Goodall, wrote about this aspect of the work in her article about the project: "Women's lifestyles tend to contain small time-scales, brief moments—we need flexibility to deal with the tiny important moments that children, friends, lovers, present."[43] The miniature scale of the work was also a consequence of the lack of materials to hand (and the lack of funds to buy proper art materials) and the type of objects used. Caroline Tisdall, in her review of the show in London at the ICA, commented on the tiny size of much of the work: "Hundreds of tiny things make for a niggling feeling, tucked away in mock suburban dressing tables, pathetic plastic boudoirs, the ever-present kitchen, all reconstructed at the ICA."[44] The diminutive stature of the work also underlines the association of "tiny" and "fragile", uniquely pertinent for the *Feministo* work, much of which was lost or destroyed rather than preserved as art objects.

In addition to Tisdall's piece, *Feministo* garnered attention in mainstream and feminist press, both during its run at the Institute of Contemporary Art in London[45] as well as further afield. One Birmingham journalist criticized the work for its lack of ideological specificity and rigidity:

> Feministo itself is a neat piece of word play on "female manifesto," yet the nearest they come to embroidering their beliefs on a banner is a collage "in a make-up tray from Boots" which simply poses the question: "I wonder what it's like to be in your kitchen, your mind, your place ..."[46]

Much like the debate over Kelly's nappies or Clark's bodily fluids, the exhibition and phenomenon of *Feministo* was treated more as a "woman's topic" than an artistic subject deserving of serious critical attention in most of the mainstream press. Journalists concentrated on the narrative elements of the story—the isolation of women, the lack of opportunities for female artists—and left the art aside. One writer never even mentioned a work of art in her review of the exhibition.[47] Other reviews are similarly general, avoiding any serious criticism of the work or the collective notion of *Feministo*.

In understandable contrast to this marginalization, the women's press, including journals and newsletters such as *Spare Rib, Shrew, Mama* and *FAN (Feminist Art News)*, considered *Feministo* an exemplar of feminist polemic. For example, Rozsika Parker quoted some of the vitriolic responses of male visitors to *Feministo*:

> "Miserable bitches," commented one man. "Bitter and twisted," said another. "I don't see what all the fuss is about." While North West Arts Association who housed their first show put up a notice reading "Unsuitable for Children".[48]

Perhaps this is where the danger lies in creating work that is conceived as a result of a political movement. The tenuous border between art and propaganda is often transgressed, with the viewer seeing only the political statement rather than an artistic merit (or lack thereof) in the work.

What is particularly striking about *Feministo* is that much of the work has been lost. None of it has gone into public collections that could preserve and archive such art.[49] This case study supports the thesis that when art practice moves into the domestic space it is not valued, and clearly deemed unsuitable for a gallery or museum.[50] Although the *Feministo* project was eventually collated and shown at a major London venue, it was not valued for its importance as objects or cultural artifacts. It was instead treated as ephemera, and is therefore unappreciated in the dialogue of art history today.[51] All that remains is the documentation of the work, and in some cases, only the memory of it. Walker commented on this, saying, "Some of it was stolen, some of it fell apart, some of it was thrown away. All of the work went back to the original makers so they did with it what they wanted to."[52] In deliberately avoiding the commercial system, artists involved in *Feministo* would have not expected the work to be conserved and saved. Yet the project is a vital part of feminist history of art in the UK, perhaps the first large-scale, collaborative work to relocate artistic production from the studio to the domestic space.

The domestic space also became the site for performances that were sometimes never enacted for an audience, intended instead to be documented in photographs. Alexis Hunter's *Domestic Warfare* series shows a couple at home. During the course of the evening, the couple's relationship devolves from a pleasant dinner and glass of wine into a brawl where the female protagonist takes a hammer to a wall. It was shot at her flat in Camden Town with the help of Hunter's illustrator neighbor, who takes the male role, and fellow feminist artist Catherine Elwes, who plays the role of the female subject.

This work is important for its depiction of a domestic dystopia. Like other works such as Helen Chadwick's *Domestic Sanitation/Latex Rodeo* performance (discussed in the previous chapter), it defies the post-war notion of the happy housewife and provider. Instead, it presents a bleak picture of domestic life. It is evident that radical stances had to be taken by women at this time, who were challenging their accepted role in society, and seeking to redefine their identities.

Similarly, Carolee Schneemann created a domestic performance called *A Handbook of Physical Aggression for Couples* in 1971. This also examined the negative side of co-habitation, but was intended as a therapeutic approach. Conceptualized as a book, the central assumption of this project was that "an integral, vital love relationship can accommodate expressions of anger, boredom, hysteria, sexual tension, repressed agressivity (sic), irritability, nagging, hopelessness, and depression".[53] The artist's idea was for couples to enact physical actions that could release and defuse repressed feelings. In this series, which exists now in photographic documentation, Schneemann and her partner Anthony McCall (who was himself an artist and also frequently documented her work) are seen pushing, pulling and manipulating each other's bodies in their London home. Like Hunter's series above, this was not intended as performance art, but rather a static series that required performative actions to create.

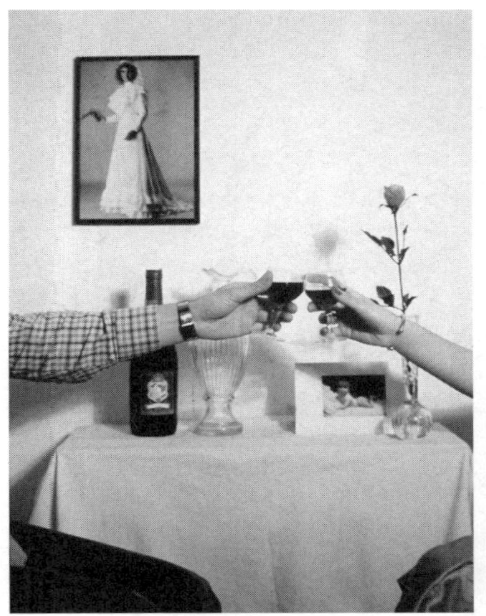 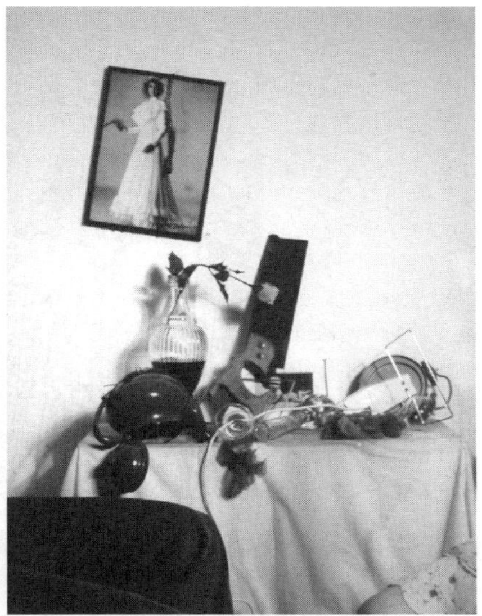

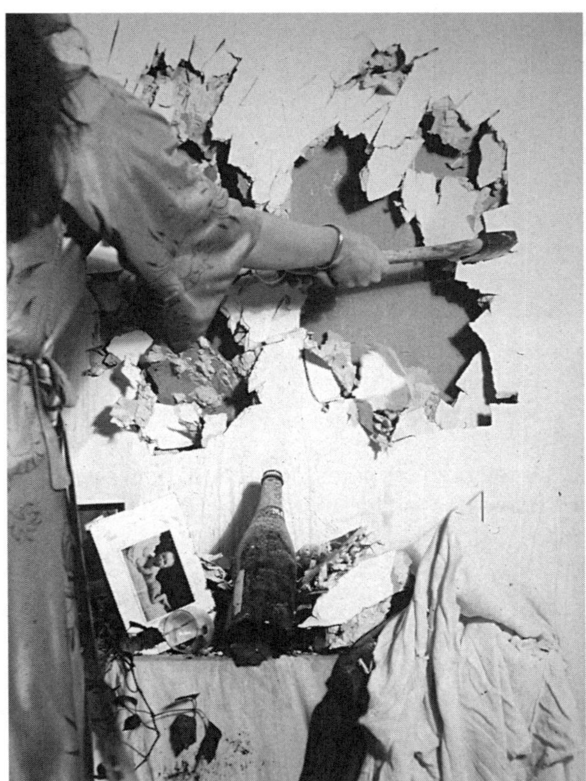

Figure 3.12
Scenes from Domestic Warfare, 1979, Alexis Hunter. Courtesy of Richard Saltoun, London.

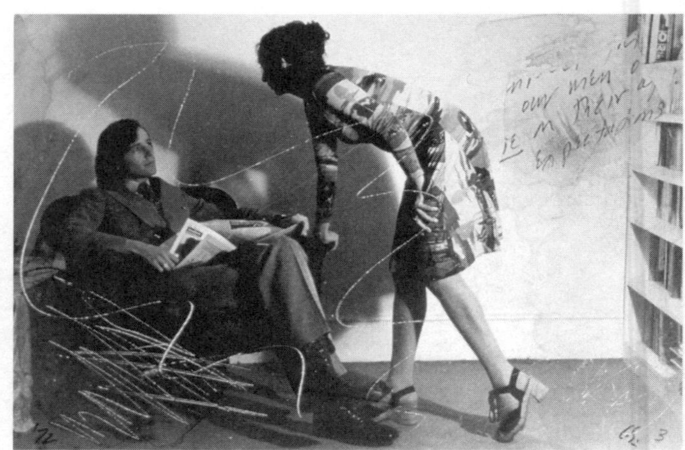

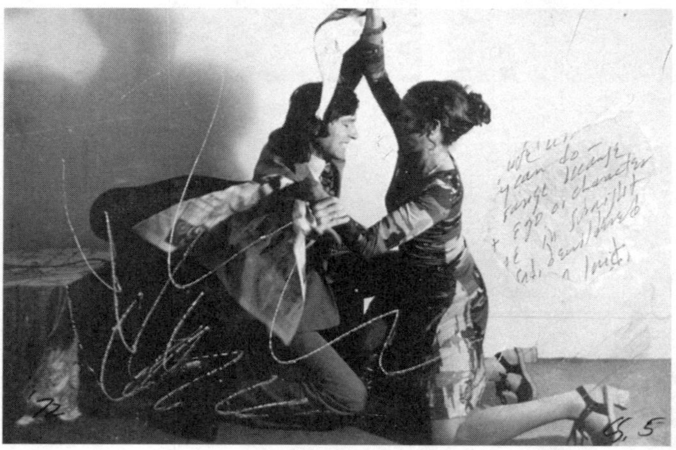

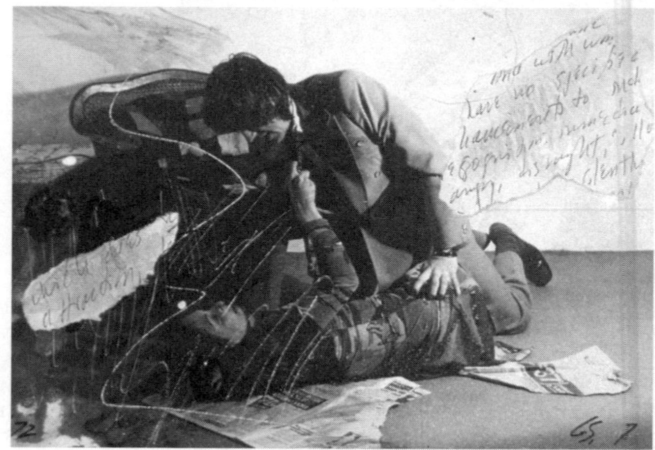

*Figure 3.13
Aggression
for Couples*,
1972, Carolee
Schneemann.
Courtesy of
the artist. A
discussion of
domestic issues
documented by
photography in
the 1970s.

A discussion of domestic issues documented by photography in 1970s London could not be complete without mention of Jo Spence and the Hackney Flashers. Born in 1974 out of an initial group (the Photography Workshop) the Hackney Flashers was named after Hackney, then a working-class neighborhood of East London. The group entailed several members[54] over the course of 1974 to the early 1980s. Spence described the Hackney Flashers as "an agitprop group which produced exhibitions and posters around issues of women, work and domesticity—moving from simple 'window on the world' techniques to ask questions about mediation and ideology."[55] One of the group's greatest contributions included a slide pack for teaching and an archive of images around class and gender. The group promoted self-reliance by imparting photographic skills. One of their mission statements was "To encourage the photographic recording of personal, group and local history by people themselves, with or without the assistance of professional photographers."[56] Posters such as the one reproduced here were used as consciousness raising devices. Like *Feministo*, this group of practitioners was interested in exploring themes previously unacknowledged in art, including domestic labor.

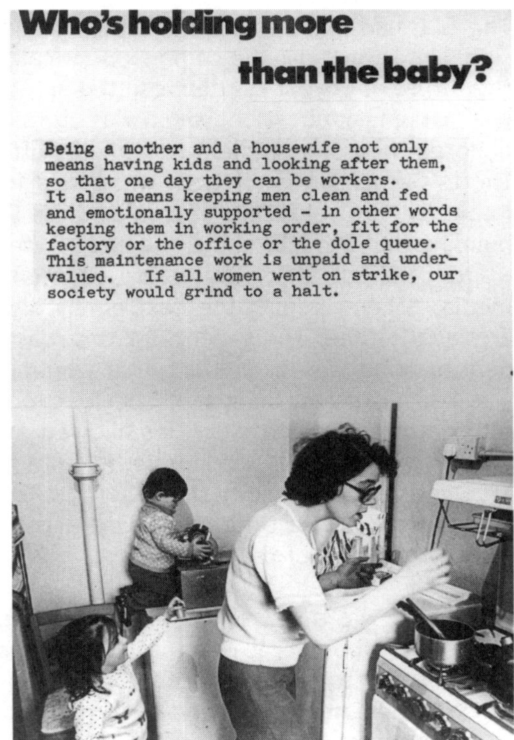

Figure 3.14
Holding baby poster, *ca* 1974. Jo Spence and the Hackney Flashers. Copyright Estate of Jo Spence. Courtesy Richard Saltoun, London.

NOT SO WELL HUNG:
LONDON'S ALTERNATIVE GALLERIES

London had several alternative spaces for showing art in the 1970s.[57] These were important sites for the burgeoning contemporary art scene, and especially feminist practice. Curious as it may seem today, with the dominance of the East End of London as a locus for production and reception of contemporary art practice, Covent Garden was the site for many of these earlier enterprises. Three of the alternative galleries that showed important exhibitions of work by feminist artists were located in this section of London.

The Acme Gallery

The Acme Gallery was a natural extension of the work of the Acme Housing Association Limited, a charitable organization that provided artists with inexpensive studios and living spaces in London.[58] The Housing Association had been operating for over three years when the gallery came into being. Acme developed from a small, self-help group into a larger body that dealt with the practical needs of artists. As such, the need for a non-commercial gallery space, when articulated by these artists, was the next logical step. In the summer of 1974 the Directors of Acme were offered a building at 43–45 Shorts Gardens, in Covent Garden. The GLC had made the offer of the building subject to planning permission. Unfortunately, the complex political situation at the time regarding the future of Covent Garden resulted in a 15-month wait for a decision on the planning application, which was ultimately denied. However, the GLC honored their commitment to Acme by offering another building, also on Shorts Gardens, where there was space for a large and flexible gallery. Ironically, five years later it would be the GLC's intention to demolish the building that brought about the end of the gallery.[59]

From the outset the gallery never intended to focus on any particular media, acknowledging the "extremely diverse field of activity"[60] in the arts at the time. The gallery, for this reason, was not fitted with permanent hanging rails or anything that would dictate a particular usage, and was kept as a neutral space,[61] perfect for presenting performances and other alternative formats. This allowed artists to create the context in which to show their work. Another key feature of Acme was that the artist was able to modify the gallery in absolutely any way that they felt was appropriate to their work. One artist spoke about this flexible attitude on the part of the gallery:

> Well it was a space where you could take over. You could rip up the floorboards. It was that kind of space. So, in a way it didn't feel like a gallery, because galleries to us represented white walls and neat floors and paintings.[62]

The reluctance to dictate a particular usage resulted in an incredibly rich range of artists and work shown at the gallery over the five years of its existence. Many performance artists were featured at Acme, including the Kipper Kids, Hesitate and Demonstrate, Anne Bean, Stuart Brisley and the Station House Opera.[63] However, more traditional work was also shown, for example, the paintings of British abstract expressionist Albert Irvin. Political and activist artists such as the "Artists for Nuclear Disarmament" were also encouraged to show their work without the fear of institutional intervention, which they might have encountered in more traditional venues. Finally, many feminist artists took over the space for various periods during its five-year run.

Long before the marriage of shopping and art[64] began to be common-place, Bobby Baker submitted her proposal to turn the ground floor gallery of Acme into an *Art Supermarket*.[65] Baker, whose work centers on the primarily maternal functions of shopping and preparing food, was at this point just beginning her professional career as an artist.[66] Her vision for the gallery included free-standing shelves stretching the length of the gallery, wire baskets, a cash register and audio accompaniments such as

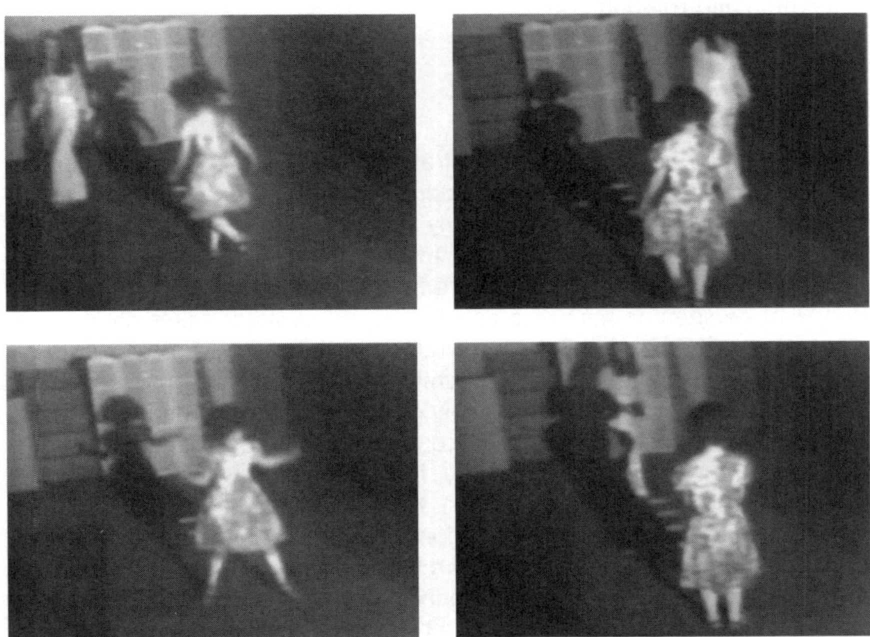

Figure 3.15
Shadow Woman, 1977. Tina Keane. Courtesy of the artist.

taped jingles, music and announcements. While Baker's installation was never actually realized, other important feminist projects took place at Acme.

One such performance was Tina Keane's *Shadow Woman* from 1977. The title was inspired by a boat trip that the artist took in the Scottish isles where she was fascinated by the shadows that the passengers cast on the water below.[67] Keane used the shadow as motif and manifestation of time's passing in several of her works, including *Shadow Woman* at Acme. Keane's daughter Emily participated in this performance where a hopscotch pattern was chalked on the floor. Each square contained text taken from an accompanying poem about the passage of time as encapsulated in the duality of mother and daughter:

> The shadow of my daughter
> Becomes the shadow of life
> As I will become the shadow of hers
> As my mother
> Grandmother and
> Great grandmother.
>
> From child to adult
> From hopscotch to maze
> From girl to woman
> From tale to labyrinth of time.[68]

Emily played hopscotch on the drawn squares while Keane remained outside the grid and recited the poem. Hopscotch, as a geometric grid that forms an inherent choreography as the player passes through it, is part of the recurring theme of children's songs and games in Keane's work.[69] Guy Brett writes, "uninhibited play, a metaphor for artistic creation, can be seen as part of a continuum ... The adult takes pleasure in rediscovering her own childhood through her daughter—the collaboration with Emily is also with herself as a child—yet fears she will pass on to her daughter the constricting social view of women imposed on her."[70] Using one's child could be considered a contentious act, even among alternative and feminist circles; Mary Kelly, for example, was insistent that her son should not appear in her work. Here Keane includes her daughter (as she would do on several occasions) to recast linear succession in a feminist light, emphasizing a matriarchal line rather than the patriarchal order and reconfiguring the traditional image of mother and child. Can a new configuration of womanhood be transposed from feminist mother to enlightened child?

Acme was an important venue for this kind of experimental work in the middle and late 1970s. While the gallery was short-lived, the Acme Trust still continues to provide housing and studios for artists, centered mostly around the East End of London.

SPACE and AIR

AIR Gallery was another space that grew out of a trust for artists. Space Studios ran a respected program that offered studios to artists including Bridget Riley[71] and Albert Irvin during the 1970s. Founded in 1968, SPACE, which stands for Space Provision (Artistic, Cultural and Educational)[72] was located in a building at St Katherine's Dock and was set up as a direct response to artists' needs for cheaper studio space. It assisted by providing inexpensive workspaces and giving information on establishing independent studios.[73] Space's contribution helped to foster a vibrant scene during the 1970s, and might be seen as typical of the politically motivated activities of the time. Michael Kenny reflected on the ethos of SPACE:

> I remember the beginnings of S.P.A.C.E. at St Katherine's Dock, the excitement, the anticipation that came with this new self-help venture. There was a weekend talk-in, I think it was 1969— self expression and self-help were very much part of the mood of the time. The year before had seen the extraordinary student sit-ins at Hornsey College of Art and Guildford School of Art, students and left-wing lecturers had taken over the buildings and were organizing lectures and debates and distributing newsletters and broadsheets. These were in turn inspired by the sit-in at the Sorbonne in Paris and the subsequent revolution in France. It was a time of heady excitement, of peace and love, of psychedelic drugs, of anti-war demonstrations, and in all of this artists, writers and musicians played a part. Visual arts were becoming conscious of their social role, gone were the days of the ivory tower. Some artists had begun to work in factories through the help of the Artist's Placement Group (A.P.G.)[74] in an attempt to forge links between art and artisanship; and now at St Katherine's Dock they were setting up their own factory through the inspired leadership of Peter Sedgeley and Bridgit Riley (sic) and others.[75]

AIR[76] Gallery was situated on the north side of Shaftesbury Avenue (numbers 125-129), close to Cambridge Circus in central London. Founded in 1975 the gallery was conveniently located near the Covent Garden galleries Acme, Garage, and PMJ Self, and was also in close proximity to several art schools including the Royal Academy, St Martin's, the Central[77] and the Slade. The idea was to treat the gallery as an open and democratic space that would enable artists to show their work regardless of their exhibition history. In fact, besides a few well-known artists, AIR only showed those who had not yet had a major

London exhibition. They did not, however, show student work as they existed to bridge the gap between art schools and professional life. Unlike other commercial galleries but similar to spaces like Acme, AIR encouraged artists "whose work breaches traditional boundaries, (eg. Performance art, installations, video, etc.)."[78] In addition to showing artists, AIR produced a monthly newsletter, which gave news and vital information to artists living in London.

Garage

Garage was the first properly organized and designed alternative gallery in London.[79] It has a complicated history with a variety of combinations of people involved in running the space, although it lasted for under two years. In 1973 Covent Garden was a run-down area of London, and the GLC were planning to flatten the area and rebuild it with an inner city rejuvenation scheme. Successful restaurateur Terence Conran[80] believed that the area could be a thriving zone for galleries, shops and restaurants. By setting up a gallery, he knew that he could help convince the GLC that Covent Garden should be kept intact.[81] He joined forces with Christina Smith and John Kasmin to set up a gallery in the ground floor at 52 Earlham Street.[82] Smith had worked for Conran, but was now importing goods from China. Kasmin was a well-respected art dealer with a gallery on Cork Street. The team of backers joined forces with Anthony Caro and Richard Smith, both of whom were represented by Kasmin.

Conran, Smith and Kasmin provided capital, while the artists each donated a work to be sold. The team would meet often to act as a kind of board of trustees. Martin Attwood, who Caro had known when he was at the British Council, was recruited to be Director of Garage.[83] Attwood then asked Anthony Stokes to be a co-director. Together they were responsible for the daily running of the gallery, whose mission was never altogether clear. Garage hovered somewhere between the commercial and publicly funded spheres.

The space was designed in the Conran style—white walls, good detailing—and was more upmarket than Acme or Space. Anthony Stokes describes its context as:

> I think in terms of commerce it fell between a publicly funded space and a commercial gallery space. It wasn't actually set up around artists. It was set up around saving the building, showing the artists who were its backers, and the policy then was to show interesting young artists in that context. That is exactly what happened.[84]

Garage resisted capitalizing on the international reputations of artists such as Caro, and concentrated on mostly emerging or cutting edge artists. The directors were keen on showing projects that may not have worked in a commercially driven environment. For example, events by Bruce McLean's pose band Nice Style and by the Moodies, which featured Anne Bean, were memorable performances.

The Moodies were a performance group made up of several women and one man: Polly Altis, Suzy Algaly, Becky Bailey, Anne Bean, Mary Ann Holiday, Rob Malvern and Annie Sloane. They had formed at Reading University for an art party, and became quite popular on the live art scene. Their events took place in a wide variety of contexts from a feminist *Spare Rib* benefit to clubs in Berlin and Amsterdam. Difficult to categorize, the group crossed the disciplines of art, music,

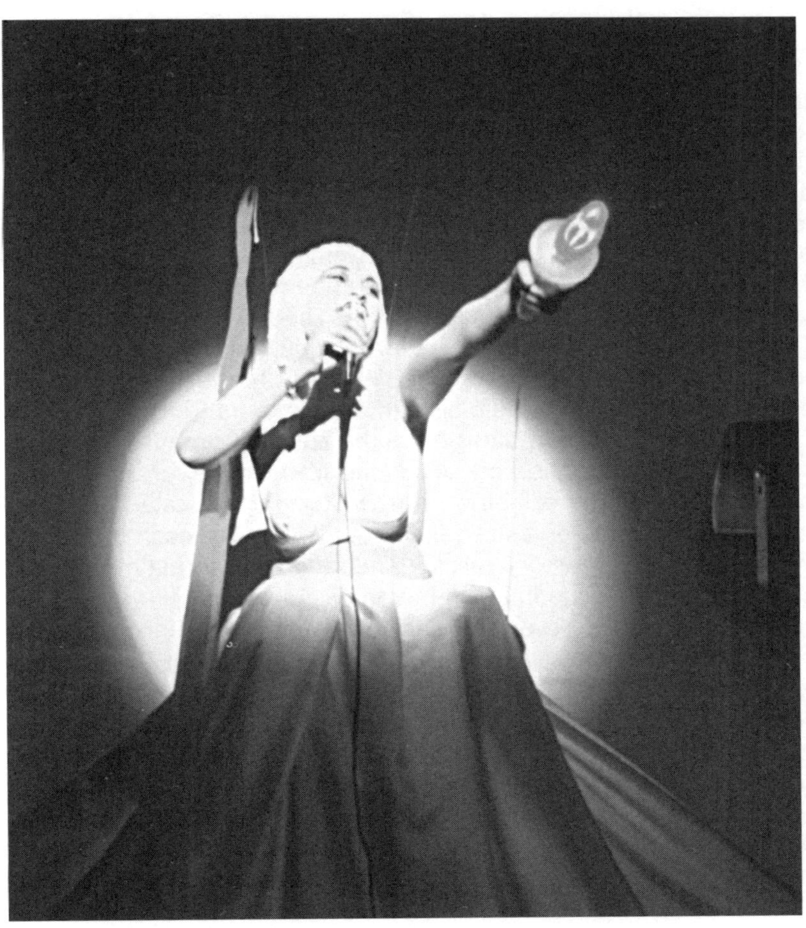

Figure 3.16
Moodies, 1974. Anne Bean. Courtesy the artist.

cabaret theater and performance. When the Moodies disintegrated because of disagreements over the direction of the group,[85] Bean formed Moodier as a second incarnation. Their 1973 performance at Garage[86] consisted of playing renditions of songs from different eras; these were a combination of homage and critique simultaneously. For example, they would sing "Stupid Cupid" to the accompaniment of ping pong bats making the rhythm section. This was accompanied by a short, plump violinist, who was dressed in a Cupid costume. Attached to his bow was a string of fairy lights, which lit as he played. Garage could afford to support such interdisciplinary work because they had wealthy backers such as Terence Conran. This, combined with an intention to show the best emerging art, resulted in an exciting but short-lived program.

Ca. 7500

The year following Judy Clark's landmark *Issues* exhibition at Garage, Stokes and Garage would help realize a show curated by American art critic Lucy Lippard. *Ca. 7500* took its name from the population of Valencia, California, where the idea for the exhibition originated.[87] It was created in response to the comment, made at the time, that there were no female conceptual artists. Lippard assembled a show made up entirely of conceptual art made by women, and one which could fit into a box, making travel easy and keeping costs low. The show was originally meant to take place at the Royal College of Art, which in the end pulled out of the show. Likewise, the Arts Council rejected the idea. Anthony Stokes and Garage stepped in to help bring the show to its fruition.

The show took place in Garage and the adjacent premises, 48 Earlham Street,[88] and included the work of 26 American female conceptual artists. The catalogue for the exhibition was similarly small-scale, and took the form of 28 randomly organized index cards, one for each of the artists as well as two introductory cards.[89] The random ordering meant readers could use the catalogue in a non-hierarchical fashion.

Ca. 7500 included several artists that went on to become members of the canon of feminist and conceptual art, including Laurie Anderson, Eleanor Antin, Hanne Darboven, Nancy Holt, Adrian Piper and Merle Laderman Ukeles. Although many of these artists had already established professional reputations, and Lippard was quite well known, she was accused of creating a further marginalization for women artists. Caroline Tisdall wrote in the *Guardian* that the show "stinks of the ghetto" and that her "overall impression ... [was] of a long, tedious gripe."[90] Tisdall, long a champion of women's art in her role as art critic for a major newspaper, found the work to be lacking in quality. Griselda Pollock, a champion of women's art in Britain, defended her American colleague Lippard in a response to the *Guardian*, asserting that Tisdall's quote in itself proved that there was a need for such an exhibition.[91] She also made an important observation about women's art exhibitions:

> All male exhibitions are frequent and are seen as "art"; sex is irrelevant. All female exhibitions are not treated in the same way, but are taken as a self conscious (sic) statement about women's art. This exposes the male norm of culture for what it is.[92]

Pollock's differentiation is especially important when one reads the introduction to Lippard's catalogue, which clearly states "the artists in the show are of no single ideological persuasion. Some are feminists, some are not. All are artists."[93] Garage, in hosting shows such as *ca. 7500* and *Issues* played an important role in supporting such work and represents a key site for a discourse on inclusion of feminist artists within art history.

The London Film-makers Co-operative

The London Film-makers Co-op was founded in 1966 as a response to the growing interest in underground artists' films. It was based upon the artist-led distribution center in the United States created by Jonas Mekas and the New American Cinema Group. Both had an open policy, but the London center was unique in offering production, distribution and exhibition facilities in the same central London site. Some members— Peter Gidal and Malcolm Le Grice—went on to become internationally celebrated, while others such as Annabel Nicholson and Jeff Keen worked across the boundaries of film and performance. Many of the works shown there fell between the worlds of film and fine art, and sat uncomfortably in either cinema or gallery spaces.[94] Writer Michael Newman recently described the co-op as a state of mind focused on collective teaching and studying rather than a physical space.[95]

While not specifically set up to function as a gallery, it nevertheless was an important nexus for many artists in the 1970s, whose work did not fit into traditional categories. The Berwick Street Film-makers Co-op, which was an offshoot, spawned the important film *Nightcleaners*, which Mary Kelly worked on with, among others, the well-respected director Mark Karlin. Also, the Co-op became a meeting point for discussions on structuralist cinema, psychoanalysis, and new media including performance. Anne Bean had performed there, and Liz Rhodes showed her groundbreaking films, such as *Light Music*; Anthony McCall's iconic work *Line Describing a Cone* was first screened there. Carolee Schneemann, McCall's partner, also performed one of her best-known works there while she lived in London.

Schneemann had come to London after a serious breakdown left her dysfunctional in New York. A friend suggested she come to Europe, and

Schneemann moved over, with her cat, which would become part of several of her works including *Fuses* and *Infinity Kisses*. Schneemann used London as a place of exile, and recuperated through psychoanalyis, as well as through making and performing work. Frustrated by the practical demands of involving groups of people in her live events such as *Meat Joy*, Schneemann attempted to create work that eliminated the training and hierarchies of performance. She also attempted to address a way of producing imagery "without being the image, to make this connection back to the gesture, the stroke, of painting and drawing."[96] Her well-known work *Up to and Including Her Limits*, performed in 1973, was the result.

In the notes for the Berkeley incarnation of this performance Schneemann wrote, "The architectural space of the museum: political and personal"; she also wrote "My intentions were TO DO AWAY WITH: (1) Performance, (2) A fixed audience, (3) Rehearsals, (4) Improvisation, (5) Sequences (6) Conscious intention, (7) Technical cues, (8) A central metaphor or theme. What was left?"[97] In this action, Schneemann hangs from a harness like a pendulum, as she creates drawings across large paper surfaces surrounding the area. The artist said that she "had to find a physicalised circumstance which could induce and produce the stroke. So that became the suspension on the rope, which by the time I got back to the United States I realized I could do a tree surgeon's knot and get myself up and down."[98] The marks are created randomly by the artist who swings from the rope. It was like using the body as a fulcrum. Dan Cameron writes that the work was "a casting out of unnecessary accoutrements, a rejection of the props and artifice of Happenings and spectacles, and a return to the most basic tools of the visual artist: the sensate self, a surface, a mark."[99]

For the duration of the performance the artist was illuminated by projections of light. Schneemann said, "The projector is very important because the light of the projector was both the way of having a portable illumination, also to question—because I was working on film intensively at the time—where film existed. Could I become a hyperfilm in the light of this projector?"[100] It is precisely this combination of film projection, the use of the body, performance and drawing that must have been compelling for an audience at the London Film-makers Co-op.[101] *Up to and Including Her Limits* is now seen as one of Schneemann's most celebrated and iconic works.

A ROOM OF ONE'S OWN:
SPACES FOR WOMEN'S ART

Women isolated from the commercial system in the 1970s gathered forces and attempted to create, organize or occupy spaces to show their work. These ranged from short-term occupations of women's centers to veritable institutions created for the sole purpose of showing women's art. Exhibiting in spaces allocated for women's art solved the dilemma of finding a suitable venue for feminist art work. Suddenly women could mobilize their work and present it to sympathetic audiences.

One of the founders of *Feministo*, Kate Walker, also helped to create A Woman's Place, a center for women in south-east London.[102] The council gave the house to the group on a low rent to enable a women's advice center. Walker says, "We got hold of this tiny house, three stories high, unreclaimed, unrestored, fairly scruffy, and we did it up and it was an office."[103] Walker's group may be considered a more radical faction of the women's liberation movement in London, and this may account at least in part for why it has not been well documented in the history of this period. However, it is an important example of women working outside of traditional spaces for showing art.

An advertisement for the center in *Feminist Art News* described it as "a Women's Liberation information service" offering services such as:

> Apart from the collating of information about feminist and related groups and activities, we also have information on other relevant services offering practical help and advice ... We currently have three meeting rooms available for women's groups to book, and duplicating and scanning facilities, which are used weekly by the London Women's Liberation Newsletter collective, amongst other groups.[104]

As a local center, women could drop in and have a drink, and pick up relevant information relating to the movement. It was self-sufficient, funding itself by selling books while members worked inexhaustibly to keep the center running.[105]

Walker met Sue Madden at the Peckham Group, which was one of many consciousness-raising women's groups. It was through Madden that she learned about *Womanhouse*,[106] a project that was done in 1972 by American artists Judy Chicago and Miriam Schapiro, and their students at the Feminist Art Program at Fresno State.[107] In this project the students, under the tutelage of Chicago and Miriam Schapiro, took over a derelict house in Los Angeles, devising installations and performances in its rooms. Thus, they were able to utilize spaces that were loaded with feminist ideology, such as the bathroom, bedroom, kitchen and even the dollhouse. Schapiro wrote about the students' and tutors' examination of domestic spaces. She said:

> We asked ourselves what it would be like to work out of our closest associative memories—the home. Our home, which we as a culture of women have been identified with for centuries, has always been the area where we nourished and were nourished. It has been the base of operations out of which we fought and

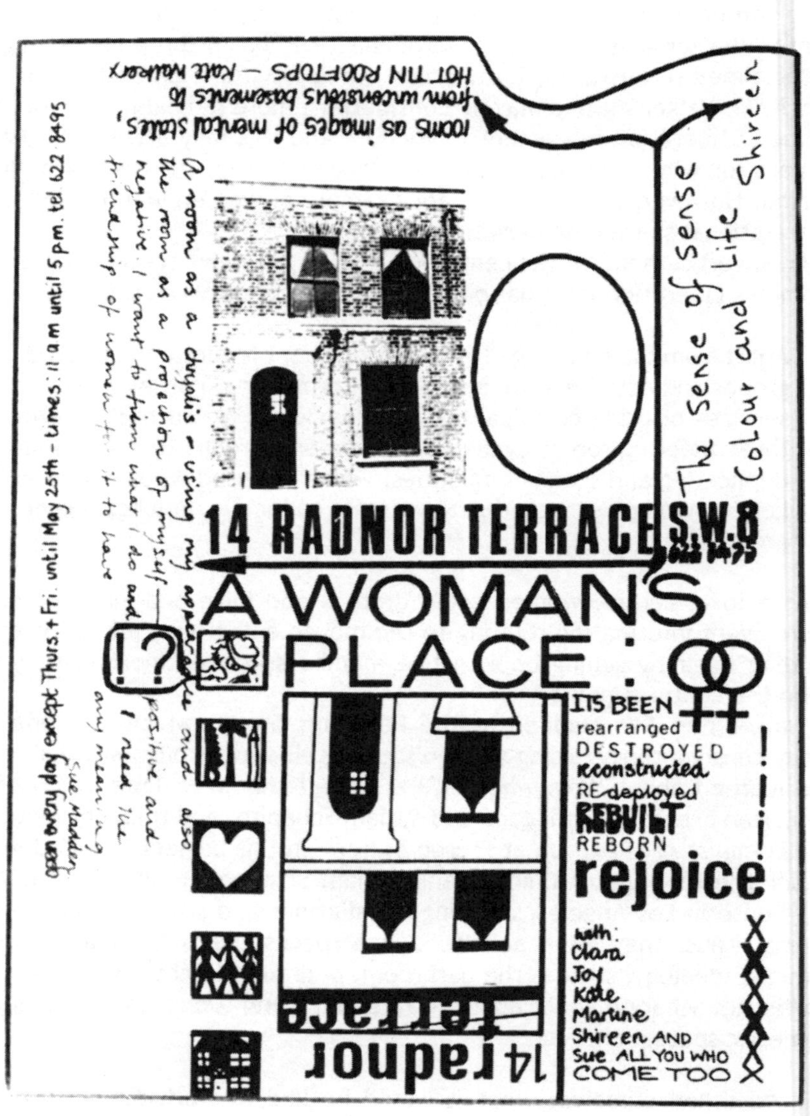

Figure 3.17
A Woman's Place poster, 1974.

struggled with ourselves to please others. What would happen, we asked, if we created a home in which we pleased no one but ourselves? What if each woman were to develop her own dreams and fantasies in one room of that home?[108]

For example, the kitchen was transformed into an installation featuring breasts protruding from the walls, and in Sandy Orgel's *Linen Closet* was a tongue in cheek comment on the role of women in the domestic division of labor. Works such as this one, made by a young feminist student, helped to instill confidence in participants, and gave them the space to experiment and express themselves in a site that was located outside of the traditional art school setting, and presumably, away from the male-dominated faculty.

Womanhouse became the inspiration for Walker and her British colleagues, who took over Radnor Terrace women's center for a similar installation. Phil Goodall, Patricia Hull, Catherine Nicholson, Su Richardson, Monica Ross and Suzy Varty, along with Walker, transformed the house into various exhibition spaces. Walker's installation occupied several rooms on the ground floor and centered on the figure of the bride. In her nightmarish kitchen footsteps, on the floor marked an endless traversing from sink to stove and refrigerator. A wedding cake was in the gas oven, and beneath this a woman in full bridal gear half-submerged in a heap of garbage. Strewn around the figure were traces of adolescent female identity: old dolls, colored pages from a Cinderella book, and in general dirty and sordid ephemera such as milk and cider bottles.

Walker's installation was a sardonic comment on the artifice of the women's image. A candlelit performance accompanied the installation during the evening hours on certain nights, including the opening. During this event Walker would perform a reverse strip-tease. Beginning naked, she would dress in more and more clothes, including housewife pinafores, and other symbolic guises. Finally she dressed as a man and left the house.[109] She notes, "Of course the fire authorities would have had a heart attack. It was all completely alternative and underground and all kinds of mad things were going on."[110]

The house was on view for two months, during which time, many people made the journey to south London to see the installations, including Nicholas Serota, who would later become Director of the Tate and Sandy Nairne,[111] who would be Director of the National Portrait Gallery in London. A review of the exhibition by Rozsika Parker serves as an important recollection of the much-forgotten events. In this piece she quotes Sue Madden, whose work was installed on the first floor of the house. Madden felt that the artistic project was premature because the women participating were lacking sufficient emotional commitment and contact: "I think for women to build up any significant working situation they must first commit themselves to developing close contact and communication between themselves."[112] Parker notes that the project was a test case and was bound to have its pitfalls:

> As an exhibition it was light years away from the art market and conventional shows. It was initiated by the artists themselves not for profit but as an experiment in working together. In fact it was the way they got the show together as much as the content of the house which overturned the accepted idea of a women's relationship to the home. They worked on the home as a group instead of in isolation, creating a public instead of private environment.[113]

Radnor Terrace and *Womanhouse* were necessary steps in the progression of an art concerned with women's liberation. For what gallery at the time would have allowed this type of work? In addition, what gallery would offer the loaded set of symbols that a house does? Like the *Feministo* postal project examined above, *A Woman's Place* is fascinating

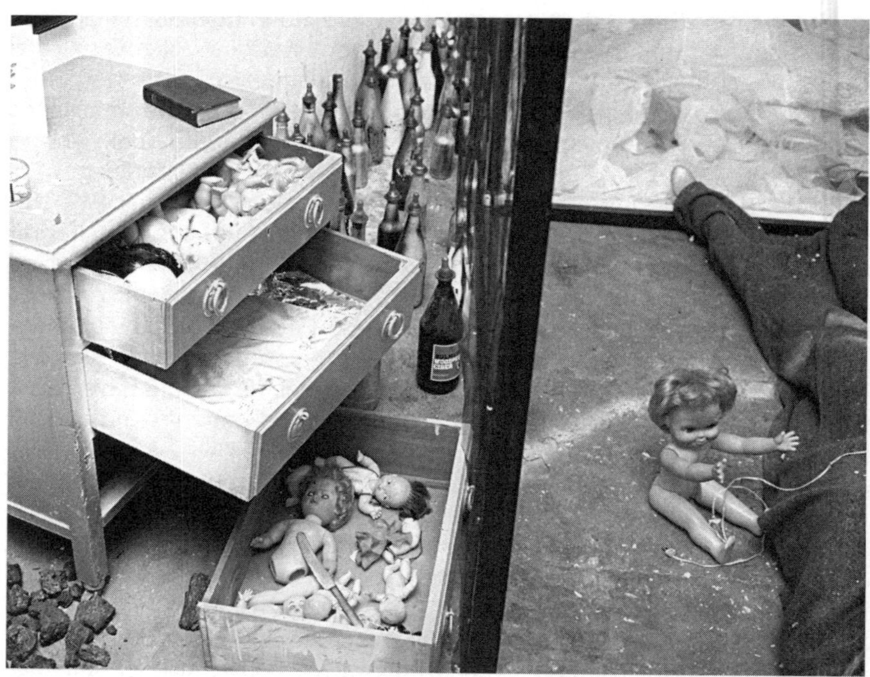

Figure 3.18
Death of a Housewife (detail), Women's Centre, Radnor Terrace, London 1974.
Kate Walker. Courtesy of the Women's Art Library/Make.

for its position in the periphery of society, and for the expression of a radical polemic.

Using a domestic space as a site for showing work allowed for a more powerful and uncompromising statement about women's issues. The domestic as a theme had been inserted into contemporary art practice since the Independent Group's examination of it during the 1950s; artists such as Eduardo Paolozzi and Richard Hamilton interrogated the post-war economic expansion and elevated the domestic as subject matter in emblematic works such as *Just What is it that Makes Today's Homes so Different, so Appealing?* However, feminist artists, such as those involved in A *Woman's Place*, went beyond the domestic as subject matter, elevating it to the site of the artwork. Herein lies the truly radical element of this project.

Women's (Free) Arts Alliance[114]

Walker repeated her installation and performance at the Women's Free Arts Alliance,[115] in North London. This was a center dedicated to a plethora of women's issues and interests, which grew out of the unanimous recognition amongst various feminist artists groups that there was a need for a space to meet and show work. It was similar to other spaces in England and the United States[116] that dealt with local issues and offered support to women artists. Kathy Nairne and Joanna Walton began work in 1972 and opened their first premises in Chalk Farm in 1975. This was the setting for *Sweet Sixteen and Never Been Shown*, the exhibition that brought together various media as well as performance, and showcased Walker's work discussed above. Later that year they moved to a site near Regent's Park.[117]

One of the original posters for Women's Arts Alliance mentions "it is run by an open collective" and lists the functions of the center as gallery, meeting space, events, darkroom, women's shop, and workshops. Clearly the remit of the center was quite wide, and the notion of an open collective is one that allows for many conflicting opinions and views about what it could be. What it definitely could not be was a resource for men. Catherine Elwes comments on the kind of discussions that took place at the time:

> Because it was a women's only venue, men were not allowed in. They were allowed in to see the exhibitions … but they couldn't come in to the meeting rooms. … I just remember this absolutely ridiculous conversation—debate—in which we had to try to decide at what point a baby or a small child becomes a man. … We tried to decide at what point this poor little boy becomes a monster called a man, and should therefore be debarred. It was absurd.[118]

Figure 3.19
Women's Art Alliance poster,
1978. Courtesy of Women's
Art Library

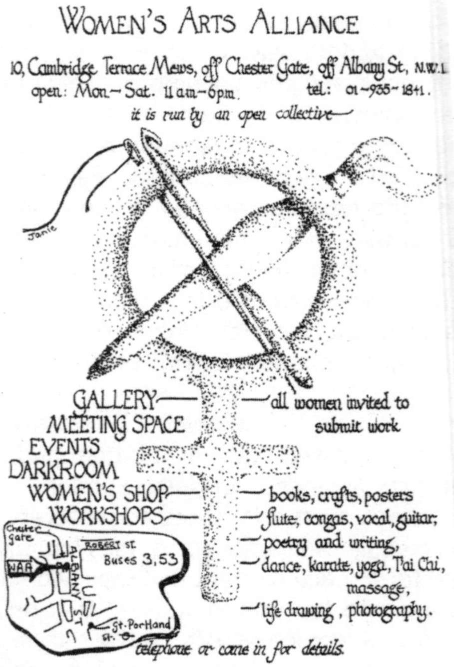

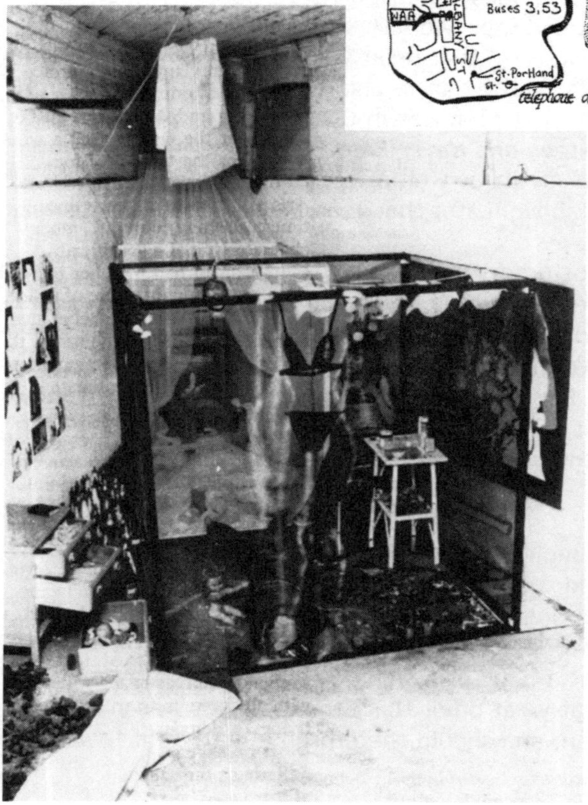

Figure 3.20
Sweet Sixteen, 1975.
Kate Walker.
Courtesy of Women's
Art Library.

While the Women's Arts Alliance provided an important outlet for many artists, it was a project beset by confusion over what it should be, as the quotation above illustrates. The problem with creating centers or galleries dedicated to women is that it creates a policy of isolation.

Elwes exhibited work at the Alliance with her colleague Annie Wright. Their exhibition in 1978 was a continuation of collaborative work they had done at the Slade School of Art. They had made a performance there in 1977 called *Female Into Male,* which consisted of the artists dressing as men in order to experience male privilege.[119]

Some were critical of their performance. One of their tutors said:

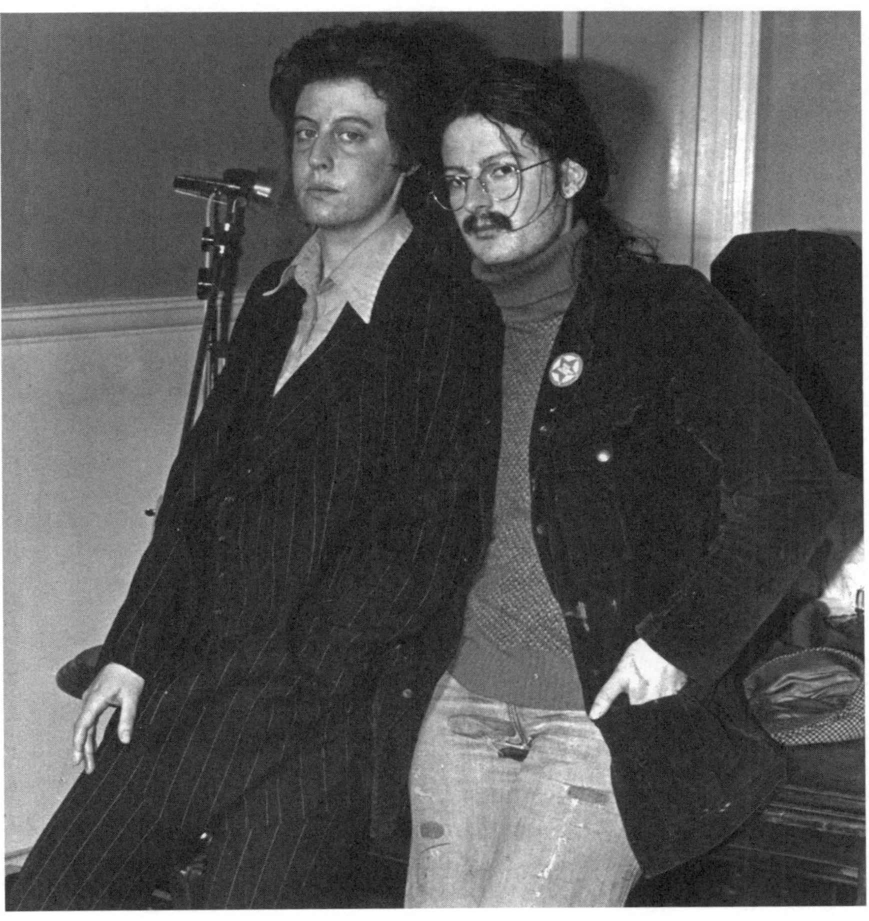

Figure 3.21
Female Into Male, 1977. Catherine Elwes and Annie Wright.
Courtesy of Women's Art Library.

> In a world that seems to be in the throes of a feminist takeover,
> something should be said in defence of the male sex. I understand
> that the purpose of the experiment was for Cate and Annie to
> disguise themselves as men. Men? Perhaps we should substitute
> that word for "dirty, oily and thoroughly unwholesome, depraved
> persons".[120]

Elwes and Wright's project admittedly is based on a clichéd and narrow conception of the male gender. However, the experiment was important in the formulation of their practice, which was largely based on sexual identity.

On Show, a series of photographs of the artists' bodies which were meant to accentuate their inadequacies, were presented as part of the Women's Arts Alliance show. For this series Wright and Elwes photographed parts of their bodies that did not conform to the ideal of feminine beauty, for example, sagging breasts and fat thighs. By accentuating their shortcomings, the artists attempted to adopt an aggressive stance towards sexual objectification.

However, despite how they saw themselves, there was still an element of sexuality and attractiveness in their youthful bodies. Their naivete was proven when Wright and Elwes took their show to Kvindegalleriet, a women's art gallery, in Copenhagen in 1978. All the photographs were purchased by one male collector, who Elwes feels missed the point of the piece, which was to underline their shortcomings as ideal feminine bodies. "He bought them for all the wrong reasons and we took the money and went back to England and pondered deeply about what we'd done. We felt we had totally compromised our ideals."[121]

This anecdote demonstrates the danger of creating work that relies on nude imagery to convey feminist ideology. Like the performance artists discussed in the previous chapter, where they hovered on the border

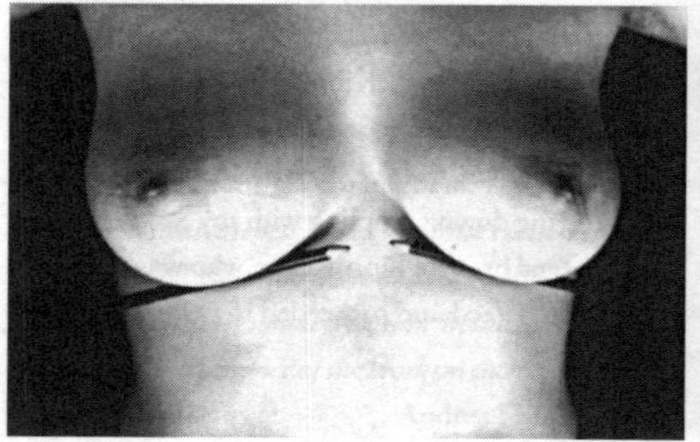
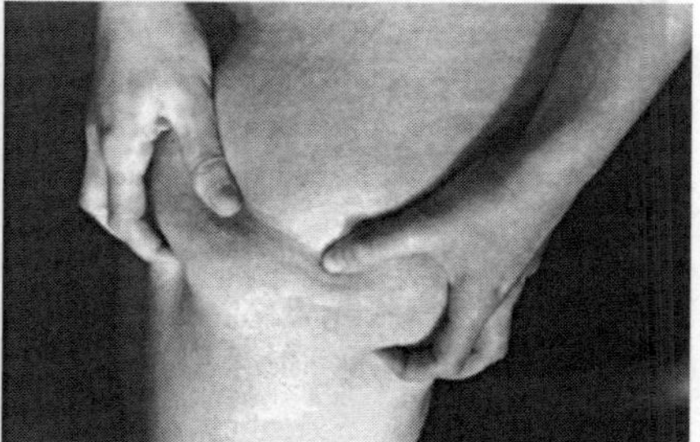

Figure 3.22
On Show, 1978. Catherine Elwes & Annie Wright.
Courtesy of Women's Art Library.

between titillation and provocation, it is in the end the viewer who makes the decision about how the work is perceived. However, by showing the work in a supportive arena for women artists, the work could be seen and discussed by their colleagues. The Women's (Free) Arts Alliance provided an ideal setting for feminist artists, with strident politics, to show work that wouldn't have been exhibited in a mainstream gallery.

<h2 style="text-align:center">RED RAGS:
JOURNALS AS ALTERNATIVE SITES</h2>

Concurrent to the activities discussed above journals and independent publications became alternative sites for feminist activism and art. While some artists organized themselves and exhibited in the spaces discussed above, this work was often supported by a range of publications: *Red Rag*, *Shrew*, *FAN* (*Feminist Arts News*), *Spare Rib* and *WIRES* became important sites for reading about women's work. While more mainstream respected publications such as *Studio* dedicated an issue to women's art, these were usually one-off ventures and there nevertheless was the audience and the need for a burgeoning literature on feminist activity. These publications were written by sympathetic commentators who were also engaged in the liberation movement. Importantly, they were also distributed and read by a public who were open to this type of activity. Looking back at these publications provides a glimpse into a time of tremendous political upheaval as well as self-initiated responses. These responses generally fell into three broad categories, exemplified by various different journals.

Spare Rib

Spare Rib was the best known and most accessible of the feminist journals. It was like a glossy magazine, with advertisements, professionally designed. It promoted a view of feminism as a positive and constructive movement. Ann Scott, in an editorial called "Why is your magazine so depressing?" discussed the remit of *Spare Rib*:

> The magazine gives women who are involved in Women's liberation one way of reaching out to women who would otherwise have no access to the movement. We are confronting the media image of women's liberation, of bra-burning and test-tube babies, on its own ground. We are fighting the media with media of our own.[122]

Spare Rib was one of the most successful feminist publications at appealing to a mass audience. It grew out of a realization on the editor's part that there were no publications that reflected the vital issues at the time. Thus, *Spare Rib* would contain a wide variety of editorial, from articles on conferences and political protests to exhibition reviews of feminist artists. One typical issue contained one of the few positive reviews of

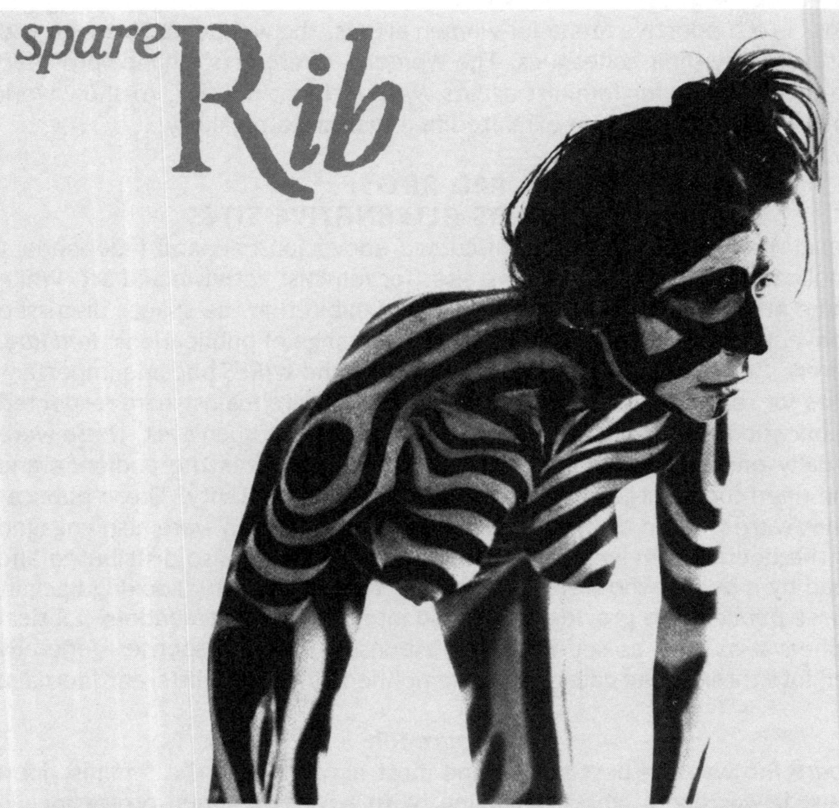

Figure 3.23
Spare Rib cover 1977. Hannah O'Shea. Courtesy of
Women's Art Library.

Kelly's *Post-Partum Document*, written by Laura Mulvey, alongside an art-historical article on Marie Bashkirtseff, a nineteenth-century painter, and an article on Navajo women artists. This wide range of subject matter meant that it appealed to women who might be just dabbling with the women's liberation movement, and wanting to learn more.

Red Rag

Red Rag was another feminist journal, with a more academic and less populist approach than *Spare Rib*. The editorial team, which billed itself as a "Marxist Feminist collective" included well-known academics and writers with serious political agendas.[123] While it contained some esoteric material such as "love poems" it featured important articles about the wider political problems of mid-1970s Britain: for example, an illustrated article on the financial decline of Britain as well as a piece on women and the National Front. Sally Alexander wrote an extensive article on the *Nightcleaners* campaign and there were reviews of feminist conferences. These important political and social debates were highlighted with editorial produced by and distributed to women. *Red Rag* also became a site for the support and critical assessment of feminist art, for example, the review of the Hayward Annual by Valerie Charlton. As in *Spare Rib*, *Red Rag* became a site where women could consolidate and educate each other without the interference of male authority. Like the alternative spaces for showing art discussed above, *Red Rag* operated outside of the mainstream conservative media system.

The *Red Rag* editorial team wrote candidly about itself in an issue from the early 1970s:

> alongside and woven in with the positive aspects of our being together, we have also had a number of upheavals, ongoing disagreements and problems. ... Whether we print a piece or not, we try to reach a collective political decision, which often takes ages, and we sometimes make mistakes and will undoubtedly do so again, because we ourselves are in the process of working out our common politics.[124]

This quote captures so succinctly the problems inherent to feminism as a larger cultural phenomenon. The multiplicity of views and concerns, which were often the cause of strife between feminists, were embraced by *Red Rag*. In this way the journal can be seen as one of the most important sites for feminist political activism at the time.

WIRES

WIRES (Women's Information Referral and Enquiry Service) billed itself as the Women's Liberation Movement Newsletter for Women Only and was one of the radical, underground journals. Created on a typewriter and photocopied, *WIRES* was sold at a cheap price (20p) and was intended as agitprop material. A far cry from *Spare Rib*, it had a handspun feel and was intended for women only. In one of its issues it reads: "The *WIRES* newsletter is for women only as it is the internal newsletter of the women's liberation movement and we ask all of you to respect this and not make it available to men."[125] Like the Women's (Free) Arts Alliance, *WIRES* necessarily distanced itself from a male audience, thereby enhancing the marginalization of women. However, it served an important purpose of keeping local groups in touch with each other and reporting activities. It reviewed events such as the Socialist Feminist Conference and advertised lesbian nights out. While by today's standards it seems makeshift and in places hilarious, it provides a fascinating view into radical feminist politics and activities of the late 1970s.

LIBERATION AND MARGINALIZATION: THE IMPACT OF ALTERNATIVE ART SPACES

The history of the early 1970s is replete with events staged and work presented in alternative spaces. In social terms this was frequently no more than a recognition that non-mainstream work—be it in art, dance, music, etc.—would have to find non-mainstream physical venues. This practical exigency should not be confused with the fact that alternative spaces were often chosen specifically with an eye to transgressing the "normal" artistic space. The avoidance of traditional middle-class containers for culture—theater, gallery, hall—in the first stage could be considered as a deliberate movement away from the normal, but was also rooted in an exploration of how the work itself might respond to a different setting. For example, Kate Walker's reverse striptease would have had a fraction of the impact had it been performed in a white cube, mainstream gallery. The residential house provided the ideal site for work based on the issues of marriage and family, as well as allowing those artists imprisoned inside conventional domesticity to turn their cage into a gallery.

Women artists during the liberation movement in 1970s London were reliant on Acme, AIR, Space, Garage and Women's (Free) Arts Alliance to provide exhibition space and journals such as *Red Rag* and *Spare Rib* to provide a forum to discuss such work. Without these organizations, much of the creative energy of feminist art would have been lost. However, it is important to recognize that much of the work that happened in these sites was not properly documented or archived. At best there are descriptions of performances and occasionally photographs or video, as in the case of *Domestic Sanitation/Latex Rodeo*. These have to stand in for the work itself in any history of the period and hence journals such as *Red Rag, Shrew, FAN* and *WIRES* are important artefacts and chronicles of this period of political and economic upheaval. While this is a logical outcome of radical work, it also opens 1970s women's art up to the danger of being erased from the cultural record. Perhaps it is now time to look back and put on record some of these events.

It is also important to acknowledge that feminist activity in alternative spaces, although born out of necessity rather than coherent theoretical conviction, helped provide a model for future activities. Julie Ault writes that "many founders of alternative art organizations derived their impetus from feminist models of critique and organization."[126] Juli Carson has also reflected on the broader effect of feminist practice, which shifted the site of activism from the political space of an institution to the more discursive site of representation.[127] The activities discussed in this chapter can be considered as forerunners for such self-organized activities in the 1980s and 1990s.

In the 1990s there was a resurgence of artist-run spaces, many of which became epicenters of London culture.[128] Artists such as Tracey Emin, Sarah Lucas, Keith Coventry and Paul Noble have again created a system for showing work that exists outside of mainstream commercial galleries. In the next chapter I examine how themes of the initial wave of feminist art practice have found their legacy in contemporary women's practice. From notions of the domestic to the artist's body, today younger generations of women are re-staging (consciously and unconsciously) debates that happened in these alternative spaces in 1970s London.

Chapter 4

FEMINIST THEMES IN CONTEMPORARY PRACTICE

INTRODUCTION

In this book I have examined themes and issues around feminist practice in 1970s London. To restate, the topics have included the body and performance art, the necessity of working outside of the mainstream gallery system, as well as the domestic as a theme and a locus for artistic activity. Some of the events and exhibitions described herein are well documented in the annals of art history, such as Mary Kelly's *Post-Partum Document* and Carolee Schneemann's *Meat Joy*. But many others have largely been ignored by art historians and curators, such as the work of Judy Clark, Kate Walker and Cosey Fanni Tutti as well as lesser-known works such as Carolee Schneemann's *Blood Diary* or Mary Kelly's *Antepartum*.

Seen from the distance of 30 years, the period described herein is relevant to work being produced today. However, female artists working in London today are enjoying a level of success that was unobtainable to previous generations of women artists. Gillian Wearing, Tomma Abts, and Susan Philipsz have won the Turner Prize, Tracey Emin has been nominated for it, and artists such as Sarah Lucas, Jemima Stehli and Hayley Newman have had solo shows in major public spaces.[1] What, if any, is the legacy from the 1970s that these artists have inherited? How have themes from the women's work of the 1970s filtered down into today's art practice and market? And are there connections between generations that are openly acknowledged?

Recently art practice has seen the resurgence of the politicized female artist. International artists such as Elke Krystufek,[2] Andrea Bowers, Patti Chang and Rachel Lachowicz[3] are unsettling the art world with visceral, subversive and challenging work that features their bodies as the central element. The difference is that this work is seen at commercial galleries and international art fairs. The same can be said for the generation of British artists discussed above. Their practice, although focused on the body, performance and in some cases alternative sites, is not, for the most part, considered as feminist. Yet, in every case mentioned above, the work involves tactics and themes deriving from earlier women's work.

This chapter examines the residue of issues exploited by subsequent generations of female artists. For example, I do not propose that Tracey Emin is a direct product of 1970s feminist art; however, her work, with its interest in craft and exploration of the personal, could not have existed without the art that has come before. What is evident in the examination of a younger generation of British women artists, is that they have no formalized historical framework for feminist artists of the 1970s, because in most cases it is not taught at art school or shown in major institutions.[4]

THE ARTIST'S BODY

In the first chapter I examined the use of the female body as a central concern in feminist practice in London during the 1970s. From Judy Clark's bodily traces to Cosey Fanni Tutti and Carolee Schneemarn's performances, artists took a firm stance regarding the incorporation or the rejection of the female figure in their work. Around the turn of the millennium there were a number of female artists who use their bodies as the predominant source material for their work. From photographs to performances, the body appears as a central and powerful subject in these works.

Averting the gaze

Jemima Stehli's[5] work revolves around the portrayal of herself in photo-graphic images. In *Chair* 1998–99 the artist appropriated Allen Jones's *Chair* 1969.[6] In Stehli's work the artist appears naked, except for fetish-ised black spike-heeled boots, lying on her back with her legs in the air, with a cushion strapped to her, seemingly inviting the viewer to contem-plate sitting on her.[7] In Jones's original image, the painted fibreglass cast of a female was contorted into the same position. In the earlier work the mannequin wore black knickers and long black evening gloves and was positioned on a white fur rug; the face, adorned with heavy makeup and a wig, highlights the artificiality of the woman. Stehli has opted for a more minimal composition, wearing only the black boots and placing herself directly on the floor, and opting for black and white film.

In the same series Stehli adopts identical poses to others in Jones's oeuvre. In *Table I* 1997–98 Stehli lies on her back supporting a plane of glass with her hands and the bottom part of her legs and in *Table II* 1997-98 Stehli is on her hands and knees, supporting the glass plane with her back and head. In each of these she is naked except for footwear.[8]

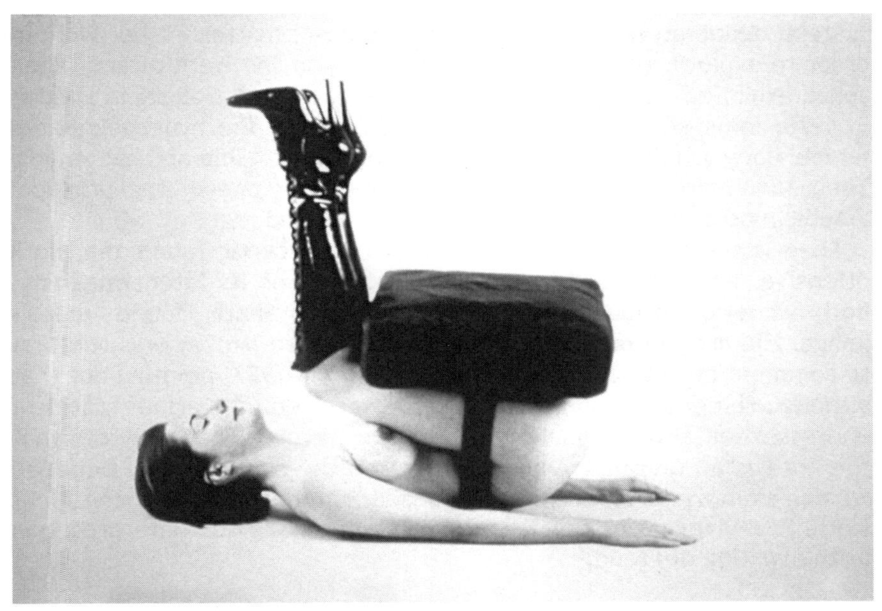

Figure 4.1a
Chair, 1998–99. Jemima Stehli. Courtesy Lisson Gallery.

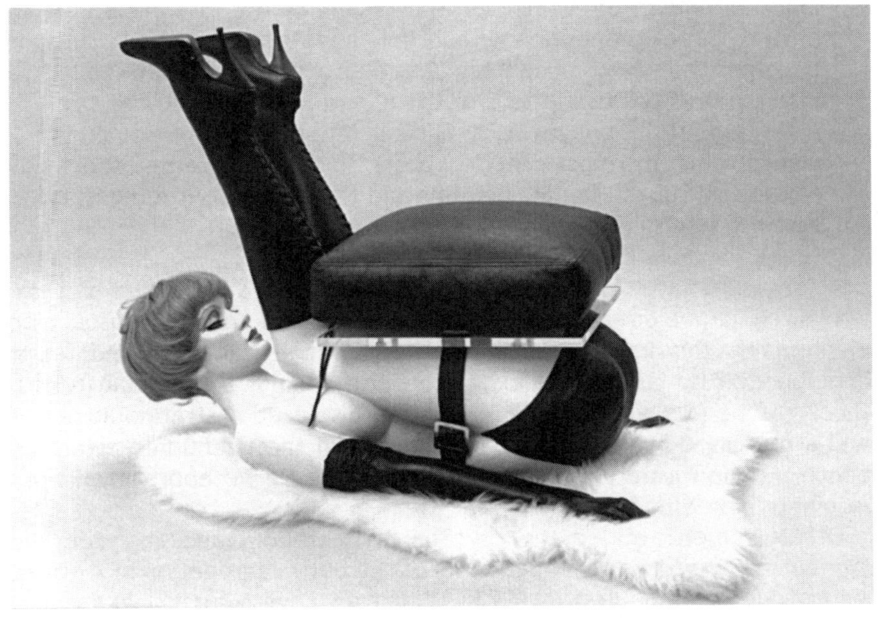

Figure 4.1b
Chair, 1969, Allen Jones. Courtesy Tate Gallery.

Stehli deliberately chose controversial subject matter for her work in order to explore the role of the female body in the work of art. When Jones exhibited his *Women as Furniture* at the Tooth Gallery in London in 1970, feminists were outraged over the use of the hyper-sexualized female body as functional objects including chairs, table and hat stands. Their sado-masochistic clothing, an extension of one of the principal graphic motifs of Jones's paintings, further elicited rage.[9]

Theorists such as Laura Mulvey and Lisa Tickner found the work offensive, and delighted in deconstructing it for its latent meaning. Both writers, although writing a few years apart, found Jones's imagery indicative of a fear of castration. Laura Mulvey was the first to comment on the artist's work in *Spare Rib* in 1973, pointing out that although the doll-like life-sized women were seen in various states of undress, their actual female genitals were never seen. She wrote that this threw "an unusually vivid spotlight on the contradiction between woman's fantasy presence and real absence from the male unconscious world."[10] Mulvey ultimately sees Jones's work as a visual interpretation of the writing of Freud:

> Fetishism, Freud first pointed out, involves displacing the sight of woman's imaginary castration onto a variety of reassuring but often surprising objects—shoes, corsets, rubber gloves, belts, knickers and so on—which serve as *signs* for the lost penis but have no direct connection with it. For the fetishist, the sign itself becomes the source of fantasy (whether actual fetish objects or else pictures or descriptions of them) and in every case the sign is the sign of the phallus. It is man's narcissistic fear of losing his own phallus, his most precious possession, which causes shock at the sight of the female genitals and the subsequent fetishistic attempt to disguise or divert attention from them.[11]

A few years later Lisa Tickner continued Mulvey's critique when she wrote, "It is not difficult to see both the sadistic and the masochistic elements in this imagery as projections of male fantasies and fears, compounded by guilt or an exaggerated awe, and, in Freudian terms, these can be recognised as dependent on displaced castration anxieties and a repressed homosexuality. This aspect of the tradition emphasises above all the *mystery* of woman … an enigma to be approached with fascination or with fear."[12]

Other women avoided the psychoanalytic theory and analyzed the *Women as Furniture* as embodiments of the daily degradation of women. Monica Sjoo commented in 1973, "When an English artist Allen Jones does degrading sculptures of women as tables, on their knees wearing black stockings and garter belts, he has the nerve to call them formale

[sic] experiments and gets away with it … but then of course anyone can go down to the nearest London tube-station and find equally degrading images of women everywhere (adverts & posters) selling everything from toothpaste to cars."[13] Indeed female imagery in advertising at the time was largely sexualized and objectified, which was one of the larger cultural debates in feminism.

Jones's work was a contentious topic for Stehli, who literally embodies Mulvey's writing by recreating the Allen Jones series with herself as model and *animateur*. But does replacing herself put her in the subjugated position of the female mannequin? And does this problem reiterate the dilemma of feminist artists who used their nude bodies in their work? In one sense, yes. Stehli's body—which happens to be well-toned and attractive—becomes the object of desire, which is seen by the viewer. Yet, she occupies the position of the viewer as well as she is the creator of the work. The success of Stehli's series relies on the moment in which the viewer must decide if the gaze has been reversed, undermined or celebrated. One contemporary writer described Stehli as "both female and male positions within the same image, not only 'woman as spectacle', 'passive object of the look,' but also as active voyeur, controller of the gaze."[14] The work deliberately resides on the tenuous line between power and subjugation.

Similar to Schneemann's critics who found the use of her eroticized body problematic, Stehli elicits uncomfortable responses. One writer commented that "what draws such a rancorous reaction is that Stehli undermines the basis of her own critique by displaying the female body as a glamorous object."[15] Her fellow artist David Burrows writes:

> An encounter with Jemima Stehli can be unnerving. She often appears naked or half-dressed, lifeless or passive; or behind a camera, creating complex relationships between viewer, artist and model in which to enmesh her audience. Most unnerving though, is the way Stehli confuses critique and pleasure. In Stehli's photographs it is difficult to separate her exhibitionism from her examination of objectification, the pleasures of voyeurism and narcissism from an analysis of the gaze, and the artist's own ambition from the way she lays bare the structures of power at play in the work of galleries, dealers, curators and critics.[16]

Burrows elucidates the ambivalence that makes the work so intriguing. Is she commenting on the nature of the objectified female body? Is she also undermining the images that she appropriates? Or is she celebrating the earlier work? Stehli's project, like some of her predecessors discussed in this dissertation, also reflects the eroticism and the pleasure of being looked at. As Catherine Elwes stated, artists often thrive on the attention of the spectators. Stehli plays on the erotic charge, both of the viewer as well as herself.

Stehli similarly appropriated sexually charged images from the fashion photographer Helmut Newton. In *Here They Come*, 1999, she transformed herself into a Newton model, emulating the clothes, hairstyle and makeup of the original. In this work the cable release signals Stehli as both artist and model. Charlotte Cotton writes:

> Stehli not only emulates the position of one of the models in Newton's original photograph but also his stylistic signature of black and white, her authorship of both made evident in the shutter-release cable that she presses with her left hand. As in Cindy Sherman *Untitled Film Stills*, Stehli's strategy for critiquing (and to some degree reclaiming) Newton's iconic images hinges on her being both the subject and the object of her work. It generates its own form of objectification and visual stereotyping and also marks the shift in the years between Newton's and Stehli's photographs from the magazine page to the gallery wall.[17]

Cotton argues that Stehli's work generates its own problem, which concerns objectification of the self. Like the work of feminist artists such as Schneemann, Wilke or Elwes, Stehli deliberately places herself in erotically charged situations within her work to question the politics of representation and authorship. Also, as Cotton points out, Stehli questions the visual language of advertisements, moving this debate into the space of the gallery.

In Stehli's *Strip* series, 1999–2000, she went a step further in questioning the erotics of spectatorship when she invited a group of men — two art critics, a curator, an artist, a dealer and an arts presenter[18] — to photograph her while she stripped for them. Each man was given the shutter release, and was instructed to take photographs of the artist, at their discretion, at various points in the striptease.

The final composition of the series is dependent upon the gaze of the art world male. They watch while the artist undresses. They snap the pictures, and thus seem to be in control. And the artist literally prostitutes herself for her work. However, what is presented to the viewer is essentially a photograph of the man looking at the artist. Thus, the viewer's gaze is directed at the man rather than the artist. The gaze between subject and object, then, takes place in two directions: the viewer sees the man who sees the artist; the artist sees the man who sees her. Ultimately the artist creates a complicated relationship with her subjects as she relinquishes artistic control in the photographs.[19] Suddenly they become responsible for the photographs rather than Stehli. As Stella Santacatterina writes,

> "In this situation all the protagonists become objects and subjects being watched. Here the artist was exposed to her own gaze as well as that of the other."[20]

While Stehli is invested in the work of Laura Mulvey and the ideology of the gaze in art, she does not profess to create feminist work.[21] She is more interested in posing (figuratively and literally) a problem for the viewer.[22] Burrows, who was one of the men in the *Strip* series, writes "Despite feminism's analysis of objectification, it seems more than ever that women, and men too, are posed as models for us to look at, desire and identify with. The issue of objectification is still a live one."[23] Thirty years after the women's movement in London, women—and men—are still being objectified in advertising and other popular media. Perhaps what Burrows and Stehli acknowledge is the pleasure of looking and being looked at, an intrinsic desire that cannot be eliminated from human behavior.

Another British artist has dedicated the majority of her career thus far to works that incorporate her body. Hayley Newman has acknowledged her work's debt to earlier performance, in particular what she "considers to be a revolutionary moment in art: the break both from theatrical performance and from object-based visual art, that can be recognised in the emergence of performance art in Europe during the 1960s and 1970s."[24] Newman left Britain for a period of study in Marina Abramović's class in Germany because she felt that the British performance scene "had become increasingly theater-based and that she wanted to redis-cover performance roots in Europe—Marina [Abramović] & Ulay, [Joseph] Beuys, Valie Export, Ulrike Rosenbach."[25]

While in Germany she performed the piece *Microphone Skirt* in several locations between 1995 and 1997.[26] In this work she go-go danced eroti-cally wearing a T-shirt, knickers and a skirt comprised of 20 microphones. As she moved, the jostling of the microphones created a cacophony of feedback and sound. The references in the work are layered. First the microphone can be considered as phallic imagery. As in Finn-Kelcey's *The Boilermaker's Assistant* the microphone becomes a symbol of power that is reclaimed by the female artist. Also, the microphones' auto-erotic possibilities are highlighted in Newman's performance as they jostle and knock against her midriff and groin. The visual spectacle is a sign of vora-cious female power and energy, while the sound element is disturbing in its intensity.

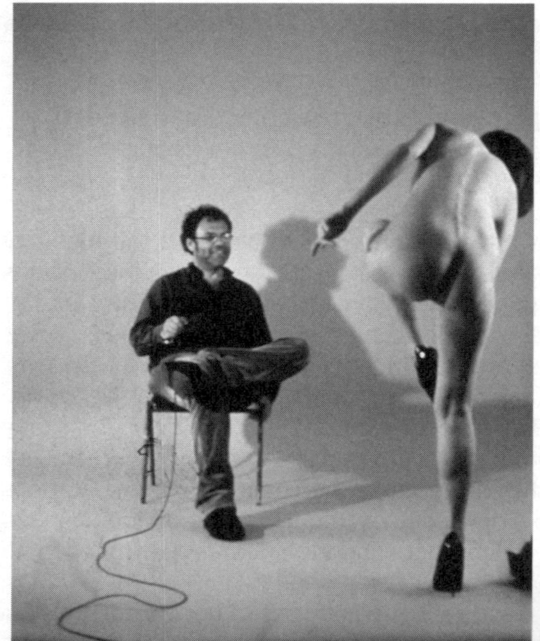

Figures 4.2 (a-d)
a) *Strip no.3*, Critic, 2000;
b) *Strip no.4*, Curator, 1999;
c) *Strip no.5*, Dealer, 1999;
d) *Strip no.6*, Critic, 2000.
Jemima Stehli.
Courtesy Lisson gallery

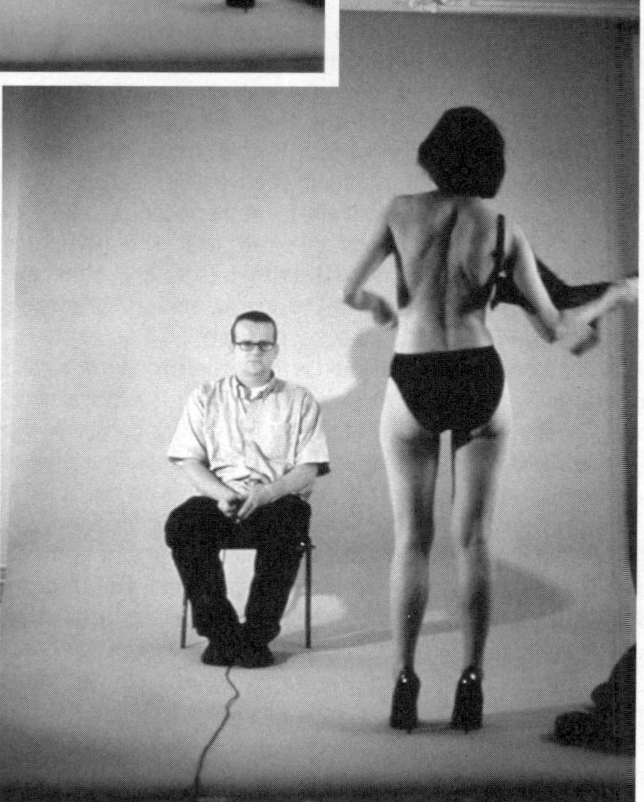

(c)

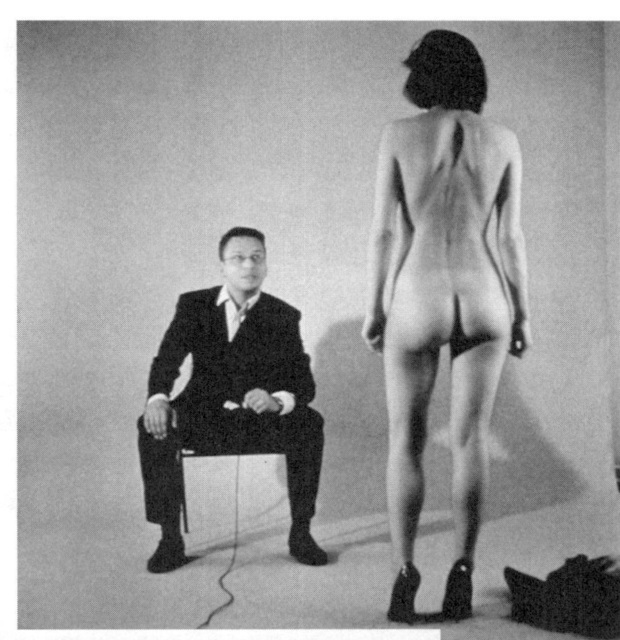

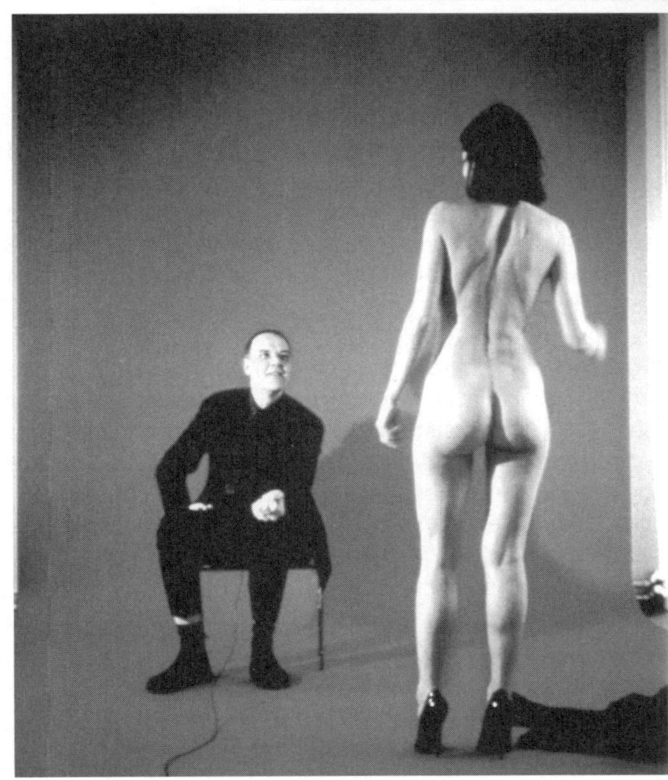
(d)

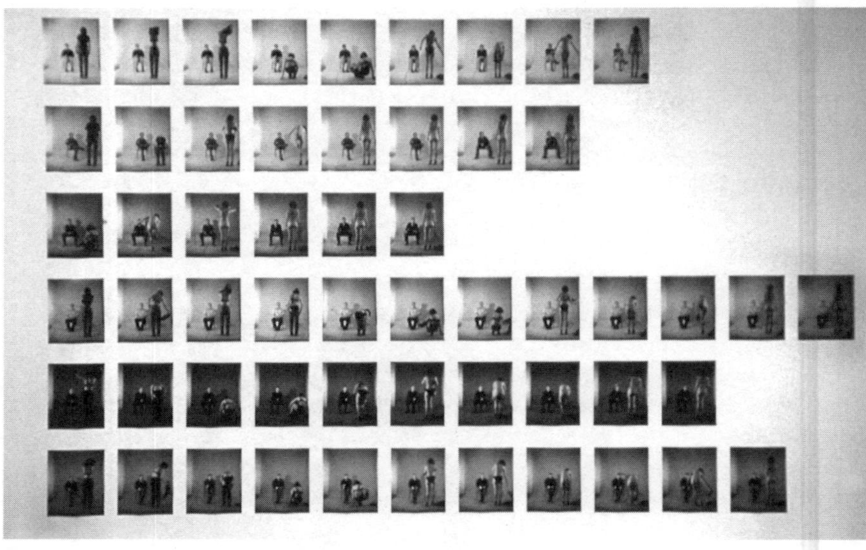

Figure 4.3
Strip Series, 1999–2000. Jemima Stehli. Courtesy Lisson Gallery.

REVISITING THE PERFORMANCE:
DOCUMENTATION AND CONTEMPORARY ART

One of the critical debates that raged in the 1970s and still exists around performance art concerns documentation. As seen in discussions of feminist performance in the 1970s, some of the artists examined here were wary of documentation because of its inadequacy in conveying the charge and immediacy of performance. For example, Anne Bean has said that an integral part of the performance was that things disappeared. She said, "It was okay if it was just in people's memory."[27]

In the late 1990s Newman made a series of works around the issue of documentation, trace and memory. In this series the artist created photographs, with the assistance of photographer Casey Orr, that appear to be documentary evidence from performances, and are further enhanced by the lengthy titles, dates, locations and captions for each work. In each of these Newman's body plays the central role and seems to authenticate the work by its presence within it. The photographs, however, are staged, and were created over one week in 1998. Thus, the dates, locations and captions are fictitious. The artist's words explain her strategy:

> As a form, performance is often mediated through the documentary image, video, film, text or by word of mouth and rumour.

With so few existing networks for the distribution of performance works, it is the image and its supporting text that is given privilege in publications on the subject, creating a handful of historical performances that have become notorious through their own documentation, leaving others behind that have not made the translation into the single image.[28]

One need only think of the iconic images of Schneemann's *Meat Joy* or Catherine Elwes' *Menstruation* performances to see Newman's point. In these earlier works one or two photographs have come to represent the performances for future generations, who only experience the work through these images. When *Meat Joy* was recently recreated in London, it was evident how much times have changed: what seemed radical and Bacchanalian in the 1960s seems quite tame now.

Newman's *Connotations* series challenges the notion of the camera as the figure of authority for the performance and the artist's body as object. Instead of the document replacing the performance, the document actually becomes the performance. For example, *Lock-jaw Lecture Series* is dated 1997–98. The accompanying caption explains that for a year Newman gave invited lectures after she had been to a dentist, who anaesthetized her mouth, rendering it virtually immobile. A list of locations for lectures helps to authenticate her claims. However, it is a fictional construction. The same thing can be said for the *Meditation on Gender Difference* photograph, dated 21 July 1996, which shows the nude artist, seated, with a severe sunburn, only in the bikini areas. The caption beside the photograph explains that the artist cut the bikini area out of a suit, and sat in her garden to obtain the sunburn. Like Stehli's work, Newman refers here to an earlier action by American conceptual artist Dennis Oppenheim, *Reading Position for Second Degree Burn* 1970. Newman parodies the self-destructive tendency found in some performance art with her faked sunburn.

Newman's *Stealth* is a black and white photograph that depicts the artist in the air, legs and arms akimbo, while nude. The accompanying caption explains that the artist jumped up and down on a trampoline for three hours in complete darkness, with a small red flashing light attached to her body. Most importantly, it reads, "Prior to the event I had instructed its organizer to enter at any point during the three hour long performance and take a single photograph with a flash to document the work. This is the only image of the work as no other photography was allowed."[29] These words echo those of the generation of artists who used performance in their practice during the 1960s and 1970s. Artists such as Catherine Elwes, Rose Finn-Kelcey and Rose English were wary of photography during the performance, and thus, many of these events are now recorded in history as a single iconic image, or not at all.

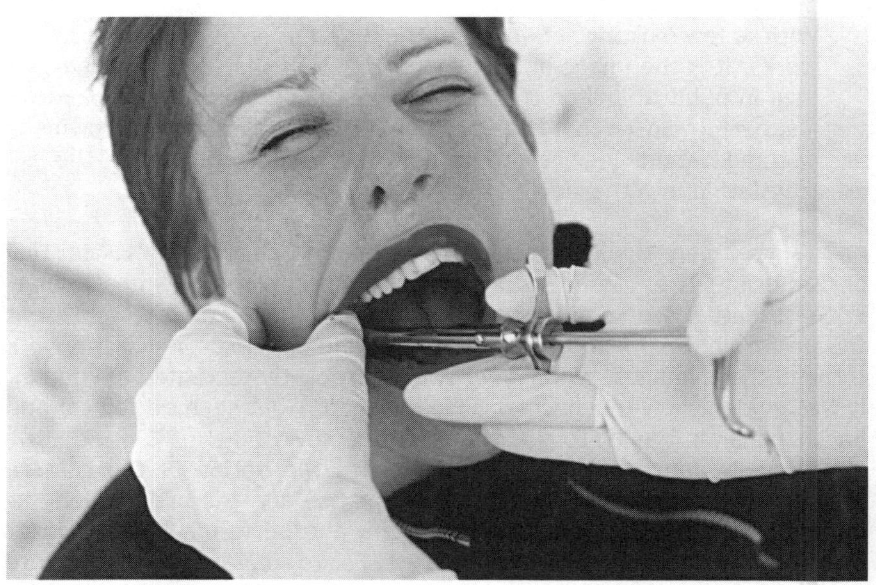

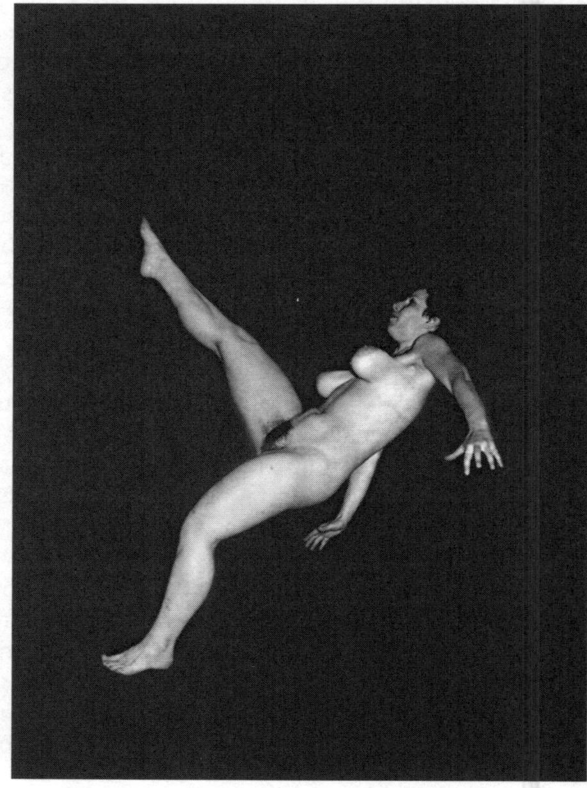

Figure 4.4
Connotations Series.
Hayley Newman.
(Above) *Lockjaw*
Lecture, 1997–98.
(Right) *Stealth,* 1996

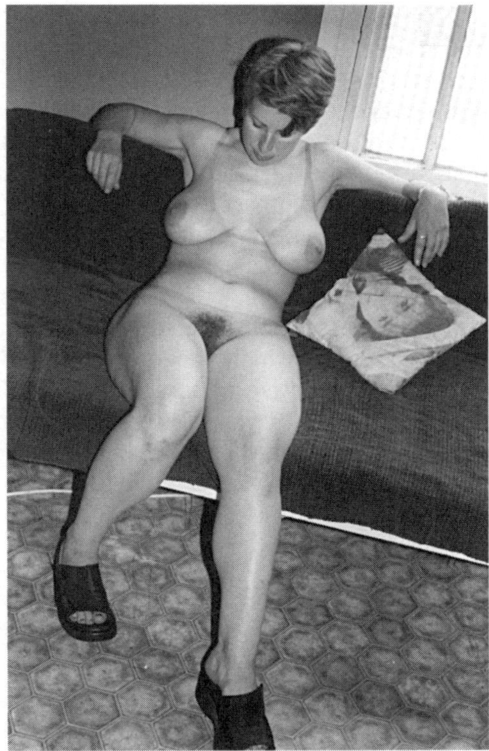

Figure 4.5
Connotations Series. Hayley
Newman. *Meditation on Gender
Difference*, 1996.

Newman described how the series was instigated by looking at documentation of her own performances:

> It's a very simple thought that started it off, which was when I get these photos back after a performance they don't speak of the performance to me, or they don't speak of that experience. Or they speak of it in a very different way and after a period of time your memory of the performance fades but the photograph comes to the surface. That's how you then remember it. The experience gets absorbed and recycled and becomes a part of something else.[30]

Newman's work explores how documentation reconfigures performance in history. She confronts the slippage between event and record of that event. Her work poses important questions about the legacy of performance practice, such as: Does the documentary evidence become predominant over the live event? And, what role does performance play in a women's art practice?

THE DOMESTIC IN CONTEMPORARY ART

The domestic as subject matter was one of the abiding themes of feminist art. As discussed in Chapters One, Two and Three, artists such as Bobby Baker, Cate Elwes, Mary Kelly and Judy Clark turned to the home for inspiration as well as a site to make and show work. Domestic subject matter has resurfaced in work produced by today's generation of younger women artists. For example, film-maker Sarah Pucill's work has largely relied upon domestic imagery, including teapot spouts that double as phalluses and the projection of herself onto household items such as cups and saucers. In her 16mm film from 1990 titled *You Be Mother*[31] domestic objects on a table take on a nightmarish quality. The accompanying sound, which ranges from ambient noise to bursts of ceramic clangs, is suggestive of something dark lying underneath the surface of normality in the home. This reflects the tone of Baker's *An Edible Family in a Mobile Home*, where a lurking sense of menace undermined the idea of woman as care-giver and nurturer.

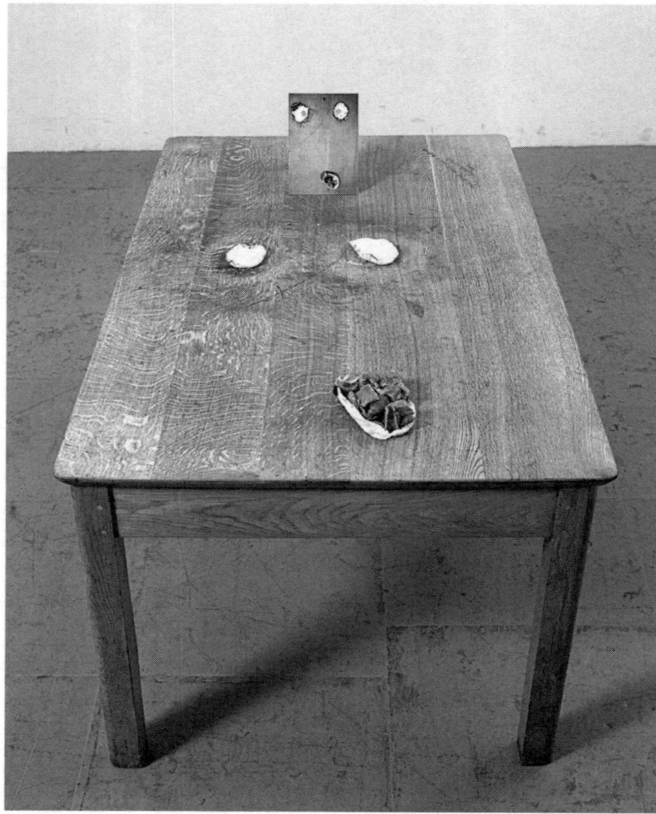

Figure 4.6
Sarah Lucas.
Courtesy of
Sadie Coles
HQ, London.
Copyright the
artist.

One of the most well-known examples of the legacy of domestic materials is Sarah Lucas.[32] Her *Two Fried Eggs and a Kebab,* 1992, consists of little more than what the title indicates: two fried eggs and a kebab placed on a bare dining table with a photograph.[33] The placing of the objects on the table is suggestive of female sex organs and the crudely naive look of the sculpture adds to the aggressive tone of the piece. It echoes the work of Su Richardson, for example, her *Crocheted Breakfast* from the *Feministo* project. The use of food in *Two Fried Eggs and a Kebab* can also be compared to Bobby Baker's cakes and Carolee Schneemann's use of mackerel and chickens in *Meat Joy.* Lucas' meat and eggs continually putrefy and need replacing, similar to Baker's cakes, which went off during the course of her installation. But Lucas' food becomes anthropomorphic, suggesting body parts of a woman. Matthew Collings writes, Lucas' sculpture differs from its precedents in that it is "not soppy, solemn or frenzied, but dry, witty, clever and sly."[34] This is an unfair criticism of earlier work; many of Lucas' predecessors, such as Walker and Baker, used humor in their work.

Lucas' *Au naturel,* 1994, is a sculpture that lies directly on the floor, which consists of a mattress, propped against a wall. A cucumber sticking directly up into space, flanked by two oranges—clearly a reference to male genitalia—and a bucket and two large melons, are strategically placed to suggest a vagina and breasts. Juxtaposed on the dirty mattress, the shapes represent the basest form of expressing gender, the kind of tabloid division of the sexes: women as big-breasted sexualized creatures and men as penises. Again Lucas mimics earlier examples of the use of food that exhibits anthropomorphic qualities while the dirty mattress conjures up dark images of domestic life.

One writer has described the artist's strategy here as, "to exaggerate grossly the reduction of the contrasting 'objects of desire' in a manner that is both aggressive and jocular, although outright laughter sticks in the throat because the artist's staged objectification of sexuality is too mundane."[35] It is this everyday character of the work that looks back to feminist strategies of the 1970s in London. Works such as Kate Walker's *Keep Smiling Chocs,* from the *Feministo* project, are forerunners of Lucas' simply constructed sculpture. In this work Walker created chocolates that replicate vaginal forms and labeled them with suggestive titles such as "Orange Cream", "Coffee Cream" and "Liquid Cherry". The simplicity of materials and the lack of reverence for traditional skills-based work give the work a vernacular appearance and an aggressive tone. However, Lucas, unlike her predecessors, is celebrated for this attitude. Whereas the women in *Feministo* were called "miserable bitches"[36] by one visitor to the show, Lucas is today hailed as one of Britain's most important artists.[37] This leads one to re-evaluate women artists' position in the current art market: they have gone from the furthest margins to the center of art dealing. Feminism's overtly politicized stance and its diffi-cult imagery helped pave the way for artists such as Lucas to succeed.

What is the cultural shift that brought about the change in attitude toward aggressive work by female artists? Clearly the work does not differ greatly in strategy, materials, or presentation. The difference, then, must lie in the viewer's relationship to the work. Today's art-viewing public is accustomed to controversy, for example, as seen annually in the Turner Prize. Another important difference is that women of the yBa generation, Lucas in particular, were respected and supported by male peers. For example, when Damien Hirst curated the *Freeze*[38] exhibition after gradu-ating from Goldsmiths College, he included Lucas' work in the exhibition. This sent out an important signal to his peers, as well as to critics and dealers. One can only imagine what would have happened if successful male artists promoted their feminist colleagues in the 1970s; however, at the time the women may not have co-operated, as it was part of their political ideology to create their own alternative systems for making and showing work. After all, some organizations, such as the Women's Arts Alliance, didn't allow men.[39]

One of the most notorious examples of the use of the domestic in contemporary art is Tracey Emin's[40] *My Bed* 1999. Exhibited as part of the Turner Prize exhibition at Tate Britain in 1999, Emin's installation elicited controversy[41] and a wealth of press coverage.[42] This work has become a signature work of Emin's and is now part of the Saatchi Collection in London. However, Emin's *My Bed* is not the first time an artist has moved her domestic environment into the Tate. In 1985 Hannah O'Shea created *Hannah's at Home,* an installation and series of performances where she moved her entire domestic surroundings into the gallery. Her bed was juxtaposed with clothing lines and O'Shea conducted performances in which she wore tampons for earrings, drawing on the aspects of feminine experience that were considered offensive to the general public in much the same way as Emin has done recently.[43] (Emin actually shows blood-stained knickers as part of this installation.) The resurgence of domestic subject matter into a public gallery space is testament to the notion that some aspects of a woman's experience—sex and drug taking in the case of Emin's bed—are still considered unacceptable to some of the art viewing audience. It is also testament to feminist artists as forerunners for concerns that would continue to be debated by contemporary artists.

ALTERNATIVE SITES

The Radnor Terrace project[44] discussed in Chapter Three was important as a British answer to the successful feminist project *Womanhouse,* led by Miriam Schapiro and Judy Chicago. The Radnor Terrace project, like most of the radical feminist activity in Britain during the 1970s, is largely unheard of today. It is doubtful that if you asked any young female artist

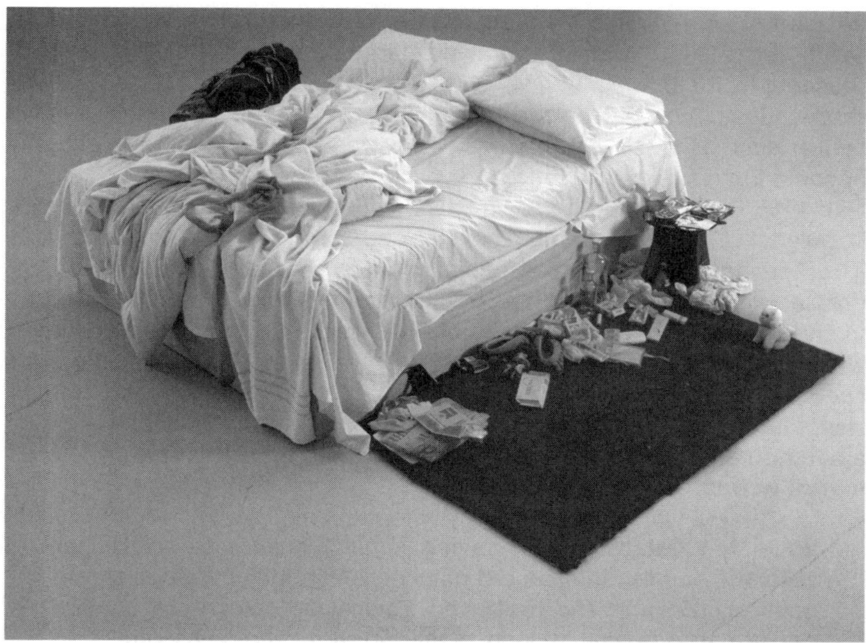

Figure 4.7
© Tracey Emin. All rights reserved, DACS 2012.

practicing in London today that they would know, or would have been formally taught about, this project. Likewise, Bobby Baker's *An Edible Family in a Mobile Home* project is written out of conventional art history. However, the idea of using domestic space as a public venue has seen a rebirth of late.[45] In the 1990s artists in London were determined to take matters into their own hands. Like the women who organized the *A Woman's Place*, Emin decided to take her domestic space and single-handedly turn it into a gallery, thus transforming her life into a work of art by blurring the boundary between public and private life.

Emin funded her early work by "friends of Tracey" contributions. These took the form of Tracey Emin bonds that could be swapped for works of art.[46] For a small fee, it was also possible to regularly receive letters written by the artist. In return for a cash fee the supporter would be guaranteed to receive four letters from Emin. She called this the "Eminway School of Art."[47] Then Emin met fellow artist Sarah Lucas[48] and together they decided to open a shop in a dilapidated Victorian house in the East End of London[49] where they sold various bits of ephemeral art including ashtrays with Damien Hirst's face printed on the bottom, Rothko blankets, and other hand-crafted merchandise. Sarah Lucas said, "A lot of the merchandise was crap, but the seeds of subsequent ideas were sown—both in my work and in Tracey's."[50] Their shop/gallery[51] was patronized by some of the most important art world figures such as Hirst, and his dealer Jay Jopling, who would eventually become Emin's dealer.

In 1995 Emin opened her own space called the Tracey Emin Museum. Located in South London,[52] the self-dedicated museum was actually a rented flat in a converted minicab office squeezed between a hair-dresser and a dentist.[53] While the museum is now closed, it lives on in the legend that has become Emin's career. Art critic Esther Pierini wrote about her experience at the museum, where she viewed *How it Feels*, a documentary-style video about Emin's abortion and miscar-riage. Emin had become pregnant after being told she was infertile, had a botched abortion, and suffered a horrific miscarriage a few days later. Pierini writes:

> While the details are harrowing, Emin manages to relate her rage and anguish in a candid manner which falls between sordid public confession and art-styled ironical autobiography. ... The performance begins as soon as you arrive at the "museum", and the overwhelming sensation for an audience member is that no matter how much Emin exposes of herself, her process of crea-tivity and dissection is incessant; audience response in the Emin Museum is taken for cataloguing and filing for future reference like any other subject under the microscope.[54]

Pierini's account of her visit brings two issues to the surface. First, the idea of self-confession, and second, the experience of being an audi-ence member there. Like her videos, poems, performances, drawings and installations, the museum is a hyperbolic form of self-confession and self-obsession. And thus, it is difficult to separate the person from the work. Indeed, it is impossible. Adrian Searle wrote of Emin's solipsism[55] while Richard Dorment has written, "In a performance of monstrous audacity, she expects her audience to be interested in virtually everything that has ever happened to her."[56] But what he neglects to write is that Emin's personal exploration seems to capture the attention of audiences, as her work continues to grow in interest.[57] Also, Emin's excavation is a contem-porary incarnation of the feminist slogan "the personal is political". However, in Emin's personal story there is no celebratory female experi-ence, no earth goddess imagery, no optimism. For her, the personal is a disaster. This lack of optimism may be closer to the truth of many women's situations than the celebratory feminism of an artist like Judy Chicago.

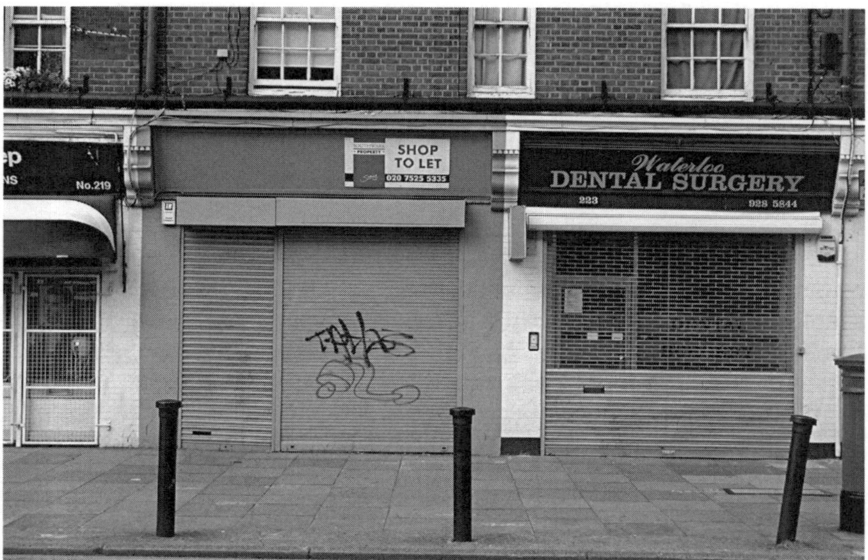

Figure 4.8
The vacant site of the Tracey Emin Museum. Photograph: Nigel Talamo.

Emin's tactics of confession and personal revelation had played a major role in the feminist work made by women artists in the 1970s. Take for example, the rape plays performed by the women on the feminist art program that staged *Womanhouse*. Similarly in this country, projects such as *Feministo* encouraged women to express themselves and many of the participating artists made work based on their domestic situations. Take, for example, Monica Ross' piece in *Feministo*, in which stuffed babies suggest an underlying discomfort with her domestic situation. Likewise in *A Woman's Place* Kate Walker's performance conveys the horrific side of being a bride and wife. At the time when these works were made, women artists unwittingly created a ghetto, which resulted in their ostracism from the mainstream art world.

The Bond Street dealers and other blue chip galleries did not represent aggressively political work at the time, nor do they now. However, conditions for young women artists are radically different today. Why does the commercial art world today accommodate women artists with political and radical stances? Carolee Schneemann believes that it is fashion driven:

> Well, it's all so chic. Every smart gallery says "Hey, I need a bad-mouthed cunt. Who's wild and crazy? I need one. Don't give me two. Just one." … But the initiating artists, they don't want to fuck us, so they don't want to show us either. Once you're not a fuckable female then you have to wait to be eighty.[58]

Schneemann's words have a particular relevance when seen in the light of an artist such as Emin. She is, after all, a sexually charged woman[59] who is open about her abortions, love affairs, masturbation and suicide attempts. It is precisely this candor that is so unsettling for some and yet simultaneously so attractive to others. Her antics on television during the Turner Prize debate on Channel 4 in December 1997 have made her a kind of anti-hero for the yBa generation.[60] This has led to her modeling for top fashion designer Vivienne Westwood and writing a column for a men's lifestyle magazine. Indeed, Emin is a celebrity based on her acerbic personality. Richard Gott writes that Emin "brings with her something of the fame and aura of a rock musician."[61] This is an interesting statement when compared with the fact that Anne Bean didn't want the Moodies to become represented by Malcolm McLaren because she feared it would be too fashionable. Clearly today's younger artists, raised under Thatcherite politics, have to be more interested in self-promotion and financial success, as government grants for such work have greatly diminished.

Emin's most sexually charged work to date has been her *Everyone I Have Ever Slept With 1963-1995*, a tent which lists the names of everyone that she's ever slept with. Emin's embroidered sculpture contains almost one-hundred names, including her nan, her twin and her teddy bear. It was made for the *Minky Manky* show at South London Gallery in 1995, which was curated by Emin's then boyfriend, Carl Freedman.[62] Indeed his name is stitched on to the tent flap. Provocative as it may be, her use of textiles and stitching seems to refer to generations of traditional "women's work". Emin sewed each name on to patches of fabric and then applied the fabric to the canvas of the tent. Janis Jefferies writes of the piece, "While quilting and embroidery techniques are employed, Emin's gigantic patchwork adorned tent refuses the first wave of a woman's celebratory experience, cited earlier through the example of Judy Chicago's *The Dinner Party*."[63] Jefferies' point about the rejection of celebratory women's experience is an important one. Emin's expression of personal crises contrasts with the celebratory collaborative spirit of Chicago's project. However, Emin's use of sewing and stitchwork was not consciously derivative of an earlier feminist project. When questioned about the relationship between the domestic and her textile pieces she said, "I sew simply because I sew and I am actually quite good at it. It's not like I'm trying to come up with some kind of grand female statement. And I like the humbleness of sewing."[64] However, it is

important to acknowledge that she does return to a traditionally feminine medium. Her patchworked pieces have many historical anteced-
ents, more recently the AIDS quilts projects, as well as those made by
Kate Walker in the early 1970s.

Clive Phillpot discussed this matter of what I call "unconscious
appropriation":

> Because the times are as they are certain things will happen
> and they'll happen regardless of the fact that someone's done
> it before. ... And these people are doing it, as I say, innocently,
> because they don't know the history very often. And then some
> do know the history and build on it. But a lot of it is totally
> unconscious. And it just confirms to me this rupture as you call
> it, this change that I see is ongoing.[65]

If Emin was unaware of Walker's work (and I hasten to add that it
doesn't really matter whether she was or was not) it is because the
latter belongs to a generation of under-recognized artists from Britain.
The influence of 1970s feminist practice on contemporary art is not
direct; rather, it comes more indirectly through their modes of practice. Feminist artists such as Kelly, Clark and Baker, in their critique of
conceptual practice, inserted subjectivity into the artistic debate. This
concern with subjectivity continues to be one of the dominant themes
in contemporary art practice, and is witnessed in the work of artists
like Emin and Newman.

CONCLUSION

The artists in this chapter adopt strategies similar to feminist artists;
however, they are not labeled as such, as these techniques and motifs
have found their way into the mainstream. The Tate Modern have dedicated a room to the work of Sarah Lucas, and have acquired several
works for the Tate's collection. Yet they have only a handful of feminist works from the 1970s in their collection. The younger generation, it
seems, have thrived without any association with the women's liberation
movement, although many of the latter's themes are implicit in their
work. This generation's work has broken sales records at auctions, and
demands prices equal to that of male artists. Compare this to women in
the 1970s, who survived largely by teaching or with the help of their part-
ners, or in the case of Kate Walker, have had to forge a different career
path to ensure financial stability.

Clearly though, the work made by visual artists during the women's
liberation movement in London was powerful and evocative, if at times
slightly mawkish or naive. The use of the female artist's body in making
work resurged in the 1990s with the practice of Jemima Stehli and Hayley

Newman as well as artists from abroad such as Vanessa Beecroft, Elke Krystufek, Patty Chang and Rachel Lachowicz. Using the body has helped women artists to break with the confines of traditional media such as painting or sculpture. At times it has also served as a continuation and reconfiguration of those media, for example, in the case of Schneemann's actions, which grew out of her paintings and installations. Contemporary performance artists, though, are largely supported by a mainstream gallery system, with documentation in the form of photographs or videos now sold on the market.[66]

This chapter concludes a book that did not attempt to create a comprehensive history of the feminist artists working during the 1970s. Rather it begins the effort that is needed to document, preserve and understand works made by women in the 1970s in London, and to understand how this work is relevant to contemporary practice. The ephemeral nature of much of the earlier work, while it is part of its strength, has also proved problematic. Herein lies the problem with women who chose to work in radical or alternative systems: it necessarily excluded them from the mainstream organizations that help promote and conserve works. However, this is also what makes much of the work in this study unique. Its momentary and fleeting nature means that being there can never be replaced, and that it can never be repeated, packaged or sold as a commodity.

It is important to remember the context of much of the work presented in this book. Mary Kelly, Rose Finn-Kelcey, Bobby Baker and others emerged from art schools that were dominated by the breakdown of media, and troubled by confusion over what should comprise an art education. Art schools were vulnerable to external circumstances, such as politics. Take for example, the sit-ins at Hornsey and other colleges. This political climate led to institutional confusion, aesthetic openness and a degradation of technique.

The history of women's art prior to the 1970s had been a history of women replicating men's work. Take for example, Artemisia Gentileschi, Angelika Kauffman or Mary Cassatt. Although their subject matter may have been more particular to their femininity, their paintings are quite conventional for the periods in which they were executed. One can argue that there has been a certain male-ness attached to painting, in the way one might say about bull-fighting. Painting has been associated with figures such as Picasso and Pollock, men considered artistic geniuses. We could say now that we live in a period of the aesthetic women. Artists such as Eva Hesse, Rebecca Horn, Annette Messager and Cindy Sherman have established a kind of female activity of making art work which makes monumental work such as Anish Kapoor or Anthony Gormley seem overblown. This new female aesthetic, I would argue, has also filtered down into men's practice, especially in the work of West Coast American artists such as Mike Kelley and Tony Oursler.

One of the factors that differentiates 1970s and contemporary women artists from their art historical predecessors is their use of the body. During the period examined in this book, the body became another material for artists to engage with and a site for art work. Rose Finn-Kelcey, Carolee Schneemann, Catherine Elwes and Anne Bean among others, used their bodies in performances. Others such as Mary Kelly and Judy Clark necessarily implicated their bodies in the work. This allowed for a radical re-alignment of what a work of art could be.

In contemporary examples, it can be seen as rethinking of the women artist's body. Hayley Newman relies almost entirely on her body to create works, which question the hierarchy of performance and documentation. Her work poses the question that art historians are now grappling with in terms of earlier performance art: When does the documentation override the original performance, supplanting the live event as a proof of activity? Jemima Stehli's use of her body represents a different approach. Her work questions the role of the female nude in art. After some feminist artists denounced using female nude imagery, and others such as Schneemann and Wilke were criticized for doing so, Stehli re-opens this discussion. She dares to ask tough questions in her art regarding the status of the artist's body. With Stehli, along with other contemporary artists such as Stelarc, Orlan or Franko B, one sees that the body is still a topic for debate.

The domestic is another theme from feminist art that is relevant to today's practice. Feminist artists' interrogation of the domestic, as both subject matter and site, paved the way for future generations of artists to further examine this theme. From Louise Bourgeois and Bobby Baker to Tracey Emin and Sarah Lucas, artists have continued to examine themes around the home, from its architecture to the idea of it as the site for oppressive familial structures.[67]

This book has attempted to situate previously under-recognized artists such as Bobby Baker, Alexis Hunter, Kate Walker and Judy Clark among better known artists, such as Mary Kelly and Carolee Schneemann, in the context of 1970s feminist activity. The primary goal has been to excavate works, and to attempt an understanding of why they have not been institutionally supported and acknowledged. This project only breaks the surface of understanding this period. There are countless other events, exhibitions and artists to be discussed and examined.

The book was structured in a manner that was best able to encompass a range of activities and artists, while still being able to get deeper into issues. A comparison could be drawn to literature of the period: while there are countless books on feminist politics, there are hardly any retrospective looks at feminist art in Britain. Rozsika Parker and Griselda Pollock's *Framing Feminism* was an attempt, but is it is almost three decades since its original publication. This book tries to address this inadequacy, by bringing things back into consciousness. These things, as illustrated in this chapter, are still relevant and floating on the surface of contemporary art practice. The book is an attempt to make visible the invisible and to give it a public life and a permanence.

NOTES

Introduction

1 Amelia Jones, ed, *Sexual Politics: Judy Chicago's Dinner Party in Feminist Art History*, Los Angeles: UCLA at the Armand Hammer Museum of Art and Berkeley: University of California Press, 1996.

2 Jane Rendell, "Introduction" in Jane Rendell, Barbara Penner and Iain Borden, *Gender, Space, Architecture,* London: Routledge, 231-3.

3 Linda Nochlin, "Feminism & Art, 9 Views," *Artforum,* October 2003, 141.

4 Amelia Jones, "Feminism & Art, 9 Views," 143.

5 See Carson's interview with Mary Kelly in *Rereading Post-Partum Document: Mary Kelly* and "Two Walls 1989", Ken Ehrlich and Brandon LaBelle, eds, *Surface Tension,* Los Angeles: Errant Bodies, 2003; *Excavating Discursivity: Post-Partum Document in the Conceptualist, Feminist and Psychoanalytic Fields,* PhD Thesis: Massachusetts Institute of Technology, 2000.

6 From a talk that William Furlong gave as part of the London Consortium Summer School at Tate Modern on 30 July 2003. Furlong is one of the founders of *Audio Arts,* a magazine that takes the form of a cassette tape with artist interviews.

7 Griselda Pollock, "Trouble in the Archives: Introduction," in *Differences: A Journal of Feminist Cultural Studies,* 4:3, 1992, x.

8 See Jacques Derrida, *Archive Fever: A Freudian Impression,* Eric Prenowitz, trans, Chicago: University of Chicago Press, 1998, 2-3.

9 For example, in the beginning of the research I had assumptions about the binary between "essential" and conceptual feminist art. By the end of this project I acknowledged a much more fluid relationship between approaches.

10 Joan W. Scott has written on the difficulty of historical recovery that relies on experience, especially for historians documenting the lives of those overlooked in the past. She writes, "What counts as experience is neither self-evident nor straightforward: it is always contested, always therefore political." See Joan W. Scott, "Experience", Judith Butler and Joan W. Scott, eds, *Feminists Theorize the Political,* New York: Routledge, 1992, 37.

11 In New York Jasper Johns and Robert Rauschenberg were situated in a predominantly gay circle of young American artists. Both drew on the work of predecessors such as Philip Guston, Jackson Pollock, Clyfford Still, while expanding the boundaries of the canvas with sculptural elements and new techniques such as encaustic and assemblage.

12   See Tariq Ali and Susan Watkins, *1968: Marching in the Streets*, London: Bloomsbury, 1998; and Matthew Higgs and Paul Noble, *Protest and Survive*, London, Whitechapel Art Gallery, 2000.

13   See Joanna Frueh, *Hannah Wilke: A Retrospective*, Missouri: University of Missouri Press, 1989; Hannah Wilke, *Intra Venus*, New York: Ronald Feldman Fine Arts, 1995; Nancy Princenthal, *Hannah Wilke*, New York, Prestel, 2010; Tracy Fitzpatrick, "Hannah Wilke Gestures", New York, Neuberger Museum of Art, Purchase College, State University of New York, 2009; Carolee Schneemann, *Imaging Her Erotics: Essays, Interviews, Projects*, Cambridge: MIT Press, 2002; and *Carolee Schneemann: Up To and Including her Limits*, New York: New Museum of Contemporary Art, 1996.

14   Kelly has spoken on several occasions of her reluctance to include her body in early work. See Mary Kelly, "Re-Viewing Modernist Criticism", *Screen*, 1981, reprinted in Brian Wallis, ed, *Art after Modernism: Rethinking Representation*, New York: New Museum of Contemporary Art, 1984; Mary Kelly, "That Obscure Subject of Desire: An Interview with Mary Kelly by Hal Foster," *Imaging Desire*, London: MIT Press, 1996, 169-70; and "Mary Kelly in conversation with Juli Carson", Sabine Breitwieser, ed, *Rereading Post-Partum Document*, Vienna: Generali Foundation, 1999, 204.

15   A notable exception in Hiller's work is her piece *Ten Months*, 1977-79, which documents her belly during pregnancy. This is presented in ten units, where the curve of her abdomen resembles a moon. See Barbara Einzig, ed, *Thinking About Art: Conversations with Susan Hiller*, Manchester: Manchester University Press, 1996, 47-50.

16   Carolee Schneemann, Interview with the author, 18 April 2002.

17   Rose Finn-Kelcey, Interview with the author, 16 June 2000. This will be discussed further in Chapter Two.

18   Jones 24. Jones seems to have Mary Kelly in mind in this discussion, as she goes on to quote her.

19   Betty Friedan, *The Feminine Mystique*, (1963), London: Penguin Books, 1992.

20   Germaine Greer, *The Female Eunuch*, (1970), London: Grafton, 1986.

21   Jane Rendell, "Introduction: Gender," in Rendell, Barbara Penner and Iain Borden, eds, *Gender, Space, Architecture: An Interdisciplinary Introduction*, London: Routledge, 2000, 16.

22   Today this debate is still relevant, especially when taken in regard to the Republican Party's controversial beliefs about women's reproductive rights, a battle that is still being fought today in the United States.

23   One example of this is Robert Morris' performance *Site*, 1964, which featured Carolee Schneemann dressed as Manet's Olympia. Morris, like Schneemann, was involved with the Judson Dance Theatre in New York during the 1960s. Schneemann's performance, *Meat Joy*, 1964, involved a number of participants in each of its manifestations.

24   See Henry Bial, ed, *The Performance Studies Reader*, London: Routledge, 2004, 145, and J.L. Austin, *How to Do Things with Words*, London: Oxford University Press, 1976 (1962). See also Andrew Parker and Eve Kosofsky Sedgwick, "Introduction to Performativity and Performance," in Bial, 167-74.

25   There was much debate over the meaning of the terms performance and performativity in an event with Martha Rosler and Carey Young chaired by Judith Williamson at the Whitechapel during their "Short History of Performance, Part Two" in February 2004. A member of the audience asked for people to consider the terms in relation to the work presented that evening. Others protested, saying it was a form of artspeak and not relevant to the discussion.

26   Michael Fried, "Art and Objecthood," in *Art and Objecthood: Essays and Reviews*, Chicago: University of Chicago Press, 1998.

27   Amelia Jones, *Body Art: Performing the Subject*, 55.

28   See Pepe Karmel, "Pollock at Work: The Films and Photographs of Hans Nemuth," in Kirk Varnedoe and Pepe Karmel, *Jackson Pollock*, London: Tate Gallery, 1988 (originally New York, Museum of Modern Art, 1998, 87-137); Rosalind Krauss, *The Optical Unconscious*, Cambridge: MIT Press, 1993; Briony Fer, *On Abstract Art*, New Haven: Yale University Press, 1997, 93-7.

29   Judith Butler, *Gender Trouble: Feminism and the Subversion of Identity*, New York: Routledge, 1990, viii.

30   Butler quotes Simone de Beauvoir in her "Performative Acts and Gender Constitution: An Essay in Phenomenology and Feminist Theory", in Bial, 154. For a discussion on gender as constructed through culture and through difference see also Catherine Hall, *White, Male and Middle-Class: Explorations in Feminism and History*, London: Polity Press, 1992, 13-15.

31   Butler 156.

32   See Jeffrey Kastner and Brian Wallis, eds, *Land and Environmental Art*, London: Phaidon Press Limited, 1998; Gilles A. Tiberghien, *Land Art*, New York: Princeton Architectural Press, 1996; Brian Aldiss, *Earthworks*, New York: Doubleday and Co, 1996; Ann Morris Reynolds, *Robert Smithson, Learning from New Jersey and Elsewhere*, London: MIT Press, 2002; Michael Heizer, et al, *Double Negative*, New York: Rizzoli, 1992; Anne Seymour et al, *Richard Long: Walking in Circles*, London: George Braziller, 1991.

33   See Dan Graham, "Homes For America," *Arts Magazine*, 1966.

34   See Kathy Battista, "Domestic Crisis: Women Artists in South London, 1974-1995," in Brandon Labelle and Ken Ehrlich, eds, *Surface Tension*, Los Angeles: Errant Bodies, 2003; Judy Chicago, *Through the Flower: My Struggle as a Woman Artist*, New York: Penguin Books, 1975, 112-32; Judy Chicago, *The Dinner Party*, New York: Viking Press, 1996. Also, see Alan Moore, "Art Gangs: Protest and Counterculture in New York City", New York: Autonomedia, 2011.

35   For an excellent discussion of these see "A Chronology of Selected Alternative Structures, Spaces, Artists' Groups, and Organizations in New York City, 1965-1985," in Julie Ault, ed, *Alternative Art New York*, Minneapolis and New York: University of Minnesota Press and The Drawing Center, 2002, 17-76.

36   Brian O"Doherty, *Inside The White Cube: The Ideology of the Gallery Space*, Berkeley: University of California Press, 1986.

37   See Carol Duncan, *Civilizing Rituals: Inside Public Art Museums*, New York: Routledge, 1995.

38   For an excellent discussion on the gendering of space see Jane Rendell, "Introduction: Gender, Space," in Rendell, Penner, Borden.

39   Doreen Massey, "Space, Place and Gender," in Rendell, Penner, Borden 129.

40   Lisa Tickner, "Questions of Feminism: Question 1," *October* 71, Winter 1995, 44.

41   Cottingham, *Seeing Through the Seventies*, VII-VIII.

42   Amelia Jones, "Introduction" in *The Feminism and Visual Culture Reader*, London: Routledge, 2003, 1. Andreas Huyssen makes a similar point in his work on postmodernism and women. He argues that the turn to subjectivity, issues of identity and the foregrounding of gender found in postmodern art, particularly video and performance art, is indebted to the work of the 1970s, particularly that produced by feminists. See Huyssen, "Mass Culture as Woman: Modernism's Other," in *After the Great Divide: Modernism, Mass Culture, Postmodernism*, Bloomington and Indianapolis: Indiana University Press, 1986, 61-2.

1 Women's Work

1   Barry Barker, interview with the author, 26 April 2000.
2   For example, most of the artists, critics and gallerists that I interviewed would ask whose work I was examining and would say, "Of course you will look at Mary Kelly."
3   Catherine Elwes, interview with the author, 6 April 2001.
4   Kelly's film *Antepartum*, 1970, did use the body of the artist. This will be discussed as a counterpart to *Post-Partum Document*.
5   Kelly today would not want to be labeled as a feminist artist. However, as the piece was influenced by the women's movement and has been widely read as a feminist piece, I call it as such here. Kelly has said, "Well even though I used the term feminist art myself in the early days, now you know I strongly object to that and I say "art informed by feminism." Because I don't think there's a style. There's not a feminist art the way that there's a conceptual art. And I just find the awkwardness of say, well you wouldn't say Socialist Art. This being political ideology, some of it linked to a movement, I think you have to be careful about who and what is identified as feminist, but that is completely different from art that doesn't want to acknowledge it. I think now that it's important to acknowledge that art which was informed by feminism was very much a part of the epistemological rupture of postmodernism." Mary Kelly, interview with the author, 10 January 2001.
6   It would be another four years before this public institution would host a season of feminist exhibitions, from 1979–80, under the leadership of Director Sandy Nairne.
7   Barrie and Barker were teaching colleagues at the London College of Furniture Design in the early 1970s.
8   Barry Barker, interview with the artist, 26 April 2000.
9   Barker was made Director of the ICA proper, but he "always described himself as Director of Exhibitions" as Roland Penrose was President at the time. Eventually, Ted Little joined him as Director of the downstairs gallery.
10 Spanning from 1973–78, the work was shown in progress at several stages in its development. Previous to the exhibition at the ICA, "Documentation I" was shown at the Northern Arts Gallery in Newcastle. After the ICA show sections would be exhibited on a regular basis in various curatorial manifestations, including under the rubric of feminist art, conceptual art, self-portraiture and even creative writing. For the most comprehensive exhibition history of this work see "List of Exhibitions of Post-Partum Document" in Sabine Breitwieser, ed, *Rereading Post-Partum Document Mary Kelly*, Vienna: Generali Foundation, 1999, 279–81.
11 Eventually these notes would be collated, along with images of each unit in the work, and published as a book with an introduction by Lucy Lippard. See Mary Kelly, *Post-Partum Document*, London: Routledge & Kegan Paul, 1981.
12 Kelly and her partner Barrie discussed the name of the baby in their communal household. They decided to name the child "Kelly Barrie" in order to circumvent traditional patriarchal hierarchy of the so-called *nom du père*. Instead of taking the name of the father, the baby takes the name of both parents, thus inserting the *nom de la mère*. Kelly, interview with the author.
13 It is interesting that Carolee Schneemann, also an American artist living in London during this period, made a quasi-scientific work called *Sexual Parameters*. For a brief description of this work see Kristine Stiles, ed, *Correspondence Course: An Epistolary History of Carolee Schneemann and \ Her Circle*, Durham: Duke University Press, 145–6.

14   It is important here to consider the idea of the "public". Surely it is impossible to gauge the response of all members of the viewing public. In my use, I term as public the written record of reactions to this piece as well as a general audience apart from the art world.

15   Mary Kelly, "Notes for Reading *Post-Partum Document*," in *Mary Kelly: Post-Partum Document*, London: Routledge & Kegan Paul, 1981, 9.

16   Despite his populist appeal, Spock was aligned with the left wing, having protested the Vietnam War in America and been publicly arrested on a number of occasions. Spock had also been a Presidential Candidate in 1972 and Vice Presidential Candidate in 1976 for the People's Party, a coalition of left-wing organizations. See Eric Pace, "Benjamin Spock, World's Pediatrician, Dies at 94," *New York Times*, March 17, 1998; Mark M. Meinero, "Drs. Spock, Salk Seen as Playing Key Role in 20th Century American Parenting", *Parent News*, December 24, 2000; Dwight Garner, "The Spock Touch," *Mothers Who Think*, March 1998. My thanks to Dr John Tercier for his assistance with this information.

17   Although some feminists took exception to Spock's continually placing childcare duties in the female's role, in retrospect, he was quite a liberal and progressive doctor.

18   "Douglas Crimp in conversation with Mary Kelly," in *Mary Kelly*, London: Phaidon Press Limited, 1997, 15-16.

19   Mulvey would later go on to publish *Fetishism and Curiosity*, London: British Film Institute, 1996.

20   It is perhaps interesting to note here that another female artist at the time, Judy Clark, was also making work based on the trace of things related to the presence of the body. However, Clark was not steeped in psychoanalysis, but more aligned with the cultural analysis of Mary Douglas as found in her groundbreaking *Purity and Danger*.

21   "S" stands for Sally Alexander, the historian whose house Kelly and her partner lived in. Kelly has spoken of this communal household in an interview with the author. Kelly, interview with the author, 26 April 2001.

22   Dan Graham, "Statements," in Sabine Breitwieser, ed, *Rereading Post-Partum Document Mary Kelly*, 151.

23   If this Documentation is performative, however, the sound element is lacking. There is no voice, either of mother or child, present in this section. It is therefore a silent performance, which reinforces the "silent" or invisible domestic labor of the mother. In later sections of *Post-Partum Document* one hears, or more accurately, reads the voice—of the artist, the child and the father—which is not present in this section.

24   During the 1970s Phillpot was librarian at Chelsea School of Art and played a key role in amassing a collection of artists' books for the school. He went on to be the chief librarian at the Museum of Modern Art New York, returning to England to take a post as librarian at the British Council.

25   Clive Phillpot, interview with the author, 23 January 2002. Phillpot included Kelly's work in the exhibition *Live in Your Head: Concept and Experiment in Britain 1965-75* at the Whitechapel Art Gallery, 4 February-2 April 2000. This exhibition centered on conceptual, rather than feminist, practice. See Clive Phillpot and Andrea Tarsia, ed, *Live in Your Head: Concept and Experiment in Britain 1965-75*, London: Whitechaptel, 2000.

26   Kelly regards them as "readymades" in a certain sense. Kelly, interview with the author, 10 April 2000.

27   Even more liberal newspapers, such as the *Guardian*, got into the fray. Their problem with the work was less about the nappies and more about the status of art, for example, is this art or is it sociology? The tabloids, however, also

played on concerns about the rise of feminism and the use of public money to fund art.

28   Curiously this debate resurfaced recently when British artist Chris Offili's paintings, which include dried elephant dung, were shown in the *Sensation* exhibition at the Brooklyn Museum of Art in New York in 1998. Republican mayor Rudolf Giuliani moved to close down the show. When the museum would not comply with his demands he threatened their future funding.

29   Roger Bray, *Evening Standard*, London, 14 October 1976.

30   The other exhibition reviewed by Richard Cork was by an artist called David Dye.

31   Richard Cork, "Big brother—and Mary Kelly's baby," *Evening Standard*, 14 October 1976, 22-3.

32   Cork 22-3.

33   This space will be discussed at further length in Chapter Three.

34   *Issues* took place from 28 November–16 December 1973. It is an obvious point, but one worth noting, that Clark's work pre-dates much of the London-based feminist activity. The invite to Clark's show is a striking predecessor of Damien Hirst's obsession with the forensic, including scientific instruments. The invite looks as contemporary today as it would have almost 40 years ago. (See the Introduction for an image of the invite.)

35   Judy Clark, interview with the author, 12 July 2001.

36   Here Clark speaks about her time at Portsmouth College, *ca* 1968, where there was a small student uprising, similar to the events at Hornsey and Guilford, as well as further afield, for example, at Kent State in Ohio.

37   Clark, interview with the author.

38   Shortly after the exhibition at the Slade, the Galerie Rackerman in Cologne actually consigned these pieces, all of which are now sold or lost.

39   Lisa Tickner mentioned that Clark had created a portrait of her by requesting locks of hair, nail clippings, etc. Tickner, in discussion with the author.

40   Clark, interview with the author.

41   Artists in London knew about Chicago's activities. Kelly gave a lecture on *Womanhouse* at an Artists Union meeting in 1976. This is discussed further in Chapter Two.

42   *Fuses* had a lot of attention in London, including several screenings, at the ICA and the Roundhouse, for example.

43   Rozsika Parker, "Body Works", *Spare Rib*, 1974 (23): 37-8, reprinted in Parker and Griselda Pollock, 280.

44   Kelly has cited Godard and Straub Huillet as favorites and was an avid reader of the journal *Screen*. In addition, her personal relationships with film-makers such as Laura Mulvey and Peter Wollen had an influence on her work. In particular, Wollen and Mulvey's use of chapters and framing can be seen as formative upon the structure of *Post-Partum Document*. Kelly even appeared in their film *Riddles of the Sphinx*. For more information on Mulvey and Wollen see Margaret Dickinson, ed, *Rogue Reels: Oppositional Film in Britain 1945 to 1990*, London: British Film Institute, 1999. For information on Kelly's engagement with film theory and practice see Judith Mastai, ed, *Social Process/Collaborative Action: Mary Kelly 1970-75*, Vancouver: Charles H. Scott Gallery, 1997.

45   Douglas Crimp and Mary Kelly 11-13.

46   Kelly also made films with her students at London College of Furniture and Camberwell School of Art in the early 1970s.

47   Kelly made *Nightcleaners* in collaboration with Mark Karlin and the Berwick Street Film Collective. It followed the campaign for better working

conditions for London night cleaners. See Claire Johnston and Paul Willemen, *"Nightcleaners*: Brecht and Political Film-making Practice,"* Judith Mastai, ed, *Social Process/Collaborative Action: Mary Kelly 1970-75*, 95-104; John Wyver, "Mark Karlin," *The Thursday Review, Independent*, 28 January 1999; Sheila Rowbotham, "Reel dreams and real lives", *Guardian*, January 1999.

48   *Antepartum* was only shown once when it was first made, Kelly thinks at Trent Polytechnic, but can't remember precisely. In recent years it's been shown at the Generali Foundation in Vienna (1999), and at Robert Sandelson Gallery in London (2001) and at Queens Nails in San Francisco in 2008.

49   See Stiles *Correspondence Course* for Schneemann's lifelong exchanges with Stan Brakhage and his wife.

50   Many feminist artists were working with the topic of menstruation and repro-duction at the time. Helen Chadwick, discussed at further length in Chapter Three, has several notes in her notebook from 1975-8 that bear a striking simi-larity to both Clark and Schneemann, including "cycle of blood loss", "blood cycle-series 10 towels stained with blood", etc. See http://www.henry-moore.org/hmi/archive/turning-the-pages--helen-chadwick-notebooks.

51   Carolee Schneemann, interview with the author, 18 April 2002.

52   McCall was a film-maker and a key player in the London Film-makers Co-op, which is discussed below. Today his work is shown mostly in the context of art institutions. McCall was also a collaborator and documented many of Schneemann's performances. From a discussion with the author, 4 September 2010.

53   Marina Vaizey, "Judy Clark," *Financial Times*, 1973 (found in WAL artist file).

54   Caroline Tisdall, "Bodyworks," *Guardian*, 1973 (undated, found in WAL artist file).

55   Althea Greenan, "Judy Clark," in *Judy Clark: The Occupier and Other Works*. Chichester: Pallant House Gallery, 1998, unpaginated.

56   For example, the significant publications *Wack* and *Art & Feminism*, omit any discussion of Clark's work, although she is one of the few feminist artists in the Tate collection. See Cornelia H. Butler and Lisa Gabrielle Mark, *Wack! Art and the Feminist Revolution*, Cambridge: MIT Press, 2007 and Helena Rickett, ed, *Art & Feminism*. London: Phaidon Press Ltd, 2001.

57   Judy Clark, "Letter to Althea Greenan at the Women Artists Slide Library," 21 May 1997.

58   Ewa Lajer-Bucharth, "The Archaeologist of the Self: A Conversation with Mary Kelly", in Milada Slizinska, *Mary Kelly: Words are Things*, Warsaw: Center for Contemporary Art Ujazdowski Castle, 2008, 28-9.

59   Charles Harrison, interview with the author, 11 April 2000.

60   Charles Harrison, "The Trouble with Writing," in *Conceptual Art and Painting: Further Essays on Art & Language*, Cambridge, Massachusetts: MIT Press, 2002, 25.

61   Kelly taught a class called "The New Art," which was a pun on an exhibi-tion at the Hayward Gallery in 1972 titled *The New Art*, which featured conceptual artists. Mary said, "Instead of just doing the conceptual guys I included women, obviously, and everything else, lots of performance and *Womanhouse*, everything that was going on at the time." Kelly, interview with the author, 21 April 2001.

62   *The New Art* was at the Hayward Gallery, 17 August-24 September 1972 and included 14 British artists, all male.

63   "Mary Kelly in conversation with Juli Carson," *Rereading Post-Partum Document*, 185.

64   Kelly and Carson 185.

65   It is not until the child can syntactically construct phrases and sentences that we can consider its move into language. When the child utters single words, they can be considered as signs rather than language.

66   The photograph, which is a contemporary reworking of a pieta theme, echoes postcard images that Kelly saved in her archive. This now iconic photo with her son was set up to parody the Michelangelo Tondo. As a student in Rome Kelly was fascinated by pieta images. She has pondered, "How would I get around the sentimental representation of the Madonna? How could I get that affect without privileging the iconic sign?" See Kelly and Carson 204.

67   Kelly has spoken fondly of her time in this communal house, where there were strict schedules of cooking and cleaning, and one could expect up to 25 people for dinner on any day. It was over such meetings that they discussed, art, politics, child-rearing, etc. Living in this house contributed to Kelly being able to actually make *Post-Partum Document* because it was possible to share childcare with her partner Ray Barrie and her friend Sally Alexander, who also had a small child. Kelly, interview with the author.

68   Kelly, interview with the author.

69   This kind of reference to scientific methodology will surface later in the *Post-Partum Document*, particularly in "Documentation V", which is not discussed in this book because it was not included in the ICA show, where she parodies natural history museums' display techniques.

70   Carson 51.

71   Kelly, interview with the author.

72   Helen Molesworth, *At Home with Duchamp: The Readymade and Domesticity*, PhD Thesis: Cornell University, 1998.

73   Margaret Iverson, "Visualising the Unconscious: Mary Kelly's Installations," in *Mary Kelly*, London: Phaidon Press Limited, 1997, 35.

74   Her earlier collaborative pieces *Nightcleaners* and *Women & Work* are testament to the artist's interests in series-based work.

75   Kelly, interview with the author.

76   Here Kelly speaks of Benjamin Buchloh, who wrote one of the seminal pieces on conceptual art, "Conceptual Art 1962-9: From the Aesthetic of Administration to the Critique of Institutions," originally published in *October* 55 (Winter 1990), reprinted in Alexander Alberro and Blake Stimson, eds, *Conceptual Art: A Critical Anthology*, Cambridge, Massachusetts: the MIT Press, 1999, 514-37.

77   Juli Carson, *Excavating Discursivity: Post-Partum Document in the Conceptualist, Feminist, and Psychoanalytic Fields*, PhD Thesis: Massachusetts Institute of Technology, February 2000.

78   Kelly's problem at the ICA echoed Carl Andre's incident earlier that year. Tate had purchased Andre's *Equivalent VIII* (1966) in 1972, which consisted of 120 cream colored American firebricks and assembly instructions. When tabloid journalists discovered the price tag for such a work, they exposed the Tate's "folly" to the public. In addition to the price of the piece, the press was outraged by the fact that they were not the original pile. Andre's piece, originally made in 1966, did not find a buyer in America, and hence he returned the bricks to the brickyard. When the Tate showed interest in acquiring the work, Andre was undeterred and simply bought 120 new bricks. An amateur artist threw dye on Andre's sculpture, claiming it as his own work, when it was exhibited. Feminist artist Bobby Baker made a sugar icing painting about the incident as part of her modern masters series.

79   See Simon Ford, "Myth Making, The yBa," *Art Monthly* (194), March 1996, 3-9.

80 For an excellent account of this group see Simon Ford, *Wreckers of Civilisation: The Story of Coum Transmissions & Throbbing Gristle*, London: Black Dog Publishing Limited, 1999.

81 In 2004 the ICA revisited this theme with an evening of talks and events called erotICA. Topics included how to start a sex magazine and the politics of lap dancing. The panel discussions were complemented by a burlesque show by the Whoopee Club. The mainstream press picked up on it with articles in the *Guardian* and *The Times*.

82 Ibid, 6.19

83 Interestingly, in the Tate archive there are two binders full of clippings from *Prostitution*, which amount to hundreds of articles. There is only a handful on Kelly's *Post-Partum Document*. (It is unclear whether this is because there was less coverage, or because there were fewer articles saved.)

84 They had received £52.50 for travel to Rottweil for a performance and £273.58 for the Paris Biennale.

85 Barker, interview with the author.

86 Cosey Fanni Tutti is a play on the Mozart opera *Cosi fan tutte*. The artist was born Christine Carol Newby in Hull 1951.

87 Ford, 6.4.

88 See Chapter Three for more on Space and AIR, their gallery.

89 The debate over pornography was central to the women's movement as a *cause célèbre*. One only need think of the work of writers such as Andrea Dworkin or Catharine MacKinnon to see the opposite position to Cosey's extreme liberalism.

90 Simon Ford, "Subject & (Sex) Object," *make*, London, Women's Art Library, June-August 1998, 4.

91 Ford 4.

92 Lisa Tickner, "The Body Politic: Female Sexuality and Women Artists since 1970", *Art History* 1:2 (June 1978): 246. Tickner was not the only one to see this problem. Many female artists who use their bodies have long been criticized for hovering on the edge of titillation, for example the work of American artists Carolee Schneemann and Hannah Wilke.

93 Mulvey was working on this while Kelly worked on the *Document*. It was eventually published in *Screen* 16, 3 Autumn 1975, and was reprinted in a collection of her writings, *Visual and Other Pleasures*, London: Macmillan, 1989.

94 Another important example of this would be the body of work—*Untitled Film Stills*—produced by Cindy Sherman in the late 1970s and early 1980s.

95 Tutti's images have featured in two recent exhibitions in London: *Live In Your Head* at the Whitechapel Art Gallery, and *Protest & Survive*, also at the Whitechapel Art Gallery later that year.

96 In the former, Hirst's sheep in formaldehyde was attacked by a visitor who—in a gesture reminiscent of Andre and Baker—poured ink into the tank when the sculpture was shown at the Serpentine Gallery. See "Sheep exhibit attack "an artistic statement"," *Daily Telegraph*, London, 17 August 1994. For a thorough selection of reactionary press on Hirst see Damien Hirst, *i want to spend the rest of my life everywhere, with everyone, one to one, always, forever, now*, London: Booth-Clibborn editions, 1997. *Bed*, which was discussed by some writers for its adherence to the legacy of artists such as Mary Kelly, saw Emin put her bed, and all its assorted accoutrements, including stained knickers, used condoms, fluffy toys, discarded clothes and over the counter drugs, on display. Finally, Smith's piece was discussed for its disparaging comments, which were left by the public and exhibited by the artist. The public were offended in particular by comments made toward

the Queen Mother, who was at the time celebrating her 100th birthday. See Emine Saner, "Tate exhibition shows abuse of Queen Mother," *Sunday Times*, August 6, 2000.

97 This is especially ironic in the case of the Tate, who hosted Emin's *Bed*. They seem keener to flirt with controversy than to actually commit to collecting this kind of work. *Bed* is now part of the Saatchi Collection in London.

98 Barker, interview with the author.

99 The vests were actually a present from Branka Magash, who had worked on *New Left Review*.

100 Mary Kelly, *Post-Partum Document, Introduction*. 1976. Today this work is found in the Norton Family Foundation, Santa Monica, California.

101 Less well-known is Shirley Cameron, the performance artist who often performed events with her children.

102 Kelly, interview with the author, 10 April 2000.

103 Kelly, 10 April 2000, interview with the author, 137.

104 For an introduction and breakdown of Schema L, see Elizabeth Grosz, *Jacques Lacan: A Feminist Introduction*, London: Routledge, 1990, 73–4. See also Jacques Lacan (trans. Alan Sheridan), *Écrits*, London: Routledge, 1977, (orig. pub 1966, Éditions du Seuil), 193–4.

105 Kelly spoke of her interests at that time in an interview with Carson, who curated the 1999 exhibition of *Post-Partum Document* in its entirety at the Generali Foundation in Vienna: "This moment was also the beginning of my collaboration with Claire Johnston, Jacqueline Rose, Elizabeth Cowie, Cora Kaplan, and Marie Yates. We tried to bring the question of representation into the general arena for feminist theory and to introduce notions of psychoanalysis and semiotics at the National Socialist Feminist Conference. See Kelly and Carson 198.

106 See for example, Juli Carson's doctoral dissertation (MIT Department of Architecture and Art) and her article in *Rereading Post-Partum Document*; Margaret Iverson in *Mary Kelly*.

107 Craig Owens, "Feminists and Postmodernism," in Hal Foster, ed, *Postmodern Culture*, London: Pluto Press, 1985, 63.

108 Catherine Elwes, interview with the author, 6 April 2001.

109 It was organized by a collective from various study groups who realized there was a need to communicate with each other. The group raised £120 profit from the conference and used this money to publish their papers in a small Xeroxed booklet. See Sue Cooper, Sara Crowley, Charlotte Holtram, *Papers on Patriarchy Conference*, Sussex: Women's Publishing Collective, December 1976.

110 Dalston Study Group, *Papers on Patriarchy Conference*, 76.

111 The work was shown recently (in 2001) at Robert Sandelson Gallery in London. See Kathy Battista, "Mea Culpa", *Third Text*, Winter 2002.

2 The Body and Performance Art

1 Amelia Jones, *Body Art: Performing the Subject*, Minneapolis: University of Minnesota Press, 1998, 5.

2 I must thank Catherine Elwes for a discussion on performance art, and its use by male and female artists, which provided me with an important point of view.

3 McCarthy is a West Coast-based American artist, trained at CalArts, whose performances used ketchup, mayonnaise, mud and other visceral material to suggest blood, semen, faeces and other normally taboo substances. See

Kristine Stiles, et al, *Paul McCarthy*, London: Phaidon, 1996. See also Dan Cameron, et al, *Paul McCarthy*, New York and Ostfildern-Ruit: New Museum of Contemporary Art and Hatje Cantz Verlag, 2000.

4   Brisley is one of the most celebrated British performance artists. When the Arts Council set up substantial bursaries for live arts at the end of the 1970s, Brisley was the first person to receive one. For a performance artist, he was well-known and successful at the time.

5   John Latham's *Art and Culture* or *Chew and Spit*, 1967, was a piece begun as a social event where Latham and Brisley, his student at the time, encouraged Central St Martin's students to chew Greenberg's book and spit it into a vitrine. Latham then distilled the "essence of Greenberg" and returned that to the library at St Martin's, in the place of the book he had borrowed. Latham was promptly fired and never taught again. See John Walker, *John Latham: The Incidental Person, His Art and Ideas*, London: Middlesex University Press, 1995, 84; Richard Hamilton, *John Latham, Early Works: 1954-1972*, London: Lisson Gallery, 1987, 2.

6   Guy Brett, "Life Strategies: Overview and Selection Buenos Aires-London-Rio de Janeiro-Santiago de Chile, 1960-1980," Schimmel, 201.

7   One need look no further than Hans Nemuth's photographs and films of Pollock attacking his canvases to see the link between documentation and historical merit. These visual remnants of the action serve to heighten the mythology of the work, and of course add to its authenticity and worth.

8   Besides being an author, Goldberg is the founder of Performa, a biannual performance festival that takes place in New York City. See www.performa-arts.org

9   RoseLee Goldberg, *Performance Art: From Futurism to the Present*, London: Thames & Hudson, 1988, 132-3.

10   See Catherine de Zegher, *Martha Rosler: Positions in the Life World*, Cambridge, Massachusetts: MIT Press, 1999; Alex Alberro, et al, *Martha Rosler*, Birmingham, Ikon Gallery, 1998; and Martha Rosler, *Decoys and Disruptions: Selected Writings 1975-2001*, Cambridge, Massachusetts: MIT Press, 2004.

11   For a good overview of Piper's work see Maurice Berger, *Adrian Piper: A Retrospective*, New York, The New Museum of Contemporary Art, 1999, and for a collection of the artist's theoretical writings see Adrian Piper, *Out of Order, Out of Sight*, Cambridge, Massachusetts: MIT Press, 1999.

12   Kristine Stiles, "Performance Art," in Stiles and Peter Selz, 694.

13   Amelia Jones, "Survey," in Tracey Warr, ed, *The Artist's Body*, London: Phaidon, 2000, 21.

14   Jones 21.

15   For example, "performance relics" from Chris Burden's early works have been exhibited at Gagosian Gallery in London. The estate of Hannah Wilke is now represented by Alison Jacques Gallery (London) and early works by Linder are sold by Modern Art (London) and featured at art fairs.

16   Examples from contemporary practice include Patty Chang and Vanessa Beecroft, both artists who create performances in gallery spaces. Photographs and videos from these performances are sold on the international market, and in fact, most viewers know their work predominantly through the extensive documentation rather than the live performance itself.

17   Certain art galleries, however, played key roles in hosting performances. Take for example, Gilbert & George's *The Singing Sculpture* performed at Nigel Greenwood Gallery in 1968, or Bruce McLean's pose band Nice Style, who staged events at Garage in the early 1970s.

18   Silvia Ziranek, interview with the author, 17 February 2002.

19 Rose Finn-Kelcey, interview with the author, 16 June 2000.
20 Catherine Elwes, "Floating Feminity: A Look at Performance Art by Women," in *Women's Images of Men*, Sarah Kent and Jacqueline Morreau, eds. London: Writers and Readers, 1985, 164-93, reprinted in Catherine Elwes, *Video Loupe*, London: KT press, 2000, 71-84.
21 I am thinking here of the inclusion of performance in the 1979 Hayward Annual at the Hayward Gallery.
22 *About Time* was an exhibition based on performance held at the ICA 30 October-9 November 1980. See below for a discussion of Finn-Kelcey's contribution to this exhibition.
23 Writer and curator Guy Brett gave the example of Carlyle Reedy, an early performance artist who was also a poet and visual artist. Her work was centered on language, and she even invented foreign tongues. She has remained virtually unrecognized because none of the performances are recorded anywhere. Guy Brett, interview with the author, 13 April 2000.
24 Writers such as Guy Brett and Lisa Tickner both turned their attention to Finn-Kelcey's work early on, recognizing its importance not only for a feminist practice, but for an avant-garde sensibility. Guy Brett has written, "one could say that Rose Finn-Kelcey's work belongs to a movement of experimental practice in Britain which has virtually no record in official histories of art here but whose importance and durable interest is becoming increasingly evident. Brett, "Vacating the Premises," in *Rose Finn-Kelcey*, London: Chisenhale Gallery and Birmingham: Ikon Gallery, 1994, unpaginated.
25 Unlike some of the artists discussed in this dissertation, Finn-Kelcey has consistently been able to develop a career in the visual arts. Finn-Kelcey has managed to keep public interest and her work is in many important collections, including the Saatchi Collection, the Arts Council Collection and the Tate Collection.
26 She attended Chelsea School of Art in London.
27 For example, *Feminist Kunst International*, which was held in the Netherlands in 1977.
28 I write here of young artists today, for whom the stakes are very high. Take for example, British *enfant terrible* Damien Hirst, who made millions in his early thirties after skyrocketing prices of his art. In recent years he sold one sculpture to a private collector (Charles Saatchi) for one million dollars. Hirst was also behind the $50 million price tag for his diamond encrusted skull.
29 Finn-Kelcey, interview with the author. It is interesting to note that today's radical artists are embraced by the media: for example Tracey Emin has appeared in ads for Vivienne Westwood clothing as well as gin.
30 Finn-Kelcey's flag pieces, situated in public sites in London and abroad, will be discussed at further length in Chapter Three.
31 Keane is mostly known for her work in video and installation. For more information see Jean Fisher, Richard Dyer, Peter Wollen, *Electronic Shadows: The Art of Tina Keane*, London: Black Dog Press, 2004.
32 This collective was an offshoot of the Artists Union, and met every two to three weeks in a member's house to discuss the implications of being a woman artist. It was out of this collective that the Women Artists Slide Library (later to become the Women Artists Library, and finally the journal *Make*) was set up under the leadership of Pauline Barrie with a grant from the GLA (Greater London Arts, later the London Arts Board, and now London Arts). Members included Finn-Kelcey, Tina Keane, Pauline Barrie, Catherine

Elwes, Mary Kelly, Jessica York, Sonia Knox and many others. Finn-Kelcey noted that although there were frictions within the group, it provided an important network of support. There were many other groups of this nature, for example the Woman Artists Group at the Slade in the middle of the 1970s, the Women's Workshop of the Artists Union, and the important Women's Art History Collective, to which Lisa Tickner, Griselda Pollock, and Rosie Parker belonged.

33   Finn-Kelcey, interview with the author.

34   Sally Potter interviewed by Marc Chaimowicz, "Women and Performance in the UK," *Studio International* (192: 982) London, July/August, 1976: 33. Potter has now become a feature film-maker.

35   *London Calling* was the name for a yearly series of performances and concerts that took place for the most part at the Acme Gallery, which will be discussed at length in Chapter Three. In 1976 the festival was organized by John Sharkey, Artists for Democracy, Art Meeting Place, London Musicians Collective, the Art Room, and Tone Place, and featured among others, Tina Keane, Monica Sjoo, Carlyle Reedy, Marc Camille Chaimowicz and David Medalla.

36   The artist would later use the phonetic translations of 17 magpie calls in a performance called *Her Mistress's Voice* in 1977 at the Welsh Eistedfodd, one of Europe's oldest and largest cultural festivals.

37   Language was a major topic of feminist debate in the 1970s. Many women's liberation activists encouraged women to avoid being trapped into patriarchal structures as such. Lisa Tickner wrote, "The problem that all artists face to some extent, of actually externalizing an interior world in an appropriate formal language, seems to be particularly critical for women, especially because they"re worried about taking on a language which is not their own." Tickner 67.

38   Finn-Kelcey quoted in Tickner 66. For her discussion of the desire to find a woman-defined language as an alternative to one traditionally determined by men see Sally Potter in discussion with Marc Chaimowicz. See also American performance artist Joanna Frueh, *Erotic Faculties*, Berkeley, University of California Press, 1996, 6.

39   Finn-Kelcey, interview with the author.

40   Laura Mulvey, "Visual Pleasure and Narrative Cinema," *Screen* 16:3, Autumn 1975: 6-18.

41   The debate around the body was one that Finn-Kelcey was seriously investigating at the time. While teaching a course at Maidstone the artist organized women in art seminars, and began to amass slides of this kind of work. She said, "I did a lot of research into how women artists were working with the body, and made comparisons with Vito Acconci and Hannah Wilke. I would cross-refer between men and women." Finn-Kelcey, interview with the artist.

42   Even Finn-Kelcey admits that Kelly's work at times estranged her colleagues: "We were thinking why is she using Freud? Why is she so deeply entrenched in male theory—Freud and Lacan?" Finn-Kelcey, interview with the artist.

43   This series took place from 16-23 January 1978 and featured a variety of men and women artists including Tina Keane, David Medalla, Annabel Nicholson, and Carlyle Reedy.

44   H Walton, "Description of performance," artist's personal archive, dated 1978, unpaginated.

45   According to the artist, the whispers relate to Chinese whispers, and the misuse of information.

46 H. Walton, "Description of performance", artist's personal archive, 1978.

47 H. Walton, "Description of performance", artist's personal archive, 1978.

48 Finn-Kelcey says that if one does not have a "conversation" with the work, meaning leaving something to chance, then "you"re going to be an actress." Finn-Kelcey in Tickner 66.

49 Finn-Kelcey in Tickner 66.

50 Contemporary British performance artist Hayley Newman would also use the microphone as symbolic of the male in a performance over twenty years later. *Microphone Skirt,* 1995, involved the artist dancing with twenty micro-phones forming a skirt to create a kind of ambient feedback noise. See Hayley Newman, *Performancemania,* London: Matt's Gallery, 2001, 18. See Chapter Four for a lengthier discussion of Newman's work.

51 Jeni Walwin, "Close to the Horns," *Performance* (43), September/October 1986: 10.

52 Catherine Elwes, "In Praise of Older Women: Rose Finn-Kelcey and Kate Meynell," *make* (78) December 1997/March 1998: 17-19.

53 Brett, interview with the author.

54 This performance was part of *About Time,* an exhibition that showed video, performance and installation by 21 women artists, and took place at the ICA in London from 30 October-9 November 1980, clearly quite late in the day as far as the women's movement is concerned. By this time the establishment were recognizing the strength of the movement and the fact that it inspired many artists' work.

55 H. Walton, "Mind the Gap," unpublished notes on the performance, artist's personal archive.

56 Guy Brett, *Carnival of Perception: Selected Writings on Art,* London: Institute of International Visual Arts, 2004, 212.

57 Carolee Schneemann, original Naked Action Lecture script, found in the artist's personal archive, New Paltz, NY, unpaginated.

58 Unattributed review, "Happenings: The Sticking Point", found in the artist's personal archive, undated and unpaginated.

59 I use this title in homage to an exhibition held in 1978 at the ICA in London, which centered on a group of feminist artists who exchanged work through the post. This will be discussed at length in Chapter Three.

60 See especially the section on "The Happy Housewife Heroine" in Betty Friedan, *The Feminine Mystique* (1963), London: Penguin, 1992.

61 In Martha Rosler's *service: a trilogy on colonization* the artist wrote three "novels" (in fact short stories) that were sent to her mailing list as a postcard series through the postal system. In this series she created fictional narra-tives that centered on women and colonization. One woman's voice takes the character of a pampered, white, middle-class, well-traveled housewife, who wants to learn South American gourmet cuisine. Another fictional character works in a McTower restaurant, serving burgers, and becomes known for planting pot, mushrooms and aphrodisiacs in the meat. *Tijuana Maid* centers on a woman who is smuggled across the border to become a housemaid. A deadpan portrayal of politically incorrect white middle-class Americans would come as no surprise to any visitor to California, where even today Mexicans stand on corners waiting to do daily manual labor. The presentation of these stories in book form resembles a housewives' manual from the 1950s, intending to turn women into domestic goddesses. Rosler, however, uses the domestic site of each story to suggest the boredom, racism and even abuse suffered by women at the hands of men in control of their domestic situations.

62   It is perhaps important to remember here that *Post-Partum Document* was
       also steeped in the domestic and concerns over the division of labor within
       the family.
63   Chadwick's life was sadly cut short when she died suddenly at the age of
       42 in 1996. She was one of Britain's most celebrated artists whose work
       encompassed photography, sculpture and performance. Her work had been
       shown at the Museum of Modern Art in New York and the Centre Pompidou in
       Paris prior to her death and she is still acclaimed for her unorthodox use of
       materials including chocolate, snow, urine, animal organs, and plants. *Helen
       Chadwick: A Retrospective* took place at the Barbican Art Gallery in 2004.
       See Mark Sladen, ed, *Helen Chadwick*, London: Barbican Art Gallery and
       Hatje Cantz Publishers, 2004; also *Helen Chadwick: Effluvia*, Essen: Museum
       Folkwang, 1994 or Mark Holborn, ed, *Enfleshings: Helen Chadwick*, London:
       Martin Secker & Warburg Limited, 1989.
64   Mark Sladen, "A Red Mirror", in *Helen Chadwick*, London, Barbican Art
       Gallery and Hatje Cantz Publishers, 2004, p 13.
65   Repetition indeed becomes an important artistic trope at this time, in part
       influenced by the writings of Samuel Beckett. From performers such as
       Pina Bausch and Merce Cunningham, to artists including Bruce Nauman and
       Dan Graham, performing nonsensical actions became a way of exploring
       the body's incorporation into the artwork. This theme is not specific to
       performative practice, it is also of course redolent in the work of minimalist
       sculptors and painters. Two decades later, Janine Antoni deals with similar
       themes to Chadwick's in performances that convert private rituals—bathing,
       mopping, eating, sleeping—into obsessive process sculpture that exalts
       female pleasure, critiques male-dominated art forms such as minimalism
       and spoofs fine art traditions from painting to the classical bust. *Loving
       Care*, 1992-96, was performed at several sites including the Anthony D"Offay
       Gallery in London and the Matrix/129.
66   This is in fact her real name, and not a stage name as might be expected.
67   See also the work of Catherine Elwes and Judy Clark, who made perfor-
       mance and conceptual work after emerging from painting departments in
       Britain during the early 1970s.
68   Celebrated by a series of major exhibitions at the Whitechapel Art Gallery
       during the 1960s, the New Generation sculptors used industrial materials
       such as metal, fabricated from acrylic and car paint in bright colors, and
       abstract geometrical forms.
69   Bobby Baker, interview with the author, 24 May 2001.
70   Baker, interview with the author.
71   It is perhaps interesting to note that the successful young British artist Sarah
       Lucas has made a series of cakes with inkjet pornographic images on them.
       These, however, are treated more reverentially as multiple art objects, as
       the public is not invited to eat them.
72   Baker, interview with the author.
73   Bobby Baker's *Art Supermarket* was commissioned by Ted Little in the late
       1970s after Baker had done a successful piece *The Dinner Party* (this has no
       relationship to Judy Chicago's well-known installation of the same name at
       the same time) at the ICA some time earlier.
74   Baker's project might be compared to Claes Oldenberg's *Store* in New York,
       where he assembled faux consumer objects, really works of art, to be sold
       at a cheap price out of a storefront.
75   The concept of destruction, though presented in a gentle and humorous
       manner, is evocative of earlier, more male-centered movements such as the

DIAS (Destruction in art Symposium) and proponents such as Gustav Metzger and John Latham. Baker manages to present a serious subject matter—the political and in many cases unpopular notions of division of labor and capitalism—in a seemingly harmless way to the visitor.

76   Baker, interview with the artist.
77   Baker, interview with the artist.
78   Baker, interview with the author 277.
79   Marina Warner, "Bobby Baker: The Rebel at the Heart of the Joker," in *A Split Second of Paradise: Live Art, Installation and Performance*, Nicky Childs and Jeni Walwin, eds. London: Rivers Oram Press, 1998, 72.
80   Butler in Jones 397.
81   Susie Slack, "Bobby Baker at the ICA," review found in Baker's personal archive.
82   For a discussion of the 1978 Hayward Annual, also known as the "Girl's Own" annual, see Griselda Pollock and Rosie Parker, *Framing Feminism: Art and the Women's Movement 1970-1985*, London: Pandora, 1987.
83   Ziranek, like Baker, would use the domestic as inspiration in her work. Her *Very Food* is a collection of written and photographic work, all of which is satirically based on food. See Ziranek, *Very Food*, London: Book Works, 1987.
84   Cosey Fanni Tutti managed to distress the organizer of the event, Richard Francis, who was adamant about all of the things she was not allowed to do. In the end she broke all the rules by breaking eggs with her thighs and attempting to insert them into her vagina, while wearing criss-crossed baby blue ribbons up her legs, ballerina style. Ziranek, a fellow participant said, "Well Richard Francis was so agog with, I don't know artist adrenaline, call if for the sake of anything much more exciting. He was just riveted by this display of sexuality so he didn't remember that he was supposed to veto any of this." Ziranek, interview with the author.
85   Ziranek, interview with the author.
86   These recipes are in the book, *Very Food*, published by Bookworks. See reference above.
87   Ziranek, interview with the author.
88   Rebecca Schneider, *The Explicit Body in Performance*, London and New York: Routledge, 1997, 31.
89   I choose to examine Schneemann, because, as will soon be clear, besides being a seminal figure and role model for female performance artists, she also spent several years in London in the early 1970s. Two of her most well-known works, *Meat Joy* and *Up to and Including Her Limits* were staged for audiences in London. However, she is rarely associated with British feminism. During her time in London she also created new works, including a proposal for a performance piece for children, *Banana Hands*, and an artist's book called *Body House*.
90   For a discussion of Schneemann's participation in that work see David Levis-Strauss, "Love Rides Aristotle Through the Audience: Body, Image and Idea in the Work of Carolee Schneemann," in *Carolee Schneemann: Imaging Her Erotics*, Cambridge: MIT Press, 2002.
91   Elwes, interview with the author.
92   *Meat Joy* was first presented at Jean-Jacques Lebel's Festival of Free Expression in Paris, then at Dennison Hall in London and finally at Judson Church in New York, all 1964. See Tamsin Dillon's entry in *Short History of Performance*.
93   Carolee Schneemann, *More Than Meat Joy*, 1979.
94   Carolee Schneemann, interview with the author, 18 April 2002.

95 Schneemann, interview with the author. Interestingly, Schneemann wasn't the only artist who used synchronized swimming as inspiration for performance. In subsequent decades Tina Keane's *The Diver*, 1987, took the form of a live synchronized swimming performance with video and sound that took place in a pool in Banff, Canada.

96 Schneemann, interview with the author.

97 When Schneemann and a group of participants re-enacted this performance in 2002, the public reaction was not one of shock. Jonathan Jones from the *Guardian* wrote, "the first 40 minutes or so of Meat Joy seemed extraordinarily slow. Like the shambling zombies in George Romero's 1968 Night of the Living Dead, the performers were slack and clumsy, the action diffuse. You can never go back. It's never the same." Jonathan Jones, "So that was the 1960s … ," *Guardian*, London: 18 April 2002.

98 Elwes, interview with the author.

99 Dan Cameron, "In the Flesh," in *Carolee Schneemann: Up to and Including Her Limits*, New York: The New Museum of Contemporary Art, 1996, 11.

100 Amelia Jones, "Survey," in *The Artist's Body*, Tracey Warr, ed, London: Phaidon, 2000, 24.

101 Sally Potter, "On Shows," in *About Time: Video, Performance and Installation by 21 Women Artists*, London: Institute of Contemporary Arts, 1980, unpaginated.

102 Carolee Schneemann, "Letter to her parents," Getty Institute, no 950001, box 2. See also Kristine Stiles, ed, *Correspondence Course: An Epistolary History of Carolee Schneemann and her Circle*, Durham, North Carolina: Duke University Press, 2010.

103 Schneemann's American colleague Hannah Wilke would also be accused of this as she was young and attractive, and much of her work involved some form of self-representation. However, her *Intra Venus* series, a set of photographs in classical poses of female nudes, taken in the early 1990s while she was dying of cancer, can be seen as an answer to these critics. The later photographs certainly resist the ideology of idealized female nudes, showing the artist with bruises, bandages and scars. British artist Jo Spence also made photographs documenting her losing battle to breast cancer. See Elizabeth Delin Hansen, Kirsten Dybbøl, Donald Goddard, eds, *Hannah Wilke: A Retrospective*, Copenhagen: Contemporary Art Center, 1998; and Jo Spence, *Cultural Sniping: The Art of Transgression*, London: Routledge, 1995.

104 Schneemann "Public lecture," Whitechapel Art Gallery, April 2001.

105 See Andrea Dworkin, *Pornography: Men Possessing Women*, London: The Women's Press Limited, 1981.

106 Elwes was of course not the only British female artist to concern herself with taboo images. Judy Clark and Carolee Schneemann, as discussed in Chapter One, dealt with similarly controversial topics and images.

107 I use the word "radical" instead of essentialist throughout this essay as the latter has increasingly been used as a pejorative term. I am also not convinced that writers who create a dichotomy between the more theoretical and the "essential" feminist practice give either work its full credit. The various nuances, strains, and polemics make the two disparate categories inadequate. For example, Carolee Schneemann, whose work often involved her nude body and overt sexuality, was deeply steeped in psychoanalysis, but did not focus on this in her work.

108 Performance became increasingly important at the Slade under the tutelage of Brisley. It is interesting to note that there were women teaching at the

Slade at the time, most notably Rita Donagh and Tess Jaray. These women were not, however, teaching feminist practice. See Elwes, interview with the author.

109 Elwes notes that this had a number of jokes about the type of "regurgitative" performance that Brisley was known for.

110 Elwes, interview with the author. Judy Clark had actually used menstrual blood in a work shown at Garage in 1973 and Carolee Schneemann made her *Blood Diary* in 1972, although the latter was never shown in London. It is clear that Elwes wasn't aware of this work at the time. British artist Judith Higginbottom also worked on the topic of the menstrual cycle, but more in its relationship to the lunar cycle, and she and Elwes corresponded for a time.

111 Alexis Hunter, *Artscribe*, 1980, quoted in Elwes, *Video Loupe*, 56.

112 Lippard, Lucy, "The Pains and Pleasures of Rebirth," in *The Pink Glass Swan: Selected Feminist Essays on Art*, New York: The New Press, 1995, 111.

113 Ironically, in Chicago's *Red Flag* the removal of the tampon resembles a phallus, which serendipitously parallels more theoretical feminist inquiries into Lacanian theory, which examined the notion of penis envy. Thus, it is evident that the so-called "essentialist" artists had more in common with theoretical artists than is generally acknowledged.

114 A notable example of an artist who used explicit sexual imagery comes a bit later than this study. Helen Chadwick created a series of wreaths made of flowers and liquids, which in some cases clearly resemble the female sexual organs. See also the section on *Feministo* in Chapter Three of this book for a discussion of Kate Walker's chocolate box of sex organs.

115 Born 1955, Stockport, Manchester.

116 See Barbara Einzig, ed, *Thinking About Art: Conversations with Susan Hiller*, Manchester: Manchester University Press, 1996, 47-50.

117 Elwes, interview with the author.

118 I want to emphasize that Elwes has also spent most of her career producing articles and criticism that have frequently addressed the role of women's art and representation of women. Her written works can be seen as equally important to her performative pieces, and are essential to her practice. For a full bibliography and excerpts see Catherine Elwes, *Video Loupe*, London: KT Press, 2001.

119 During the 1970s Sally Potter was at various times a dancer, a choreographer, musician, film-maker, and performance artist. She has gone on to direct major feature films for the British industry, including *Orlando*, 1992, and *The Tango Lesson*, 1997, and is probably best-known for this aspect of her career.

120 As a point of interest, Bobby Baker actually made a cake for this performance, which in turn became the catalyst for her interest in live works.

121 Rose English, interview with the author, 8 March 2001.

122 English, interview with the author.

123 Part One took place on Friday 26 and Saturday 27 March 1976.

124 Rose English and Sally Potter, "Notes from *Berlin* performance," March/April 1976, 1, Rose English personal archive.

125 English and Potter, "Notes."

126 Rose English, interview with the author.

127 Marc Camille Chaimowicz, part of "347 minutes, ideas and experimentation," a one-day conference held at Conway Hall, 25 Red Lion Square, on Friday 24 March 2000. This was held in conjunction with the *Live in Your Head* exhibition at the Whitechapel Gallery, curated by Andrea Tarsia and Clive Phillpot.

128 For an excellent history of Keane's work see Jean Fisher, Richard Dyer and Peter Wollen, *Electronic Shadows: The Art of Tina Keane*, London: Black Dog Press, 2004.

129 Elwes, interview with the author.

3 Alternative Spaces for Feminist Art

1 Writing about this phenomenon in New York Julie Ault commented, "During the 1970s and early 1980s, many artist-initiated alternative spaces and group structures were established as constructive responses to the explicit and implied limitations of this commerce-oriented world." See Ault, ed, *Alternative Art New York 1965-1985*, Minneapolis: University of Minnesota Press, 2002, 3.

2 For more information on the economic and political climate as well as general cultural history of 1970s London see Jeremy Black, *Britain Since the Seventies*, London: Reaktion Books, 2004; Jonathon Green, *Days in the Life: Voices from the English Underground 1961-1971*, London: Pimlico, 1998; Sheila Rowbotham, *A Century of Women*, London: Penguin Books, 1999; Ann Kaloski, ed, *The Feminist Seventies*, London: Raw Nerve Books, 2003; and Martin Jones, *Psychedelic Decadence: Sex, Drugs and Low-Art in Sixties and Seventies Britain*, London: Cultural Vision, 2001.

3 For a critique of the widespread use of the term "patriarchy" in feminist ideology, see Parveen Adams, "Psychoanalysis and Feminism", in Adams and Elizabeth Cowie, eds, *The Woman in Question*, London: Verso, 1990, 231-2.

4 Finn-Kelcey, interview with the author.

5 For further information on the changes in art school education and the switch to a degree structure, see: Lord Eccles, "The State and the Arts," *Studio International*, (183:936), September 1971: 58-60; Philip Pilkington, Kevin Lose, David Rushton and Charles Harrison, "Some Concerns in Fine Art Education," *Studio International*, (183:937), October 1971: 120-2; Linda Morris, "Some Concerns in Fine Art Education II," *Studio International*, (182:938), November 1971: 168-9; R.H. Litherland, "Power Without Authority in Art and Design Education," *Studio International*, (182:939), December 1971: 224-5.

6 English, interview with the author.

7 Tickner, interview with the author.

8 This is not to say that male artists were not supported by this system, but there is not space here for a broader discussion.

9 Finn-Kelcey, interview with the author.

10 This was part of a series of exhibitions that took place across the country, for example "Art Spectrum Southeast," "Art Spectrum North," which happened in the early 1970s. The London exhibition at Alexandra Palace was a survey of artists in which Finn-Kelcey was invited to participate.

11 Finn-Kelcey, interview with the artist.

12 Alexandra Palace, located on one of the highest sites in London, was the site of the first public broadcast of radio, as well as the location where the first animation was done on videotape.

13 Finn-Kelcey, interview with the artist.

14 Guy Brett has also related this series of flags—or windblown objects as the artist sometimes refers to them—to the explorations of kinetic art from the 1960s. The prevailing idea of this type of art was that the artist would take decisions on form and imagery only up to a certain point and after that allow natural phenomena to prevail. See Guy Brett, *Rose Finn-Kelcey*, Birmingham and London: Ikon Gallery and Chisenhale Gallery, 1994.

15 For example, both Brisley and Latham were interested in the plight of the working classes and created work in industrial settings. Also, Latham's organization, APG, placed artists in industrial situations.
16 Artist David Medalla often staged impromptu performances as well. For more information on Medalla see Guy Brett, *Exploding Galaxies*, London: InIVA, 1996.
17 For more information see Anne Bean, interview with the author, 16 January 2002; and Tamsin Dillon, *A Short History of Performance*, London: Whitechapel Art Gallery, 2001.
18 Bean moved to London in 1973 after studying first in Cape Town then at Reading University.
19 Bean, interview with the author.
20 Bean, interview with the author.
21 Ziranek, interview with the author.
22 The element of risk was often incorporated in Bean's early performances, where she would do things such as cutting open a finger to make lipstick and then writing on a sheet of glass that she had smashed her head through. See Bean, interview with the author. The element of pain involved here may be compared to the artists Gina Pane and Marina Abramović, whose early work also centered on the limits of the body's endurance. See Klaus Biesenbach, ed, *Marina Abramović: The Artist is Present*, New York: Museum of Modern Art, 2010. For more on Gina Pane and the recording of her work, see Alice Maude-Roxby and Françoise Masson, *On Record: Advertising, Architecture and the Actions of Gina Pane*, London: Artwords Press, 2004.
23 Thank you to Silvia Ziranek for recounting this performance, which was not recorded by photography or video.
24 Ziranek has recently turned her efforts to creating "five-minute performances" for organizations including the Crafts Council, Wapping Power Station and Modern Art Oxford.
25 The Whitney Museum in New York hosted a major retrospective of Mendiata's work in 2004. For more information on Mendiata see Olga M. Viso, *Ana Mendiata*, Washington DC: Hirshhorn Museum and Sculpture Garden, 2004, and Helena Rickett, ed, *Art and Feminism*, 98.
26 This was his only published work and is considered one of the most important texts of the twentieth century.
27 Performance notes courtesy of the artist.
28 Acme was an organization (and for a short time a gallery) run by Jonathan Harvey and David Panton. It will be discussed at further length under the "Alternative Galleries" section of this chapter.
29 Bobby Baker, interview with the author, 24 May 2001.
30 It wasn't until later in the decade of the 1970s that feminism as an institution became a dominant interest for Baker, although her work has always been based on domesticity, food and role-playing, all of which are key feminist issues.
31 Baker, interview with the author.
32 Silvia Ziranek had similar comments about her time at art school under the tutelage of male professors. She said, "I had a half-dozen idiotic men, who were fairly belligerent most of the time, who were totally unsupportive, … Maybe that helped me, but at the time I could"ve done with a little support, and certainly a little female company." Ziranek, in discussion with the author. A number of the artists in this book have commented on discrimination against women in art schools during the 1970s.
33 A grant from the Arts Council helped pay for the four hundred pounds' worth of icing required to create the piece.

34   It is interesting that cannibalistic fantasy was also taken up by the well-known Canadian author, Margaret Atwood, whose novel *The Edible Woman* was first published in 1969. This book relates the story of a young woman struggling to accept her position as a future housewife and mother. Baker, however, has never acknowledged this as an inspiration; rather, it is redolent of the feminist questioning of the division of domestic labor at the time. See Margaret Atwood, *The Edible Woman*, 1969, London: Virago Press, 1980.

35   Baker, interview with the author.

36   "Working on the kitchen table was a classic. Come and see my work, it's under the kitchen table. They were always working in the corners of their lives. Not that many women had the courage to say that they were artists ... They were all being mothers and lovers and wives, and teachers ..." Elwes, interview with the author.

37   From a presentation given by Monica Ross at "347 minutes", a conference hosted by the Whitechapel on the occasion of its exhibition "Live in Your Head". Ross' presentation was billed as part of the "art activism and feminism panel", and took place on 24 March 2000. Many thanks to Monica Ross for sending me a transcript of her talk. For an example of Ross' more recent work, see Monica Ross, *Valentine*, London: Milch, 2000, an artist's book based on her performances throughout the 1990s.

38   The exhibition at the ICA in London was actually made to resemble a domestic space, with works installed in various tableaux. For example, the ICA entrance featured a fake lawn and door with a child's doll buggy and milk bottles.

39   Born 1938, Britain, Walker is one of the first generation of feminists working in Britain. At various times she has worked as an artist, single mother, housewife, designer, teacher and educator in prisons. Although she has resisted a career as a commercial artist, she is nevertheless a key player in feminist art in Britain.

40   Here I refer to the Franklin Institute Conference on Women in Art called "The Maker and the Muse," which was co-ordinated by Lisa Tickner in 1975. The Franklin Institute was located in North London, near Swiss Cottage.

41   Su Richardson, Monica Ross, Kate Walker, "Feministo—Women's Postal Art Event" notes, courtesy of Women's Art Library, *ca* 1978.

42   Kate Walker, interview, with the author, 8 August 2001.

43   Phil Goodall, "Feministo: Portrait of the Artist as a Young Woman," *Spare Rib* (49) 1976, 37.

44   Caroline Tisdall, "Anonymous was a Woman," *Guardian*, June 1977 (found in *Feministo* file at Women's Art Library).

45   The exhibition *A Portrait of the Artist as a Housewife* ran from 10 June-20 July, 1977 at the ICA in London. This was accompanied by a public discussion at the ICA on 14 July 1977. *Feministo* exhibitions were also presented at the Readers' Lounge, Central Library, Birmingham, 4-27 August, at the Academy Gallery in Liverpool from 4-18 October, 1977, and at the Edinburgh Festival of that year. Although the work varied in each exhibition, all of the shows had a similar format and were focused on the outcome of the collaborative postal network.

46   Joan Bates, "Express Delivery," *Birmingham Mail*, June 1976 (found in *Feministo* file at Women's Art Library).

47   Anne Simpson, "Feministo Puts You in the Picture", *Women's Herald*, 1976 (found in *Feministo* file at Women's Art Library).

48   Rozsika Parker, "Portrait of the Artist as a Housewife", *Spare Rib*, no. 60, 1977, 5-8, reprinted in Parker and Pollock, *Framing Feminism: Art and the Women's Movement 1970-1985*, London: Pandora, 1987.

49   For example, the Tate was buying conceptual art at the time, as seen in the example of Carl Andre's bricks.

50   An interesting counterpoint to this will be discussed in the following chapter, which speculates on contemporary artists' use of domestic themes, and the institution's desire to incorporate this work into their exhibitions and collections. (For example, Tracey Emin's *Bed*.)

51   It is interesting to think of the Fluxus art movement here. This work was largely ephemeral; however, much of it has been archived and institutionalized, unlike comparable feminist examples.

52   Walker, interview with the author.

53   Carolee Schneemann, notes from personal archive, courtesy of the artist.

54   Although the group consisted of many members, including An Dekker, Terry Dennett, Helen Grace, Sally Greenhill, Liz Heron, Gerda Jager, Neil Martinson, Maggie Millman, Michael Ann Mullen, Maggie Murray, Jini Rawlings, Ruth Burrenbaum, Christine Roche, Annette Soloman, Jo Spence, Arlene Strasberg, Sue Treweek and Julia Vellacot, the most well known of these is the late Jo Spence, an artist and activist known for her agitprop work on gender, domesticity and labor.

55   Jo Spence, *Cultural Sniping: The Art of Transgression*, London: Routledge, 1995, 89–90.

56   Spence, 92.

57   It is important to remember that there were always one or two commercial galleries who showed avant-garde work as well. Nigel Greenwood and Edward Totah could be considered examples of these.

58   Jonathan Harvey, David Panton and Shirley Read, "THE ACME GALLERY". Unpublished document, 1976 (from Acme archive).

59   Jonathan Harvey, "THE ACME GALLERY-POLICY STATEMENT", unpublished gallery statement, *ca* 1980. The directors did attempt to find other suitable gallery space, but by then it was becoming increasingly hard in London to find these kind of deals.

60   Harvey, Panton, Read.

61   See Brian O"Doherty's *Inside the White Cube* for a discussion of whether a gallery can ever be considered a neutral space.

62   Finn-Kelcey interview with the author.

63   unattributed, "MAIN PROGRAMME, THE ACME GALLERY", *ca* 1981 (Acme archive).

64   I refer here to recent projects hosted by retail stores, which include works by well-known contemporary artists. These include the Saks Fifth Avenue window exhibition program in New York and Los Angeles, where the American retail giant joined forces with museums in various cities in the late 1990s to present the work of high-calibre artists such as Vito Acconci and Charles Ray in their windows. Another recent example is Selfridge's London store wrapping itself in a specially commissioned three-storey photographic panel by Sam Taylor-Wood. And of course, there was the Art Supermarket at Harvey Nichols in London. For more on art and shopping see Kathy Battista, "The Art of Shopping: salon3 and Saks Fifth Avenue," *Public Art Journal* (1:2), October 1999: 34-5; and Kathy Battista, "London as Museum of the Twenty-first century," *World Architecture*, Beijing: World Architecture, June 2002, 106–11.

65   Bobby Baker, "Application for Gallery Space at the Acme Gallery," unpublished proposal, 1977. See the discussion of this work, which eventually was presented at the ICA, in the previous chapter.

66   See www.bobbybakersdailylife.com for more information on Baker and her archive.

67   See Guy Brett, "Tina Keane: Between Light and Dark", in *Carnival of Perception: Selected Writings on Art,* London: Institute of International Visual Arts, 2004, p 220.
68   Catherine Grant, ed, *Electronic Shadows: The Art of Tina Keane,* London: Black Dog Publishing, 2004, 14. This performance also occurred at Artists For Democray.
69   Hopscotch in fact was the title of several of Keane's works from the mid-1980s including a video and a neon installation. See Grant, 50-3.
70   Brett, 221.
71   Riley was of an older generation than most of the artists discussed in this dissertation. Although she was in London during the time of the women's movement her work was not informed by feminist ideology.
72   See unattributed, "Help Yourself to Studio Space" pamphlet, October 1975, Space archive.
73   Unattributed, "AIR & SPACE (Art Services Grants Ltd.)", document found in Space archive.
74   APG was organized by John Latham and his wife Barbara Steveni. See Chapter Three for reference notes.
75   Michael Kenny, "S.P.A.C.E. some personal recollections," May 1994, unpublished document found in Space archive. Kenny is an artist who was given a Space studio, and has kept it for over 20 years.
76   AIR stood for Artists' Information Register, which consisted of slides of work donated by artists, who sent them in. See Mary Rose Beaumont, Introduction, *10 Years at AIR: A Retrospective,* London: February 1985, unpaginated.
77   As it was known then, Central eventually united with St Martin's to create Central St Martin's College of Art and Design.
78   Unattributed, "AIR Gallery Policy 1978-9," 13 January 1978.
79   I must thank Irene Bradbury at the White Cube Gallery, for her assistance with information on the history of Garage. Access to her unpublished paper on Garage provided me with important background material, and led me to investigate the space further.
80   Conran was also owner of the Habitat shops and a chain of restaurants. He also founded the Design Museum in London. Interestingly, Conran also attended some of the Independent Group Meetings in the 1950s. (Thank you to Dr Barbara Penner at the Bartlett School of Architecture for information on Conran and the Independent Group.)
81   Irene Bradbury, "Garage," unpublished paper for the Royal College of Art, Master's Degree in Curating and Commissioning Contemporary Visual Art, 1996.
82   This building is now home to the Pepe Jeans shop, in the heart of a thriving commercial zone.
83   The name Garage came from Conran's design team because of the building's previous life as a vehicle depot for the market. You could actually get a car or lorry into the space at the time.
84   Anthony Stokes, interview with the author, 19 March 2001.
85   They had become increasingly successful and were being courted by Malcolm McLaren for management. Some members of the group, such as Bean, were opposed to Moodies becoming something packaged and choreographed. From Bean in discussion with the author.
86   The performance at Garage was repeated at a women's festival in Rotterdam.
87   The exhibition in London was the fourth in a series organized by Lippard, beginning in 1969, and including "557,087" in Seattle, "955,000" in Vancouver, and "2,974,453" in Buenos Aires. This information found in the original press release for "ca. 7500," 1974, unpaginated.

88 On Lippard's press release it only lists 48 Earlham Street as the premises for the show.

89 I am indebted to Lisa Tickner for providing me with a copy of this catalog.

90 Caroline Tisdall, "Women Artists," *Guardian*, April 1974, reprinted in Parker and Pollock, 198.

91 Griselda Pollock, "Unpublished letter to the Editor of the *Guardian*," Parker and Pollock 199.

92 Pollock 199.

93 Lucy Lippard, *ca. 7500*, card 2b, May 1973–February 1974. A review in *Spare Rib* was more sympathetic to the show, and contained descriptions of many works in the exhibition, which have proved useful as much of the work is unaccounted for.

94 Mark Weber has curated a retrospective season of works from their archive entitled "Shoot, Shoot, Shoot", which took place at the Tate Gallery, the Photographers Gallery and at 291 Gallery in May–June 2002. For more information see "Shoot, Shoot, Shoot," pamphlet published to accompany the series of events, 2002.

95 Michael Newman, "Shoot, Shoot, Shoot" Artists Panel, London, Tate Modern, 4 May 2002. Also present on the panel were Peter Gidal, Liz Rhodes, Chris Welsby and Anthony McCall.

96 Schneemann, interview with the author.

97 Carolee Schneemann, "Up to and Including Her Limits," in *Carolee Schneemann: Imaging Her Erotics*, New York, New Museum of Art, 1996, 163–4.

98 Schneemann 164.

99 Dan Cameron, "In the Flesh", *Carolee Schneemann: Up to and Including Her Limits*, New York: New Museum of Contemporary Art, 1996, 12.

100 Schneemann, interview with the author.

101 *Up to and Including Her Limits* was first performed under the title of *Trackings* at the Avant-Garde Festival #10 at Grand Central Station, New York, in 1973. It was also done at the University Art Museum, Berkeley, in 1974, as well as Artists Meeting Place in Covent Garden, London; Artists Space, New York; Anthology Film Archive New York, all 1974; the Kitchen, New York, 1976; Studiogalerie, Berlin, 1976; Basel Art Fair, 1976; and Fluxus Film Forum, Venice Biennale 1990.

102 This was located in a building normally used for domestic space on Radnor Terrace, in the Brixton neighborhood of Lambeth Borough. Radnor Terrace doesn't exist anymore; in its place there is a council estate on that site.

103 Walker, interview with the author.

104 Unattributed advertisement for A Woman's Place, *FAN: Feminist Arts News*, no. 7, 1974, 29.

105 Walker said regarding funding: "In those days there was no point in applying for funding either from private or state sources. People would just laugh in your face. I took a degree when both of my children were very young—a certificate of education—and just glued myself to that as a way of earning a living. And anything I did was for pleasure and education and entertainment, self-funded." Walker, interview with the author.

106 *Womanhouse* was also presented at a meeting the Women's Workshop at the Artists Union. Notes from a meeting held in June 1973 include a blurb about "Project Womanhouse", which speaks of the possibility of creating a London version: "We still haven't located a suitable short life house for the project as we origionally (sic) intended it, but are in touch with South London Women's Center who think they may be able to help." Members present at the meeting were Judith Adams, Alexis Hunter, Tina Keane, Jane Low,

Roberta Hunter Henderson and Alene Strausberg. On agenda for the next meeting was viewing of slides of *Womanhouse*. Obviously, although information was processed and traveled slower at that time, the project was known by some London artists. See unattributed, notes from Artists Union—Women's Workshop, Monday 4 June 1973, WAL "Women's Art Alliance/WWAU file".

107 This was the first program dedicated to feminist art practice. Their teaching methodology included consciousness-raising techniques, such as discussing personal experiences, sexuality, trauma, etc., and the use of this personal exploration in the making of feminist art. For more information on *Womanhouse* see: Amelia Jones, *Sexual Politics: Judy Chicago's Dinner Party in Feminist Art History*, Los Angeles: UCLA at the Armand Hammer Museum of Art and Cultural Center in association with the University of California Press, 1996; Peggy Phelan, "Survey," in *Art and Feminism*, London: Phaidon Press, 2001, 21-2; and Arlene Raven, "Womanhouse," in *The Power of Feminist Art*, Norma Broude and Mary D. Garrard, eds. New York: Harry N. Abrams, Inc., 1994, 48-65.

108 Miriam Schapiro, "The Education of Women as Artists: Project Womanhouse," *Art Journal*, 32, reprinted in Helena Rickett 208-9.

109 Walker, interview with the author.

110 Walker, interview with the author.

111 Thank you to Sandy Nairne for a fascinating discussion of the experience of visiting Radnor Terrace and witnessing this performance.

112 Rozsika Parker, "Housework," *Spare Rib* (26), 1975: 38, reprinted in Parker and Pollock.

113 Parker 38.

114 Women's Free Arts Alliance was eventually shortened to just Women's Arts Alliance in 1978.

115 There was also a large array of women's art centers and collectives in the United States and Europe. AIR in New York was one of the best-known, and British artists such as Alexis Hunter and Mary Kelly traveled to New York to give talks there.

116 For example, the Women's Interart Center (1969-1970) New York was a multidisciplinary workshop, community center and alternative space. Also organizations such as Women Artists in Revolution and the Ad Hoc Women Artists' Committee were examples of like-minded institutions.

117 The second site was located at 10 Cambridge Terrace Mews in NW1.

118 Elwes, interview with the author.

119 This work may be compared to other feminist and conceptual work where American artists made themselves vulnerable by enacting performances directly in the public space of the city. See Carter Radcliff, *Out of the Box: The Reinvention of Art, 1965-1975*, New York: Allworth Press, 2000, 226-31 regarding the work of Adrian Piper and Vito Acconci; and Eleanor Antin, *Eleanor Antin, Real Time Streaming*, Coventry: The Mead Gallery, 2001, 16-18.

120 Elwes, *Video Loupe*, 50.

121 Elwes, interview with the author 233.

122 Ann Scott, "Editorial," *Spare Rib*, no. 34, April 1975, 8.

123 Editorial, *Red Rag: A Magazine of Women's Liberation*, no. 4, July 1973. The collective at that time included Valerie Charlton, Linda Radford, Jackie Turner, Rosalind Delmar, Nell Myers, Lynn Segal, Elizabeth Wilson, Angela Weir, Sally Alexander, Alison Fell, Margaret Edney, Annette Muir, Nettie Pollard, Gaby Charing, Sue Cowley, Sheila Rowbotham, Bea Campbell, Micheline Wandor, Maria Loftus, Christine Peters and Gladys Brooks.

124 Editorial, *Red Rag: A Magazine of Women's Liberation*, no. 6 1973.

125 Unattributed, *Wires*, no. 74.
126 Ault 5.
127 See Carson, PhD dissertation.
128 Take for example, City Racing, which has become legendary in its ability to present new and interesting contemporary work to the public, and has achieved an excellent reputation. See Andrew Wilson, "Foreword," *City Racing: The Life and Times of an Artist-Run Gallery*, Matt Hale, Paul Noble, Pete Owen, eds, London: Black Dog, 2002, v-vii. Also, the more recent initiative "Capri", run by a collective of independent East End galleries, is indicative of the wealth of such activities at this time.

4 Feminist Themes in Contemporary Practice

1 Jemima Stehli had a solo show at Centro de Artes Visuales in Coimbra, Portugal; Hayley Newman had solo shows at Matt's Gallery and Ikon Birmingham; Sarah Lucas was the central figure in the show *In a Gadda da Vida* at Tate Britain in 2003.
2 Austrian artist, born 1970, who has made performances where the public watches her masturbate and frequently uses photographs of her own vagina juxtaposed with various objects. See Elke Krystufek, *In The Arms of Luck*, Geneva: Centre Genevois de Gravure Contemporaine, 1999, and *Elke Krystufek*, Frankfurt: Portikus, 2000.
3 Bowers, Lachowicz and Chang are all American artists, with the former two living and working in Los Angeles. Lachowicz is represented by Shoshana Wayne Gallery while Bowers is represented by Suzanne Vielmetter. Chang is based in New York and represented by Mary Boone Gallery.
4 The retrospective of Ana Mendiata's work at the Whitney is an important example of curators addressing this problem.
5 Stehli has lived in Britain for most of her life and attended art school in London, but was born in Australia in 1961.
6 It is important to note here that Jones's *Chair* was purchased by the Tate in 1981. They have not yet acquired a photograph by Stehli.
7 As an interesting aside, Kathy Temin, an Australian artist who lives in London, created a work appropriating Stehli's image of Jones's *Chair*.
8 Indeed shoes seem to have an importance for Stehli who made a photograph entitled *Wearing Shoes Chosen by the Curator* where she lay on the ground naked, except for a pair of shoes that were chosen by the curator, then exhibited it in the space that it was taken. Again, this work is a comment on the power structures between curator and artist.
9 Mulvey wrote, "The theme of *women bound* is one of the most consistent in Allen Jones's source material: at its most vestigial, the limbs of pin-up girls are bound with shiny tape, a fashion model is loaded with chains, underwear advertisements, especially for corsets, proliferate, as do rubber garments from fetishistic magazines." See Laura Mulvey "Fears, Fantasies and the Male Unconscious *or* You don't Know What is Happening, Do You, Mr Jones?," originally published in *Spare Rib*, 1973, reprinted in *Visual and Other Pleasures*, London: The Macmillan Press Ltd, 1989, 8.
10 Mulvey, "You Don't Know," 7.
11 Mulvey, "You Don't Know," 10-11.
12 Lisa Tickner, "The Body Politic: Female Sexuality and Women Artists since 1970," *Art History*, June 1978, (1:2) June 1978: 236-49, reprinted in Rozsika Parker and Griselda Pollock, eds. *Framing Feminism: Art and the Women's Movement 1970-1985*, London: Harper Collins, 1987, 263.

13   Monica Sjoo, "Some Thoughts about our Exhibition of *Womanpower: Women's Art* at the Swiss Cottage Library," originally unpublished document printed in Parker & Pollock 188-90.
14   Alison Jones, "Jemima Stehli: On All Fours Naked in High Heels—A Critical Position," *Women: A Cultural Review*, (10:3) London: Routledge, 1999, 300.
15   BS, "Jemima Stehli, Chisenhale Gallery," *Artforum*, February 2001, 164. It is a point of comparison that Hayley Newman wasn't criticized for using her nude body in her photographic series. Part of the objection to Stehli's—like that of Schneemann and Wilke—is the attractiveness of her body.
16   David Burrows, Introduction, in *Jemima Stehli*, London: ARTicle Press, 2004, 5.
17   Charlotte Cotton, *The Photograph as Contemporary Art*, London: Thames & Hudson, 2004, 197.
18   Sitters included Adrian Searle, Guardian Arts Critic; John Slyce, writer; Matthew Higgs, curator; Paul Stolper, dealer; and Matthew Collings, arts television presenter; David Burrows, artist.
19   In fact one sitter, the critic and curator Matthew Higgs, said in a public talk that he regretted being part of the photographic series and would never be in a work of art again. He felt uncomfortable with the level of scrutiny that he was subjected to by the viewer. Matthew Higgs, "Who's Afraid of Feminism," Institute of Contemporary Arts, London, 2000.
20   Stella Santacatterina, "Jemima Stehli: Subject and Object of the Gaze," *Portfolio* 33, June 2001, 28.
21   In her recent presentation at Tate Modern as part of the Women's Work course, Stehli answered to criticisms about her work, mentioning that she wasn't necessarily attempting to create feminist art. Jemima Stehli, "Artist's Talk," Tate Modern, London, 25 November 2002.
22   Another young female British artist, Janette Parris, who is a colleague of Stehli's, resides on this tenuous line in her performance work. Her recent piece *Mezzo Soprano* played on the audience's uneasiness and uncertainty about their reactions. In this work she staged a concert with a band at a music hall; however, her tone-deaf singing left the audience unsure as to how to react.
23   Burrows 5-7.
24   Aaron Williamson, Introduction, in Hayley Newman, *Performancemania*, London: Matt's Gallery, 2001, 6.
25   Williamson 6.
26   It was also performed at Beaconsfield Gallery in London and at the Hoog Huis in Arnhem during that period.
27   Bean, interview with the author.
28   Hayley Newman, *Performancemania*.
29   Newman, *Connotations*, 1998.
30   Hayley Newman, interview with the author, 31 August 2004.
31   This film was commissioned by Hull Time-Based Arts.
32   Lucas was born 1962 and works and lives in London, where she is represented by Sadie Coles HQ.
33   When the sculpture is exhibited the eggs and kebab must be changed daily.
34   Matthew Collings, *Sarah Lucas*, London: Tate Publishing, 2002, 39-40. It is interesting to note that Lucas' first major monograph has been written by a man. This would have been unheard of in the 1970s, and suggests that women artists have now achieved a level of success that was not possible in earlier generations.
35   Raimar Stange, *Women Artists in the 20th and 21st Century*, Uta Grosenick, ed. Cologne: Taschen, 2001, 330.

36   Rozsika Parker, "Portrait of the Artist as a Housewife," *Spare Rib* 60, 1977: 5-8, reprinted in Parker and Pollock, *Framing Feminism: Art and the Women's Movement 1970-1985*, London: Pandora, 1987.

37   The most obvious point of contrast is that Lucas is represented by the gallery Sadie Coles HQ, while many of the feminist artists described in the preceding chapters, do not have any representation. Lucas has had solo exhibitions in major public galleries including Portikus, in Frankfurt am Main, Germany; Museum Boijmans van Beuningen, Rotterdam; and the Freud Museum in London. She also has participated in some of the most important group exhibitions of the 1980/90s, including *Freeze* (see below), *Brilliant* at the Walker Art Center in Minneapolis, and *Sensation* at the Royal Academy of Arts in London.

38   *Freeze* was held in the Port of London Authority building in the Docklands in 1988. It was organized by the artists themselves and became a landmark show for the yBa generation. It represents a kind of "do it yourself" moment for this generation of artists, who were educated under the Thatcher regime, which saw the closing of the docks in the 1980s, as well as the miners' strikes. Self-promotion became an important vehicle for the yBas, and was begun in the *Freeze* project.

39   The *WIRES* newsletter asked female readers not to show it to men.

40   Emin was born 1961 in Margate. She left school at 13, was raped and became sexually promiscuous, and moved to London. See Stuart Morgan, "The Story of I", *frieze* (34) May 1997: 59-60 for an account of Emin's rape and subsequent promiscuity.

41   There were two protests about the installation. The first from the Stuckists, who paraded as clowns outside the Tate, calling for a return to figurative art. To this day if one visits the Stuckist gallery on Charlotte Road in London there is a bed in the middle of it with a sign saying "This is just a bed. Feel free to sit on it and enjoy the art works." The second protest was staged by two young Chinese artists.

42   Interestingly, the bed as readymade was discussed in the press in the legacy of Kelly's nappies.

43   *Hannah's "At Home"* event took place on September 30, 1985. This was a work about the interaction of working and living spaces that highlighted "the complementary, contradictory and conflict-making elements of working within the confined space of the home." Catherine Lacey, Richard Francis, Jeremy Lewison, Ann Jones, *Performance Art and Video Installation*, London: Tate Gallery, 1985, 19.

44   See Chapter Three for a full discussion of *A Woman's Place* at Radnor Terrace.

45   Recently the venue "Home" has been established in the Camberwell area of South East London. This space is run by Laura Godfrey-Isaacs.

46   See Kate Bernard, "The Women who Won't Win the Turner Prize," *Evening Standard*, London: 30 October 1996, 28.

47   Emin related to a journalist how one person sent a cheque for fifty pounds with a note that said, "Never contact me again". See Richard Gott, "Sexual in-tent," *Guardian Weekend*, 5 April 1997, 29.

48   Emin met Lucas at the latter's show at City Racing, an artist-run gallery in South London. Emin said of Lucas' work, "The feminist angle to it was quite subverted, kind of twisted." Gott 29.

49   "The Shop" was at 103 Bethnal Green Road from January-July 1993. They were originally looking for a studio space and then came up with the idea of having a shop. For an account of The Shop see Gregor Muir, "Like a Hole in the Head," *Parkett* (63), 2001: 36-8.

50 Gott 30.
51 One could compare Emin and Lucas' shop to Claus Oldenberg's Storefront in New York or even Malcolm McLaren and Vivienne Westwood's shop on the King's Road in London. These were a new breed of shop cum galleries, which sold everything from clothing to ephemera.
52 The Tracey Emin Museum was located at 221 Waterloo Road, in South East London. Emin opened her doors in 1995 and the "museum" operated for the next three years.
53 Jon Ronson, "Who wants their own museum?," *Independent, Section Two*, 9 February 1996, 8.
54 Esther Pierini, "Tracey Emin," *Flash Art*, November/December 1997: 102.
55 Adrian Searle, "Me, me, me, me," *Guardian*, 22 April 1997, 13.
56 Richard Dorment, "All about Tracey Emin," *Daily Telegraph*, 30 April 1997.
57 This voyeuristic interest in other people's lives is also reflected in the onslaught of reality television shows that have gained massive popularity in Britain in recent times. *Big Brother, Survivor* and other programs thrive on "warts and all" depictions of everyday lives. Interestingly, on each of these shows contestants are obliged to confess to the camera who they dislike in the groups and for what reason.
58 Schneemann, interview with the author. Schneemann's words resonate when one reads a piece written at the time of the first showing of Emin's tent in 1995. Her tutor from the Royal College of Art, Norbert Lynton, said "Well, I"m not on her tent. I did a quick mental check when I first heard about it." Gott 28.
59 One reporter wrote of her "quite impressive cleavage". Alastair McKay, "Art is an Eminist issue," *Scotsman*, 4 August 1998, 10.
60 In December 1997 during the post-prize-giving debate led by Waldemar Januszczak, Emin stormed out of the taping, saying "I"m leaving now. I want to be with my mum. I don't give a fuck. You people aren't relating to me now." At the time she was so drunk that she was convinced that she was in someone's house. Waldemar Januszczak, "Eminism," *Sunday Times Magazine*, 12 July 1998, 30-1.
61 Gott 27. For an interesting discussion of Emin's cultivated persona, see Robert Preece, "Artist over—*and in*—the broadsheets," *Parkett* (63) 2001: 50.
62 *Minky Manky* was at South London Gallery from 12 April-14 May 1995.
63 Janis Jefferies, "Autobiographical Patterns," *N.Paradoxa* (4) 1997.
64 Mark Gisbourne, "Life Into Art," *Contemporary Visual Arts* (20) 2000.
65 Phillpot, interview with the author 398.
66 Beecroft is represented by Gagosian, Lachowicz by Shoshana Wayne Gallery, Krystufek by Emily Tsingou Gallery and Chang by Entwistle Gallery. All of these are established, commercial galleries.
67 A good example of this is the recent project by German artist Gregor Schneider. His *Die Familie Schneider* is a project where dark family secrets are played out in two identical homes in East End London. For more information on this project see www.artangel.org.uk.

BIBLIOGRAPHY

Adams, Parveen. *The Emptiness of the Image: Psychoanalysis and Sexual Differences*. London: Routledge, 1996.

Adams, Parveen and Elizabeth Cowie, eds. *The Woman in Question: m/f*. London: Verso, 1990.

Aereen, Rasheed. *The Third Text Reader on Art, Culture and Theory*. London: Continuum, 2002.

Alberro, Alexander. *Martha Rosler*. Birmingham: Ikon Gallery, 1998.

Alberro, Alexander and Blake Stimson, eds. *Conceptual Art: A Critical Anthology*. Cambridge: Massachusetts: MIT Press, 1999.

Aldiss, Brian. *Earthworks*. New York: Doubleday and Co., 1996.

Ali, Tariq and Susan Watkins. *1968: Marching in the Streets*. London: Bloomsbury, 1998.

Antin, Eleanor. *Eleanor Antin, Real Time Streaming*. Coventry: The Mead Gallery, 2001.

"Arse for Art's Sake." *The Face*, December 2000: 146-7.

"Arts Laboratory Schedule." July 1968, Getty Research Library, Special Collections, Carolee Schneemann, no. 950001, Box 28.

Atwood, Margaret. *The Edible Woman*. 1969. London: Virago Press, 1980.

Ault, Julie, ed. *Alternative Art New York*. Minneapolis and New York: University of Minnesota Press and the Drawing Center, 2002.

Austin, J.L. *How to Do Things with Words*. London: Oxford University Press, 1976.

Bailey, David A. and Gilane Tawadros. *Veil: Veiling, Representation and Contemporary Art*. Cambridge: MIT Press, 2003.

Baker, Bobby. Personal interview. 24 May 2001.

——. "Application for Gallery Space at the Acme Gallery." Unpublished proposal, London: Acme archive, 1977.

Barber, Lynn. "Just Be Yourself—and Wear a Low Top." *Parkett* 63, December 2001: 36-43.

Barker, Barry. Personal interview. 26 April 2000.

Bates, Joan. "Express Delivery." *Birmingham Mail*. Birmingham: June 1976.

Battista, Kathy. "The Art of Shopping: salon3 and Saks Fifth Avenue." *Public Art Journal*, 1.2 October 1999: 34-5.

——. "London as Museum of the Twenty-first Century," *World Architecture*. June 2002: 106-11.

——. "Performing Feminism", *Art Monthly*, 343, February 2011.

——. "Alan Moore with Kathy Battista", *Brooklyn Rail*, April 2012.

Bean, Anne. Personal Interview. 16 January 2002.

Beaumont, Mary Rose. "Introduction." *10 Years at AIR: A Retrospective*. London: February 1985, unpaginated.

Berger, Maurice. *Adrian Piper: A Retrospective*. New York: The New Museum of Contemporary Art, 1999.

Bernard, Kate. "The women who won't win the Turner Prize." *Evening Standard*, 30 October 1996.

Bial, Henry, ed. *The Performance Studies Reader*. London: Routledge, 2004.

Black, Jeremy. *Britain since the Seventies*, London: Reaktion Books, 2004.

Bradbury, Irene. "Garage." unpublished paper for the Royal College of Art, Masters Degree in Curating and Commissioning Contemporary Visual Art, 1996.

Bray, Roger. "On View at the ICA: Dirty Nappies." *Evening Standard*, 14 October 1976.

Breitwieser, Sabine, ed. *Rereading Post-Partum Document Mary Kelly*. Vienna: Generali Foundation, 1999.

Brett, Guy. Personal interview. 13 April 2000.

——. "Vacating the Premises." *Rose Finn-Kelcey*. London: Chisenhale; Birmingham: Ikon Gallery, 1994.

——. *Exploding Galaxies*. London: InIVA, 1996.

Broude, Norma and Mary D. Garrard, eds. *The Power of Feminist Art*. New York: Harry N. Abrams, 1994.

Brown, Neal, Sarah Kent and Matthew Collings. *Tracey Emin: I Need Art Like I Need God*. London: Jay Jopling/White Cube: 1997.

BS. "Jemima Stehli, Chisenhale Gallery." *Artforum*, February 2001: 164.

Burrows, David, ed. *Jemima Stehli*. London, ARTicle Press: 2002.

Butler, Cornelia H. and Lisa Gabrielle Mark, eds, *WACK! Art and the Feminist Revolution*, Cambridge: MIT Press, 2007.

Butler, Cornelia and Alexandra Schwartz, eds, *Modern Women: Women Artists at the Museum of Modern Art*, New York: MoMA, 2010.

Butler, Judith. *Gender Trouble: Feminism and the Subversion of Identity*. New York: Routledge, 1990.

Cameron, Dan and Lisa Phillips, Amelia Jones and Anthony Vidler. *Paul McCarthy*. New York: New Museum of Contemporary Art; Ostfildern-Ruit: Hatje Cantz Verlag, 2000.

Cameron, Shirley and Roland Miller. *The Art that Moves: An Exhibition of Documents from the Development of British Performance Art, from the Sixties to the Eighties*. Sheffield: Live Art Works!, 1986.

Carson, Fiona, and Clare Pajakowszka, eds. *Feminist Visual Culture*. London: Routledge, 2001.

Carson, Juli. "(Re)Viewing Mary Kelly's *Post-Partum Document*." *Documents* (2000): 41–60.

——. *Excavating Discursivity: Post-Partum Document in the Conceptualist, Feminist and Psychoanalytic Fields*. Thesis: Massachusetts Institute of Technology, 2000.

Chadwick, Helen. *Helen Chadwick: Effluvia*. Essen: Museum Folkwang, 1994.

Chadwick, Whitney. *Women, Art, and Society*. London: Thames & Hudson Ltd, 1990 and 1996.

Charlton, Valerie, et al. "Editorial." *Red Rag: A Magazine of Women's Liberation*, 4 (July 1973).

Chicago, Judy. *Through the Flower: My Struggle as a Woman Artist*. New York: Penguin Books, 1975.
—. *The Dinner Party*. New York: Viking Press, 1996.
Childs, Nicky and Jeni Walwin, eds. *A Split Second of Paradise: Live Art, Installation and Performance*. London: Rivers Oram Press, 1998.
Clark, Judy. Personal interview. 12 July 2001.
—. Letter to Althea Greenan. 21 May 1997. Judy Clark file. Women's Art Library, London.
Collings, Matthew. *Sarah Lucas*. London: Tate Publishing, 2002.
Conley, Christine Louise. "Love Among the Runes: Allegory, Gender and the Symbolics of Loss in the Work of Three Twentieth Century Women." Thesis: University of Essex, 1998.
Cooper, Susan and Sara Crowley, Charlotte Holtam, eds. *Papers on Patriarchy Conference*. Sussex: Women's Publishing Collective, 1976.
Cork, Richard. "Big brother—and Mary Kelly's baby." *Evening Standard*, 14 October 1976: 22-3.
Cottingham, Laura. *Seeing through the Seventies: Essays on Feminism and Art*. Amsterdam: G+B Arts International, 2000.
Cotton, Charlotte. *The Photograph as Contemporary Art*. London: Thames & Hudson, 2004.
Danino, Nina and Michael Mazière. *The Undercut Reader: Critical Writings On Artists' Film and Video*. London: Wallflower Press, 2002.
Deepwell, Katy. *New Feminist Art Criticism: Critical Strategies*. Manchester: Manchester University Press, 1995.
Derrida, Jacques. *Archive Fever: A Freudian Impression*, Eric Prenowitz, trans, Chicago: University of Chicago Press, 1998.
Deutsche, Rosalyn. "Not-forgetting: Mary Kelly's *Love Songs*", *Grey Room*, no. 24, Cambridge: MIT Press, Spring 2006.
Dickinson, Margaret. *Rogue Reels: Oppositional Film in Britain 1945 to 1990*. London: British Film Institute, 1999.
Dillon, Tamsin. *A Short History of Performance*. London: Whitechapel Art Gallery, 2001.
Dorment, Richard. "All about Tracey Emin." *Daily Telegraph*, 30 April 1997.
Douglas, Mary. *Purity and Danger: An Analysis of the Concepts of Pollution and Taboo*. 1966. London: Routledge, 1993.
Doy, Glen. *Black Visual Culture: Modernity and Post-Modernity*. London: I.B.Tauris, 2000.
Duncan, Carol. *Civilizing Rituals: Inside Public Art Museums*. New York: Routledge, 1995.
Dworkin, Andrea. *Pornography: Men Possessing Women*. 1979. London: The Women's Press Ltd, 1981.
Eccles, Lord. "The State and the Arts." *Studio International*. Peter Townsend, ed. 183.936 (September 1971): 58-60.
Ehrlich, Ken and Brandon LaBelle. *Surface Tension: Problematics of Site*. Los Angeles: Errant Bodies, 2004.
Einzig, Barbara, ed. *Thinking About Art: Conversations with Susan Hiller*. Manchester: Manchester University Press, 1996.
Elwes, Catherine. *Video Loupe*. London: KT Press, 2000.

Elwes, Catherine. Personal interview. 6 April 2001.

——. "In Praise of Older Women: Rose Finn-Kelcey and Kate Meynell." *Make* 78 (December 1997/March 1998): 17-19.

English, Rose. Personal interview. 8 March 2001.

English, Rose and Sally Potter. Unpublished notes from *Berlin* performance. March/April 1976. Rose English personal archive, London.

Fer, Briony. *On Abstract Art*. New Haven: Yale University Press, 1997.

Finn-Kelcey. Personal interview. 16 June 2000.

——. "Mind the Gap." Unpublished performance notes. Rose Finn-Kelcey personal archive, London.

Fisher, Jean and Richard Dyer, Peter Wollen. *Electronic Shadows: The Art of Tina Keane*. London: Black Dog Press, 2004.

Fitzpatrick, Tracy. *Hannah Wilke: Gestures*, Purchase, NY: Neuberger Museum, 2010.

Ford, Simon. *Wreckers of Civilisation: The Story of Coum Transmissions & Throbbing Gristle*. London: Black Dog Publishing & Simon Ford, 1999.

——. "Myth Making." *Art Monthly* 194 (March 1996): 3-9.

——. "Subject & (Sex) Object." *make*. (June–August 1998): 2-7.

Freud, Sigmund. *Totem and Taboo*. 1950. London: Ark Paperbacks, 1994.

Fried, Michael. *Art and Objecthood: Essays and Reviews*. Chicago: University of Chicago Press, 1998.

Friedan, Betty. *The Feminine Mystique*. 1963. London: Penguin Books Ltd, 1992.

Frueh, Joanna. *Hannah Wilke: A Retrospective*. Missouri: University of Missouri Press, 1989.

——. *Erotic Faculties*. Berkeley: University of California Press, 1996.

Frye Burnham, Linda and Steven Durland, eds. *Citizen Artist: An Anthology from High Performance Magazine 1978-1998*. Gardiner, NY: Critical Press, 1998.

Fusco, Coco. *The Bodies that were Not Ours*. London: Routledge, 2002.

Gamman, Lorraine, and Margaret Marshment, eds. *The Female Gaze: Women as Viewers of Popular Culture*. 1988. London: The Women's Press Ltd, 1994.

Garner, Dwight. "The Spock Touch." *Mothers Who Think*. March 1998.

Gisbourne, Mark. "Life Into Art: Interview with Tracey Emin." *Contemporary Visual Arts*, 20 (2000).

Goldberg, RoseLee. *Performance Art: From Futurism to the Present*. 1979. London: Thames & Hudson, 1988.

——. ed, *Everywhere and All at Once: An Anthology of Writings on Performa 07*, Zurich and New York: JRP Ringier and Performa, 2009.

——. *Performa 09: Back to Futurism*, New York: Performa, 2011.

Goodall, Phil. "Feministo: Portrait of the Artist as a Young Woman." *Spare Rib* 49 (1976): 37.

Gott, Richard. "Sexual in-tent." *Guardian Weekend*, 5 April 1997, 28-32.

Graham, Dan. "Homes for America." *Arts Magazine*, 1966.

Green, Jonathon. *Days in the Life: Voices from the English Underground 1961-1971*. London: Pimlico, 1998.

Greenan, Althea. *Judy Clark: The Occupier and Other Works*. Chichester: Pallant House Gallery, 1998.

Greer, Germaine. *The Female Eunuch*. London: Flamingo, 1971.

Grosenick, Uta, ed. *Women Artists in the 20th and 21st Century*. Cologne: Taschen, 2001.

Grosz, Elizabeth. *Jacques Lacan: A Feminist Introduction.* 1990. London: Routledge, 1995.

Hale, Matt, Paul Noble and Pete Owen. *City Racing: The Life and Times of An Artist-Run Gallery.* London: Black Dog, 2002.

Hall, Catherine. *White, Male and Middle-Class: Explorations in Feminism and History.* Cambridge: Polity Press, 1992.

Hamilton, Richard. *John Latham, Early Works: 1954-1972.* London: Lisson Gallery, 1987.

Hammond, Harmony. *Lesbian Art in America: A Contemporary History.* New York: Rizzoli, 2000.

Hansen, Elizabeth Delin and Kirsten Dybbøl, Donald Goddard, eds. *Hannah Wilke: A Retrospective.* Copenhagen: Contemporary Art Center, 1998.

Harrison, Charles, ed. *Art & Language in Practice Vol. 2. Critical Symposium.* Barcelona: Fundació Antoni Tàpies, 1999.

—. *Conceptual Art and Painting: Further Essays on Art & Language.* Cambridge: Massachusetts: MIT Press, 2002.

—. Personal interview. 11 April 2000.

Harrison, Charles and Paul Wood. *Art in Theory 1900-1990: An Anthology of Changing Ideas.* Oxford: Blackwell Publishers, 1992.

Harvey, Jonathan. "THE ACME GALLERY-POLICY STATEMENT." Unpublished gallery statement. *ca* 1980. Acme archive, London.

Harvey, Jonathan, David Panton and Shirley Read, "THE ACME GALLERY." Unpublished document. 1976. Acme archive, London.

Heizer, Micheal et al. *Double Negative.* New York: Rizzoli, 1992.

Higgs, Matthew and Paul Noble. *Protest and Survive.* London: Whitechapel Art Gallery, 2000.

Himmelweit, Susan, Margaret McKenzie, Allison Tomlin. "Why Theory?" *Papers on Patriarchy Conference.* London: Architectural Association, 1976.

Hirst, Damien. *i want to spend the rest of my life everywhere, with everyone, one to one, always, forever, now.* London: Booth-Clibborn Editions, 1997.

Holborn, Mark, ed. *Enfleshings: Helen Chadwick.* London: Martin Secker & Warburg Limited, 1989.

Hoover, Nan. *... Barely an Instant.* London and Cambridge: Matt's Gallery & Kettle's Yard, 1986.

Hubert, Henri and Marcel Mauss. *Sacrifice: Its Nature and Functions.* E.E. Evans-Pritchard, 1964; Midway, 1981.

Huyssen, Andreas. *After the Great Divide: Modernism, Mass Culture, Postmodernism.* Bloomington and Indianapolis: Indiana University Press, 1986.

Irish, Sharon. *Suzanne Lacy: Spaces Between.* Minneapolis: University of Minnesota Press, 2010.

Iverson, Margaret, Douglas Crimp, Homi K. Bhabha. *Mary Kelly.* London: Phaidon Press Limited, 1995.

Januszczak, Waldemar. "eminism." *Sunday Times Magazine,* 12 July 1998, 30-35.

Jefferies, Janis. "Autobiographical Patterns." *N.Paradoxa,* 4 (1997).

Jones, Alison. "Jemima Stehli: On All Fours Naked in High Heels—A Critical Position?" *Women: A Cultural Review.* 10.3 London: Routledge, 1999: 297-307.

Jones, Amelia. *Body Art: Performing the Subject.* Minneapolis: The University of Minnesota Press, 1998.

Jones, Amelia. *Sexual Politics: Judy Chicago's Dinner Party in Feminist Art History*. Los Angeles: UCLA at the Armand Hammer Museum of Art and Berkeley and University of California Press, 1996.

—. "Introduction." *The Artist's Body"* Tracey Warr, ed. London: Phaidon Press Ltd, 2000.

—. "Feminism & Art (9 Views)." *Artforum* 143. October 2003.

—. *The Feminism and Visual Culture Reader.* London: Routledge, 2003.

Jones, Amelia and Andrew Stevens, eds. *Performing the Body, Performing the Text*. London: Routledge, 1999.

Jones, Jonathan. "So that was the 1960s … " *Guardian*, 18 April 2002.

Jones, Martin. *Psychedelic Decadence: Sex, Drugs and Low-Art in Sixties and Seventies Britain*. London: Cultural Vision, 2001.

Kaloski, Ann, ed. *The Feminist Seventies*, London: Raw Nerve Books, 2003.

Kastner, Jeffrey and Brian Wallis, eds. *Land and Environmental Art*. London: Phaidon Press Limited, 1998.

Kelly, Mary. Personal interview. 10 January 2001.

—. Personal interview. 21 April 2001.

—. "Introduction." *Imaging Desire*. Cambridge, Massachusetts: MIT Press, 1996. xv.

—. *Post-Partum Document*. London: Routledge & Kegan Paul, 1981.

Kent, Sarah and Jacqueline Morreau, eds. *Women's Images of Men*. London: Writers and Readers, 1985.

Krauss, Rosalind. *The Optical Unconscious*. Cambridge: MIT Press, 1993.

Krystufek, Elke. *In the Arms of Luck*. Geneva: Centre Genevois de Gravure Contemporaine, 1999.

—. *Elke Krystufek*. Frankfurt: Portikus, 2000.

Labelle, Brandon and Ken Ehrlich, eds. *Surface Tension*. Los Angeles: Errant Bodies, 2003.

Lacan, Jacques. *The Four Fundamental Concepts of Psycho-analysis*. 1973. London: Vintage, 1998.

—. (trans. Alan Sheridan). *Ecrits*. 1966. London: Routledge, 1977.

Lacey, Catherine and Richard Francis, Jeremy Lewison, Ann Jones. *Performance Art and Video Installation*. London: Tate Gallery, 1985.

Lacy, Suzanne, *Leaving Art, Writings on Performance, Politics, and Publics, 1974–2007*, Durham: Duke University Press, 2010.

Laporte, Dominique. *History of Shit*. Boston: Massachusetts Institute of Technology and Documents Magazine, Inc, 2000. Originally *Histoire de la merde (Prologue)*, 1978.

Lee, Pamela M. "Post-Feminism … Post-Gender?" *Texte zur Kunst*, Berlin, December 2011, 42-9.

Levi-Strauss, David. "Love Rides Aristotle through the Audience: Body, and Idea in the Work of Carolee Schneemann." *Carolee Schneemann, Imaging Her Erotics*. Cambridge: MIT Press, 2002.

Lippard, Lucy. *c. 7500*. London: (index card catalogue) 1973.

—. "The Pains and Pleasures of Rebirth." *The Pink Glass Swan: Selected Feminist Essays on Art*. New York: The New Press, 1995.

Litherland, R.H. "Power Without Authority in Art and Design Education." *Studio International*. Peter Townsend, ed. 182.939 (December 1971): 224-5.

MacKinnon, Catharine A. *Only Words*. Cambridge, Massachusetts: Harvard University Press, 1993.

MacRitchie, Lynn and Sally Potter, Caroline Tisdall. *About Time: Video, Performance and Installation by 21 Women Artists*. London: ICA, 1980.

Mastai, Judith, ed. *Social Process/Collaborative Action: Mary Kelly 1970-1974*. Vancouver: Charles H. Scott Gallery Emily Carr Institute Of Art and Design. 1997

McKay, Alastair. "Art is an Eminist issue." *Scotsman*, 4 August 1998, 10.

Meinero, Mark M. "Drs. Spock, Salk Seen as Playing Key Role in 20th Century American Parenting." *Parent News* (24 December 2000).

Mellor, Philip. "What a Load of Rubbish." *Daily Mirror*. London: 16 February 1976, 1.

Merck, Mandy. "The Amazons of Ancient Athens." *Perversions: Deviant Readings*. London: Virago, 1993: 121-61.

Millett, Kate. *Sexual Politics*. 1970. London: Virago Press, 1997.

Minh-ha, Trinh T. "Difference: A Special Third World Women Issue." *Feminist Review* 25: 1987.

——. *Women, Native, Other: Writing Postcoloniality and Feminism*. Indianapolis: Indiana University Press, 1989.

——. "Questions of Images and Politics." *When the Moon Waxes Red: Representation, Gender and Cultural Politics*. New York and London: Routledge, 1991.

Mitchell, Juliet. *Psychoanalysis and Feminism*. 1974. London: Penguin Books, 1986.

Mitchell, Juliet, and Ann Oakley, eds. *What is Feminism?* Oxford: Basil Blackwell Ltd, 1986.

Moi, Toril. *Sexual Textual Politics*. 1985. London: Routledge, 1994.

Molesworth, Helen. *At Home with Duchamp: The Readymade and Domesticity*. Diss: Cornell University, 1998.

Moore, Alan. *Art Gangs: Protest and Counterculture in New York City*, New York: Autonomedia, 2011.

Morgan, Robert C. "The Making of Wit: Joseph Kosuth and the Freudian Palimpsest." *Arts Magazine*, 62 (January 1988).

Morgan, Stuart. "The Story of I: Stuart Morgan talks to Tracey Emin." *Frieze* 34 (May 1997): 56-61.

Morreau, Jacqueline. Personal interview. 21 January 2002.

Morris, Linda. "Some Concerns in Fine Art Education II." *Studio International*. Peter Townsend, ed. 182.938 (November 1971): 168-9.

Muir, Gregor. "Like a Hole in the Head." *Parkett*, 63 (December 2001): 36-43.

Mulvey, Laura. *Visual and Other Pleasures*. Bloomington: Indiana University Press, 1989.

——. *Fetishism and Curiosity*. London: British Film Institute, 1996.

——. "You don't know what is happening, do you, Mr. Jones?" Rozsika Parker and Griselda Pollock., eds. *Framing Feminism: Art and the Women's Movement 1970-1985*. London: Harper Collins (1987): 127-31.

Mulvey, Laura and Peter Wollen interviewed by Claire Johnston and Paul Willemen, *Screen*, 15.3 (Autumn 1974): 121.

Nead, Lynda. *The Female Nude: Art, Obscenity and Sexuality*. London: Routledge, 1992.

Newman, Hayley. *Performancemania*. London: Matt's Gallery, 2001.

——. Personal Interview. 31 August 2004.

Nochlin, Linda. "Why Have There Been No Great Women Artists?" *ARTnews*, 69:9 (1971).

——. *Women, Art, and Power and Other Essays*. London: Thames & Hudson, 1969.

——. "Feminism & Art (9 Views)." *Artforum* 141. October 2003.

O"Doherty, Brian. *Inside the White Cube: The Ideology of the Gallery Space*. Berkeley: University of California Press, 1986.

Osborne, Peter, ed. *Conceptual Art*. London: Phaidon Press Ltd, 2002.

Pace, Eric. "Benjamin Spock, World's Pediatrician, Dies at 94." *New York Times*, 17 March 1998.

Parker, Rozsika, and Griselda Pollock, eds. *Framing Feminism: Art and the Women's Movement 1970-1985*. London: Pandora, 1987.

——. *Old Mistresses: Women, Art and Ideology*. London: Pandora, 1981.

Phillpot, Clive. Personal interview. 23 January 2001.

——. *Live in Your Head: Concept and Experiment in Britain 1965-1975*. London: Whitechapel Art Gallery, 2000.

Pierini, Esther. "Tracey Emin." *Flash Art* (November/December 1997): 102.

Pilkington, Philip, Kevin Lose, David Rushton and Charles Harrison. "Some Concerns in Fine Art Education." *Studio International*. Peter Townsend, ed. 183.937 (October 1971): 120-2.

Piper, Adrian. *Out of Order, Out of Sight*. Boston: MIT Press, 1999.

Pollock, Griselda. "Trouble in the Archives: Introduction," *Differences: A Journal of Feminist Cultural Studies* 4.3: 1992.

Potter, Sally. "On Shows." *About Time: Video, Performance and Installation by 21 Women Artists*. London: Institute of Contemporary Arts, 1980.

Potter, Sally interviewed by Marc Chaimowicz. "Women and Performance in the UK." *Studio International*. 192.982 (July/August 1976): 33.

Preece, Robert. "Artist over—*and in*—the broadsheets." *Parkett*, 63 (December 2001): 36-43.

"Profundity is a wet nappy." *Guardian*. London: 16 October 1976, 10.

Princenthal, Nancy. *Hannah Wilke*, New York: Prestel, 2010.

Radcliff, Carter. *Out of the Box: The Reinvention of Art, 1965-1975*. New York: Allworth Press, 2000.

Reedy, Carlyle. *Sculpted in This World*. London: bluff books, 1979.

Rendell, Jane, Barbara Penner and Iain Borden. *Gender, Space, Architecture*. London: Routledge, 2000.

Reckitt, Helena, and Peggy Phelan. *Art and Feminism*. London: Phaidon Press Ltd, 2001.

Respini, Eva, ed, *Cindy Sherman*, New York: Museum of Modern Art, 2012.

Ronson, Jon. "Who wants their own museum?" *Independent, Section Two*, 9 February 1996, 8.

Rorimer, Anne. *New Art in the 60s and 70s, Redefining Reality*. London: Thames & Hudson Ltd, 2001.

Rosler, Martha. *Decoys and Disruptions: Selected Writings 1975-2001*. Cambridge, Massachusetts: MIT Press, 2004.

Ross, Monica. Public presentation. 347 Minutes conference address. Whitechapel Gallery at Conway Hall, London. 2000.

——. *Valentine*. London: Milch, 2000.
Rowbotham, Sheila. *Hidden from History*. London: Pluto Press, 1973.
——. *A Century of Women*. London: Penguin Books, 1999.
——. "Reel dreams and real lives." *Guardian*, January 1999.
Reynolds, Ann Morris. *Robert Smithson: Learning from New Jersey and Elsewhere*. London: MIT Press, 2002.
Sanders, Joel. *Stud: Architecture of Masculinity*. Princeton, NJ: Princeton University Press, 1997.
Saner, Ermine. "Tate exhibition shows abuse of Queen Mother." *Sunday Times*, 6 August 2000.
Santacatterina, Stella. "Jemima Stehli: Subject and Object of the Gaze." *Portfolio* 33 (June 2001): 28.
Schimmel, Paul, ed. *Out of Actions*, Los Angeles: The Museum of Contemporary Art, 1998.
Schneemann, Carolee. *Carolee Schneemann: Up to and Including Her Limits*. New York: New Museum for Contemporary Art, 1996.
——. Personal interview. 18 April 2002.
——. "About FUSES." Getty Institute Special Collections, no. 950001, box 3.
——. *Imaging Her Erotics: Essays, Interviews, Projects*. Cambridge: MIT Press, 2002.
——. *Up To and Including Her Limits*, New York: New Museum of Contemporary Art, 1996.
Schneider, Rebecca. *The Explicit Body in Performance*. London and New York: Routledge, 1997.
Scott, Ann. "Editorial." *Spare Rib* 34, April 1975: 8.
Scott, Joan W. "Experience." Judith Butler and Joan W. Scott, eds. *Feminists Theorize the Political*, New York: Routledge, 1992.
Searle, Adrian. "Me, me, me, me." *Guardian*, 22 April 1997.
Seymour, Anne. et al. *Richard Long: Walking in Circles*. London: George Braziller, 1991.
Shuttle, Penelope and Peter Redgrove. *The Wise Wound: Menstruation and Everywomen*. 1978. London: Harper Collins Publishers, 1994.
Simpson, Anne. "Feministo puts you in the picture." *Women's Herald*. 1976.
Slack, Susie. "Bobby Baker at the ICA." *Ca* 1976. Bobby Baker personal archive, London.
Slinger, Penny. *An Exorcism*. London: Villiers Publications Ltd, 1977.
Slizinska, Milada, ed, *Mary Kelly: Words are Things*, Warsaw: Center for Contemporary Art Ujazdowski Castle, 2008.
Slyce, John. "Jemima Stehli: A Writer's Notes." *Jemima Stehli*. London: ARTicle Press, 2002.
Spence, Jo. *Cultural Sniping: The Art of Transgression*. London: Routledge, 1995.
——. *Jo Spence: Working Photography*. Cambridge: Cambridge Darkroom, 1985.
Spence, Jo and Patricia Holland, eds. *Family Snaps: The Meanings of Domestic Photography*. London: Virago Press Limited, 1991.
Stiles, Kristine, ed., *Correspondence Course: An Epistolary History of Carolee Schneemann and her Circle*, Durham: Duke University Press, 2010.
Stiles, Kristine et al. *Paul McCarthy*. London: Phaidon, 1996.
Stiles, Kristine and Peter Selz. *Theories and Documents of Contemporary Art: A Sourcebook of Artists' Writings*. Berkeley: University of California Press, 1996.

Stokes, Anthony. Personal Interview. 19 March 2001.

Tarsia, Andrea and Tamsin Dillon. *A Short History of Performance: Part One*. London: The Whitechapel Art Gallery, 2002.

Tiberghien, Gilles A. *Land Art*. New York: Princeton Architectural Press, 1996.

Tickner, Lisa. "The Body Politic: Female Sexuality and Women Artists since 1970." *Art History*. 1.2 (June 1978): 246.

——. "One for Sorrow, Two for Mirth." *The Oxford Art Journal*. April 1980.

——. "Questions of Feminism: Question 1." *October* 71. (Winter 1995): 44.

——. Personal interview. 27 June 2000.

Tisdall, Caroline. "Mary Kelly." *Guardian*, 16 October 1976: 8.

——. "Anonymous was a woman." *Guardian*, June 1977.

——. "Bodyworks." *Guardian*. London: 1973 Judy Clark file. Women Artists Library, London.

Tucker, Marcia. "PheNAUMANology." *Artforum* December 1970.

Vaizey, Marina. "Judy Clark." *Financial Times*, 1973. Judy Clark artist's file. Women Artists Library, London.

Varnedoe, Kirk and Pepe Karmel. *Jackson Pollock*. London: Tate Gallery, 1988.

Walker, John A. *Art and Outrage: Provocation, Controversy and the Visual Arts*. London: Pluto Press, 1999.

——. *John Latham: The Incidental Person, His Art and Ideas*. London: Middlesex University Press, 1995

Walker, Kate. Telephone interview. 8 August 2001.

Wallis, Brian, ed. *Art after Modernism: Rethinking Representation*. New York: New Museum of Contemporary Art, 1984.

Walwin, Jenni. "Close to the Horns." *Performance*, 43 (September/October 1986): 10.

Warner, Marina. "Bobby Baker: The Rebel at the Heart of the Joker." *A Split Second of Paradise: Live Art, Installation and Performance*. Nicky Childs and Jeni Walwin, eds. London: Rivers Oram Press, 1998.

Warr, Tracey, ed. *The Artist's Body*. London: Phaidon, 2000.

Wendler, Jack. Personal discussion. 19 April 2000.

Whitford, Margaret, ed. *The Iragaray Reader*. Oxford: Blackwell Publishers Ltd, 1991.

Wilke, Hannah. *Intra Venus*. New York: Ronald Feldman Fine Arts, 1995.

Wilson, Andrew. "Foreword." *City Racing: The Life and Times of an Artist-Run Gallery*. Matt Hale, Paul Noble, Pete Owen, eds. London: Black Dog, 2002.

Würf, Karl. *To Serve Man: A Cookbook for People*. Philadelphia: Owlswick Press, 1976.

Wyver, John. "Mark Karlin." *The Thursday Review, Independent*, 28 January 1999.

Zegher, Catherine de, ed. *Martha Rosler: Positions in the Life World*. Boston: MIT Press, 1999.

Ziranek, Silvia. *Very Food*. London: Book Works, 1987.

——. Personal interview. 17 February 2002.

INDEX